W9-BIG-182

SPECIFICATION
BY EXAMPLE

SPECIFICATION
BY EXAMPLE

How successful teams deliver the right software

Gojko Adzic

MANNING

Shelter Island

For online information and ordering of this and other Manning books, please visit
www.manning.com. The publisher offers discounts on this book when ordered in quantity.
For more information, please contact:

Special Sales Department
Manning Publications Co.
20 Baldwin Road
PO Box 261
Shelter Island, NY 11964
Email: orders@manning.com

Manning Publications Co.   Development Editor: Jeff Bleiel
20 Baldwin Road   Copyeditors: June Eding, Linda Recktenwald
PO Box 261   Illustrator: Martin Murtonen
Shelter Island, NY 11964   Designer: Leslie Haimes

Second, corrected printing August 2012
ISBN 9781617290084
Printed in the United States of America
2 3 4 5 6 7 8 9 10 – MAL – 16 15 14 13 12

Contents

PART 1   Getting Started

1   Key benefits 3

2   Key process patterns 17

3   Living documentation 29

4 Initiating the changes 36

PART 2 Key process patterns

5 Deriving scope from goals 65

6 Specifying collaboratively 77

7 Illustrating using examples 95

8 Refining the specification 114

9 Automating validation without changing specifications 136

10 Validating frequently   162

11 Evolving a documentation system 183

PART 3 Case studies

12 uSwitch 201

13 RainStor 211

14 Iowa Student Loan 217

Preface

The book you hold in your hands, or see on your screen, is the result of a series of studies of how teams all over the world specify, develop, and deliver the right software, without defects, in very short cycles. It presents the collective knowledge of about 50 projects, ranging from public websites to internal back-office systems. These projects involved diverse teams, from small ones working in the same office to groups spread across different continents, working in a range of processes including Extreme Programming (XP), Scrum, Kanban, and similar methods (often bundled together under the names *agile* and *lean*). They have one thing in common—they all got the practices of collaborating on specifications and tests right, and they got big benefits out of that.

Specification by Example

Different teams use different names for their ways of dealing with specifications and tests, yet they all share a common set of core principles and ideas, which I hold to be essentially the same thing. Some of the names that the teams used for these practices are

- Agile acceptance testing
- Acceptance Test-Driven Development
- Example-Driven Development
- Story testing
- Behavior-Driven Development
- Specification by Example

The fact that the same practices have so many names reflects the huge amount of innovation in this field at the moment. It also reflects the fact that the practices described in this book impact the ways teams approach specifications, development, and testing. To be consistent, I had to choose one name. I settled on *Specification by Example*, and I'll use that in the rest of the book. I explain this choice in detail in the "A few words on the terminology" section later in this introduction.

In the real world

I present this topic through case studies and interviews. I chose this approach so that you can see that there are real teams out there right now doing this and reaping big benefits. Specification by Example is not a dark art although some popular media might make you think that.

Almost everything in this book is from the real world, real teams, and real experiences. A small number of practices are presented as suggestions without being backed by a case study. These are ideas that I think will be important for the future, and they're clearly introduced as such.

I'm certain that the studies I conducted leading to this book and my conclusions will be dismissed for not being a serious scientific research by those skeptics who claim that agile development doesn't work and that the industry should go back to "real software engineering."[1] That's fine. The resources available to me for this book project are minute compared to what would be required for a serious scientific research. Even with those resources, I'm not a scientist, nor do I intend to present myself as such. I'm a practitioner.

Who should read this book?

If you're a practitioner, like me, and your bread and butter come from making or helping software go live, this book has a lot to offer. I primarily wrote this book for teams who have tried to implement an agile process and ran into problems that manifest themselves as poor quality, rework, and missed customer expectations. (Yes, these are problems, and plainly iterating is a workaround and not a solution.) Specification by Example, agile acceptance testing, Behavior-Driven Development, and all the alternative names for the same thing solve these problems. This book will help you get started with those practices and learn how to contribute better to your team, regardless of whether you qualify yourself as a tester, developer, analyst, or product owner.

A few years ago, most people I met at conferences hadn't heard of these ideas. Most people I meet now are somewhat aware of these practices, but many failed to implement them properly. There's very little literature on problems that teams face while implementing agile development in general, so every discouraged team thinks that they're unique and that somehow the ideas don't work in their "real world." They seem surprised how I can guess three or four of their biggest problems after just five minutes of listening to them. They are often completely astonished that many other teams have the same issues.

If you work in such a team, the first thing that this book will do for you is show you that you're not alone. The teams I interviewed for this book aren't perfect—they had tons of issues as well. Instead of quitting after they hit a brick wall, they decided to drive around it or tear it down. Knowing this is often encouraging enough for people to

---

[1] For more on the delusion that engineering rigor would help software development, as if it were some kind of second-rate branch of physics, see also http://www.semat.org. For a good counterargument, see Glenn Vanderburg's presentation "Software Engineering Doesn't Work!" at http://confreaks.net/videos/282-lsrc2010-real-software-engineering.

look at their problems in a different light. I hope that after reading the book you'll feel the same.

If you're in the process of implementing Specification by Example, this book will provide useful advice on how to get past your current problems and learn what you can expect in the future. I hope you will learn from the mistakes of others and avoid hitting some problems at all.

This book is also written for experienced practitioners, people with a relatively successful implementation of Specification by Example in their process. I started conducting the interviews expecting that I knew most of what's out there, looking for external confirmation. I ended it surprised by how many different ideas people implemented in their contexts, things I never thought about. I learned a lot from these examples, and hope you will too. The practices and the ideas described here should inspire you to try alternative solutions to your problems or realize how you can improve the process of your team once you read similar stories.

What's inside?

In part 1, I introduce Specification by Example. Instead of convincing you why you should follow the principles outlined in the book, I show you—in the true Specification by Example style—examples of benefits that teams got from this process. If you're thinking about buying this book, skim over chapter 1 and see if any of the benefits presented there would apply to your project. In chapter 2, I introduce the key process patterns and key artifacts of Specification by Example. In chapter 3, I explain the idea of living documentation in more detail. In chapter 4, I present the most common starting points for initiating the changes to process and team culture and advise what to watch out for when you start implementing the process.

One of my goals with this book is to create a consistent language for patterns, ideas, and artifacts that teams use to implement Specification by Example. The community has a dozen names for the practice as a whole and twice as many for various elements of it. Different people call the same thing feature files, story tests, BDD files, acceptance tests, and so on. For that reason, I also introduce what I think are very good names for all the key elements in chapter 2. Even if you're an experienced practitioner, I suggest you read this chapter to make sure that we have the same understanding of the key names, phrases, and patterns in this book.

In part 2, I present the key practices that the teams from the case studies used to implement the principles of Specification by Example. Teams in different contexts do very different things, sometimes even opposing or conflicting, to get to the same effect. In addition to the practices, I document the contexts in which the teams use them to implement the underlying principles. The seven chapters in part 2 are roughly broken down by process areas.

There are no best practices in software, but there are definitely good ideas that we can try to apply in different contexts. You will find thumbs-up and thumbs-down icons next to the sections in part 2, indicating practices that several teams from the survey found useful or issues they commonly faced. Treat these as suggestions to try out or avoid, not as prescriptions for something that you must follow. Arrow icons point to particularly important ideas for each practice.

Software development isn't static—teams and environments change and the process must follow. I present case studies showing the journeys of a few selected teams in part 3. I write about their processes, constraints, and contexts, analyzing how the processes evolved. These stories will help you get started with your journey or take the next step, find ideas, and discover new ways of doing things.

In the final chapter of the book, I summarize the key things I've learned from the case studies leading to this book.

Beyond the basics

On the traditional *Shu-ha-ri*[2] learning model, this book is at the *Ha* level. *Ha* is about breaking the old rules and showing that there are many successful models. In my book *Bridging the Communication Gap*, I presented my model and my experience. In this book, I try hard not to be influenced by my background. I present things from the projects I worked on only when there's an important point to make and I don't think any of the teams featured in the book had a similar situation. In that sense, Specification by Example continues where *Bridging the Communication Gap* stopped.

I introduce the basic principles briefly in chapter 2. Even if you've never heard of any of these ideas before, this should give you enough information to understand the rest of the book, but I won't go into the basics too much. I wrote about the basics of Specification by Example at length in *Bridging the Communication Gap* and have no wish to repeat myself.

If you want to go over the basics in more detail, visit http://specificationbyexample. com, register a copy of this book, and you'll get the PDF of *Bridging the Communication Gap* free.

I don't think that I'll write a follow-up on this subject on the *Ri* level—because that level is beyond books. On the other hand, I believe that this book will help you move to that level. Once you start thinking that the choice of a particular tool is irrelevant, you are there.

---

[2] Shu-ha-ri is a learning model associated with Aikido. It roughly translates to "obey-detach-leave." At the first level (Shu - "obey"), a student learns by closely following one model. At the second level (Ha - "detach"), the student learns that there are multiple models and solutions. At the third level (Ri - "leave"), the student goes beyond following models.

This book has no source code and doesn't explain any tools

This book has no source code or instructions on how to work with a particular tool. I feel compelled to mention this upfront, because I had to explain it already several times during the publishing process (typically as an answer to the question, "What do you mean? A software development book without source code? How's that possible?").

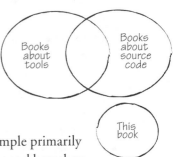

The principles and practices of Specification by Example primarily affect how people communicate in software delivery teams and how they collaborate with business uers and stakeholders. I'm sure that many tool vendors will try to sell you a technical solution for that. There are also many managers who would be happy to pay for their problem to go away instantly. Unfortunately for them, this is mostly a people problem, not a technical one.

Bill Gates said, "The first rule of any technology used in a business is that automation applied to an efficient operation will magnify the efficiency. The second is that automation applied to an inefficient operation will magnify the inefficiency." Many teams who failed with Specification by Example have magnified their process inefficiency by automating it. Instead of focusing on a particular tool, I want to address the real reasons why teams struggle to implement these ideas. Once you get the communication and collaboration right, you'll be able to choose the right tool to fit it. If you want to know more about tools that support specification by example after reading this book, go to http://specificationbyexample.com and check out the resources section.

A few words on the terminology

If this is your first contact with Specification by Example, Acceptance Test-Driven Development, agile acceptance testing, Behavior-Driven Development, or any of the other names people use for this set of practices, you've avoided years of confusion caused by misleading names. You should feel good about that, and you may skip this part of the introduction. If you have already come into contact with any of those ideas, the names I use in this book might surprise you. Read on to understand why I use those names and why you should start using them as well.

While writing this book, I had the same problem practitioners often have when writing executable specifications. The terminology has to be consistent to make sense, but we don't necessarily see that until we write things down. Because this book is the result of a series of interviews, and many people I spoke to used different names for the same thing, it was quite hard to make the story consistent with all the different names.

I realized that the practitioners of Specification by Example, myself included, have traditionally been guilty of using technical terms to confuse both ourselves and everyone else who tries to implement these practices. Then I decided that one of my goals with this book would be to change the terminology in the community. If we want to get business users more involved, which is one of the key goals of these practices, we have to use the right names for the right things and stop confusing people.

This lesson is obvious when we write our specifications, and we know that we need to keep the naming consistent and avoid misleading terms. But we don't do this when we talk about the process. For example, when we say *continuous integration* in the context of Specification by Example, we don't really mean running integration tests. So why use that term and then have to explain how acceptance tests are different from integration tests? Until I started using *specification workshop* as the name for a collaborative meeting about acceptance tests, it was difficult to convince business users to participate. But a simple change in naming made the problem go away. By using better names, we can avoid many completely meaningless discussions and get people started on the right path straightaway.

Why Specification by Example?

I first want to explain why I chose Specification by Example as the overall name for the whole set of practices, as opposed to agile acceptance testing, Behavior-Driven Development, or Acceptance Test-Driven Development.

During the Domain Driven Design eXchange 2010 conference[3] in London, Eric Evans argued that *agile* as a term has lost all meaning because anything can be called agile now. Unfortunately, he's right. I've seen too many teams who tried to implement a process that was obviously broken but slapped the name *agile* on it as if that would magically make it better. This is in spite of a huge body of available literature on how to properly implement XP, Scrum, and other less-popular agile processes.

To get around this meaningless ambiguity and arguing whether agile works or not (and what it is), I avoid using the term *agile* in this book as much as I can. I use it only when referring to teams that started implementing well-defined processes built on the principles outlined in the Agile Manifesto. So without being able to mention agile in every second sentence, agile acceptance testing as a name is out of the question.

The practices described here don't form a fully fledged software development methodology. They supplement other methodologies—both iteration and flow based—to provide rigor in specifications and testing, enhance communication between various stakeholders and members of software development teams, reduce unnecessary rework, and facilitate change. So I don't want to use any of the "Driven Development" names. Especially not Behavior-Driven Development (BDD). Don't take this as a sign that I

---

[3] http://skillsmatter.com/event/design-architecture/ddd-exchange-2010

have anything against BDD. Quite the contrary, I love BDD and consider most of what this book is about actually a central part of BDD. But BDD suffers from the naming problem as well.

What BDD actually means changes all the time. Dan North, the central authority on what BDD is and what it is not, said that BDD is a *methodology* at the Agile Specifications, BDD, and Testing Exchange 2009.[4] (Actually he called it "a second-generation, outside-in, pull-based, multiple-stakeholder, multiple-scale, high-automation, agile methodology.") To avoid any confusion and ambiguity between what North calls BDD and what I consider BDD, I don't want to use that name. This book is about a precise set of practices, which you can use within a range of methodologies, BDD included (if you accept that BDD is a methodology).

I also want to avoid using the word *test* too much. Many managers and business users unfortunately consider testing as a technical supplementary activity, not something that they want to get involved in. After all, they have dedicated testers to handle that. Specification by Example requires an active participation of stakeholders and delivery team members, including developers, testers, and analysts. Without putting *tests* in the title, story testing, agile acceptance testing, and similar names are out.

This leaves Specification by Example as the most meaningful name with the least amount of negative baggage.

Process patterns

Specification by Example consists of several process patterns, elements of the wider software development life cycle. The names I use for process patterns in this book are a result of several discussions at the UK Agile Testing user group meetings, Agile Alliance Functional Testing Tools mailing list, and workshops. Some of them have been in use for a while; some of them will be new to most readers.

A popular approach in the community is to use the name of a practice or tool to describe a part of the process. Feature Injection is a good example—it's a popular name for extracting the scope of a project from the business goals. But Feature Injection is just one technique to do that, and there are alternative ways to achieve the same goal. In order to talk about what different teams do in different contexts, we need a higher-level concept that includes all those practices. A good name describes the expected outcome and clearly points to the key differentiating element of this set of practices.

In the case of Feature Injection and similar practices, the outcome is a scope for a project or a milestone. The key differentiator from the other ways of defining the scope is that we focus on the business goals. So I propose that we talk about *deriving scope from goals*.

---

[4] http://skillsmatter.com/podcast/java-jee/how-to-sell-bdd-to-the-business

One of the biggest issues teams have with Specification by Example is who should write what and when. So we need a good name that clearly says that everyone should be involved (and that this needs to happen before the team starts programming or testing), because we want to use acceptance tests as a target for development. *Test first* is a good technical name for it, but business users don't get it, and it doesn't imply collaboration. I propose we talk about *specifying collaboratively* instead of test first or writing acceptance tests. It sounds quite normal to put every single numerical possibility into an automated functional test. Why wouldn't we do it if it's automated? But such complex tests are unusable as a communication tool, and in Specification by Example we need to use tests for communication. So instead of writing functional tests, let's talk about *illustrating using examples* and expect the output of that to be *key examples* to point out that we want only enough to explain the context properly.[5]

Key examples are raw material, but if we just talk about acceptance testing then why not just dump complicated 50-column, 100-row tables with examples into an acceptance test without any explanation? It's going to be tested by a machine anyway. With Specification by Example, the tests are for humans as well as for machines. We need to make it clear that there's a step after illustrating using examples, where we ex-tract the minimal set of attributes and examples to specify a business rule, add a title and description, and so on. I propose we call this step *refining the specification.*[6]

The result of this refinement is at the same time a specification, a target for develop-ment, an objective way to check acceptance, and a functional regression test for later. I don't want to call this an acceptance test because it makes it difficult to justify why this document needs to stay in domain language, be readable, and be easily accessible. I propose we call the result of refining a *specification with examples,* which immediately points to the fact that it needs to be based on examples but also contain more than just raw data. Calling this artifact a specification makes it obvious that everyone should care about it and that it needs to be easy to understand. Apart from that, there's a completely different argument as to whether these checks are there to automatically accept software or to automatically reject the code that doesn't satisfy what we need.[7]

I just don't want to spend any more time arguing with people who've already paid a license for QTP that it's completely unusable for acceptance tests. As long as we talk about test automation, there's always going to be a push to use whatever horrible con-traption testers already use for automation, because it's logical to managers that their teams use a single tool for test automation. Agile acceptance testing and BDD tools don't compete with QTP or tools like that; they address a completely different problem.

---

[5] Thanks to David Evans who suggested this.
[6] Thanks to Elisabeth Hendrickson who suggested this name.
[7] http://www.developsense.com/blog/2010/08/acceptance-tests-lets-change-the-title-too

A specification shouldn't be translated into something technical just for automation. Instead of talking about test automation, let's call automating a check without distorting any information *automating validation without changing specifications*. The fact that we need to automate validation without changing the original specification should help us avoid the horror of scripting and using technical libraries directly in test specifications. An executable specification should be unchanged from what it looked like on the whiteboard; it shouldn't be translated into user interface commands.

After the validation of a specification is automated, we can use it to validate the system. In effect, we get *executable specifications*.

We want to check all the specifications frequently to make sure that the system still does what it's supposed to do and, equally important, to check that the specifications still describe what the system does. If we call this regression testing, it's very hard to explain to testers why they shouldn't go and add five million other test cases to a previously nice, small, focused specification. If we talk about continuous integration, then we get into the trouble of explaining why these tests shouldn't always be run end to end and check the whole system.

The long-term payoff from Specification by Example comes from having a reference on what the system does that's as relevant as the code itself but much easier to read. That makes development much more efficient long term, facilitates collaboration with business users, leads to an alignment of software design and business models, and just makes everyone's work much easier. But to do this, the reference really has to be relevant, it has to be maintained, and it has to be consistent internally and with code. We shouldn't have silos of tests that use terms we used three years ago, and those we used a year ago, and so on. Going back and updating tests is difficult to sell to busy teams, but going back to update documentation after a big change is expected. So let's not talk about folders filled with hundreds of tests, let's talk about *evolving a living documentation system*. That makes it much easier to explain why artefacts of SBE should be self-explanatory and easy to find. It also explains why business users need access to those artefacts as well.

So there it is: I chose the names not because of previous popularity but because they make sense. The names for these process patterns should create a mental model that actually points out the important things and reduces the confusion. I hope that you'll see this and adopt this new terminology as well.

Acknowledgments

This book would not exist without the support and contributions of many people. Primarily, I'd like to thank all those who let me tap into their brains and shared their experiences: Adam Knight, André Brissette, Andrew Jackman, Aslak Hellesøy, Børge Lotre, Channing Walton, Christian Hassa, Cindy Bartz, Clare McLennan, Damon Morgan, Francesco Rizzi, Gaspar Nagy, Geoff Bache, Hemal Kuntawala, Ian Cooper, Ismo Aro, Jodie Parker, Johannes Link, Jon Neale, Jonas Bandi, Justin Davis, Kumaran Sivapathasuntharam, Lance Walton, Lisa Crispin, Marco Milone, Marta Gonzalez Ferrero, Martin Jackson, Matthew Steer, Mikael Vik, Mike Vogel, Maykel Suarez, Pascal Mestdach, Peter Janssens, Phil Cowans, Pierre Veragen, Rakesh Patel, Rob Park, Scott Berger, Stuart Ervine, Stuart Taylor, Stephen Lloyd, Suzanne Kidwell, Tim Andersen, Tony To, Wes Williams, and Xu Yi. You wrote this book; I just wrote it down.

Elisabeth Hendrickson, David Evans, Matt Wynne, Pekka Klärck, and Ran Nyman generously helped me get in touch with their colleagues, clients, and associates for this research. Adam Geras, Joseph Wilk, Markus Gärtner, Mike Stockdale, Rick Mugridge, Robert Martin, Dan North, Tom Vercauteren, and Tom Roden helped me refine all the ideas and explain them better. The following reviewed the manuscript during development and I thank them for their feedback: Bas Vodde, Craig Smith, Alex Bepple, John Stevenson, Joseph Wilk, Michele Mauro, Oleksandr Alesinskyy, Robert Martin, Robert Wenner, and Saicharan Manga. And special thanks to Rick Mugridge for his final proofread of the manuscript during production.

Jeff Bleiel, June Eding, Linda Recktenwald, Barbara Mirecki, Leslie Haimes, Martin Murtonen, and Mary Piergies from Manning were instrumental in transforming this set of stories into an actual book.

Thanks also go to Craig Larman, Jim Shore, and Harvey Wheaton for taking the time to answer my emails.

About the author

Gojko Adzic got bitten by the Specification by Example bug five years ago. Since then, he has helped numerous teams implement these practices, written two books on the subject, and contributed to several open source projects for Specification by Example. Gojko is a frequent speaker at leading software development and testing conferences and runs the UK agile testing user group.

Over the last 12 years, he has worked as a developer, architect, technical director, and consultant on projects delivering equity and energy trading, mobile positioning, e-commerce, online gaming, and complex configuration management.

Gojko runs Neuri Ltd., a UK-based consultancy that helps ambitious teams, from web startups to large financial institutions, implement Specification by Example and agile testing practices.

To get in touch, write to gojko@neuri.com or visit http://gojko.net.

Author Online

You can also contact the author through the Author Online forum run by Manning Publications at www.manning.com/SpecificationbyExample. Manning's commitment to our readers is to provide a venue where a meaningful dialogue between individual readers and between readers and the author can take place. It isn't a commitment to any specific amount of participation on the part of the author, whose contributions to the book's forum remain voluntary (and unpaid). The Author Online forum and the archives of previous discussions will remain accessible from the publisher's website as long as the book is in print.

About the cover illustration

The figure on the cover of *Specification by Example* is captioned "A Traveler" and is taken from a 19th-century edition of Sylvain Maréchal's four-volume compendium of regional dress customs published in France. Each illustration is finely drawn and colored by hand. The rich variety of Maréchal's collection reminds us vividly of how culturally apart the world's towns and countries were just 200 years ago. Isolated from each other, even if by only several miles, people spoke different dialects and languages. In the streets or in the countryside, it was easy to identify where they lived and what their trade or station in life was just by their dress.

Dress codes have changed since then and the diversity by region, so rich at the time, has faded away. It is now difficult to tell apart the inhabitants of different continents, let alone different towns or regions. Perhaps we have traded cultural diversity for a more varied personal life—certainly for a more varied and fast-paced technological life.

At a time when it is hard to tell one computer book from another, Manning celebrates the inventiveness and initiative of the computer business with book covers based on the rich diversity of regional life of two centuries ago, brought back to life by Maréchal's pictures.

PART 1

Getting started

1

Key benefits

In the internet age, delivery speed is the theme of the day in software development. A decade ago, projects lasted several years and project phases were measured in months. Today, most teams' projects are measured in months and project phases are reduced to weeks or even days. Anything that requires long-term planning is dropped, including big up-front software designs and detailed requirements analysis. Tasks that require more time than an average project phase are no longer viable. Goodbye code freezes and weeks of manual regression testing!

With such a high frequency of change, documentation quickly gets outdated. Detailed specifications and test plans require too much effort to keep current and are considered wasteful. People who relied on them for their day-to-day work, such as business analysts or testers, often become confused about what to do in this new world of weekly iterations. Software developers who thought they weren't affected by the lack of paper documents waste time on rework and maintaining functionality that's not required. Instead of spending time building big plans, they waste weeks polishing the wrong product.

In the last decade, the software development community has strived to build software the "right" way, focusing on technical practices and ideas to ensure high-quality results. But *building the product right* and *building the right product* are two different things. We need to do both in order to succeed.

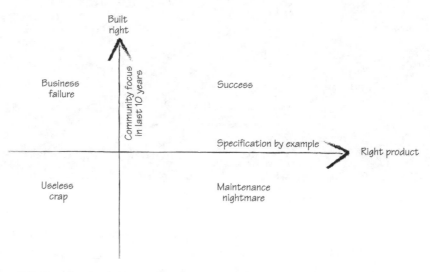

Figure 1.1 Specification by Example helps teams build the right software product, complementing technical practices that ensure that the product is built right.

To build the right product effectively, software development practices have to provide the following:

- Assurance that all stakeholders and delivery team members understand what needs to be delivered in the same way.

- Precise specifications so delivery teams avoid wasteful rework caused by ambiguities and functional gaps.

- An objective means to measure when a piece of work is complete.

- Documentation to facilitate change, in terms of both software features and team structure.

Traditionally, building the right product required big functional specifications, documentation, and long testing phases. Today, in the world of weekly software deliveries, this doesn't work. We need a solution that gives us a way to

- Avoid wasteful over-specifying; avoid spending time on details that will change before a piece of work is developed.

- Have reliable documentation that explains what the system does so we can change it easily.

- Efficiently check that a system does what the specifications say.

- Keep documentation relevant and reliable with minimal maintenance costs.

- Fit all this into short iterations and flow-based processes, so that the information on upcoming work is produced just-in-time.

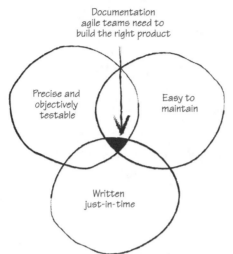

Figure 1.2 Key factors for the right kind of documentation for agile projects

Although these goals might seem in conflict at first, many teams have succeeded at fulfilling all of them. While researching this book, I interviewed 30 teams that implemented around 50 projects. I looked for patterns and common practices and identified underlying principles behind these practices. The common ideas from these projects define a good way to build the right software: *Specification by Example*.

Specification by Example is a set of process patterns that helps teams build the right software product by writing just enough documentation to facilitate change effectively in short iterations or in flow-based development. The key process patterns of Specification by Example are introduced in the next chapter. In this chapter, I'll explain the benefits of Specification by Example. I'll do so using Specification by Example style; instead of building a case for this book in a theoretical introduction, I'll present 18 real-world examples of teams that got big dividends from Specification by Example.

Before I begin, let me emphasize that it's hard to isolate the impact or effect of any single idea on a project. The practices described in this book work with—and enhance—the effectiveness of other, more established agile software development practices (such as test-driven development [TDD], continuous integration, and planning with user stories). When considering a range of projects in different contexts, patterns emerge. Some of the teams I interviewed were using an agile process before implementing Specification by Example, and some implemented Specification by Example while transitioning to an agile process. Most of the teams used iteration-based processes, such as Scrum and Extreme Programming (XP), or flow-based processes, such as Kanban— but some even used these practices in an environment that wouldn't be considered agile by any standard. Yet most reported similar benefits:

- *Implementing changes more efficiently*—They had living documentation— a reliable source of information on system functionality—which enabled them to analyze the impact of potential changes and share knowledge effectively.

- *Higher product quality*—They defined expectations clearly and made the validation process efficient.

- *Less rework*—They collaborated better on specifications and ensured a shared understanding of the expectations by all team members.

- *Better alignment of the activities of different roles on a project*—Improved collaboration led to a more regular flow of delivery.

In the next four sections, we'll take a closer look at each of these benefits using real-world examples.

Implementing changes more efficiently

In the course of researching this book, the most important lesson I learned concerned the long-term benefits of *living documentation*—in fact, I consider it one of this book's most important messages, and I cover it extensively. Living Documentation is an artefact of SBE, a source of information about system functionality that's as reliable as programming language code but much easier to access and understand. Living documentation allows teams to collaboratively analyze the impact of proposed changes and discuss potential solutions. It also allows them to make use of existing documentation by extending it for new requirements. This makes specifying and implementing changes more efficient over time. The most successful teams discovered the long-term benefit of implementing Specification by Example comes from living documentation.

The Iowa Student Loan Liquidity Corporation, based in West Des Moines, Iowa, went through a fairly significant business model change in 2009. The financial market turmoil during the previous year made it nearly impossible for lenders to find funding sources for private student loans. Because of this, many lenders were forced to leave the private student loan market or change their business models. Iowa Student Loan was able to adapt. Instead of using bond proceeds to fund private student loans, it pooled funds from banks and other financial institutions.

In order to adapt effectively, they had to perform a "dramatic overhaul of a core piece of the system," according to software analyst and developer Tim Andersen. The team used living documentation as a primary mechanism for documenting business requirements when they were developing their software. The living documentation system made it possible for them to ascertain the impact of new requirements, specify required changes, and ensure that the rest of the system works as it had before. They were able to implement fundamental change to the system and release it to production in only one month. A living documentation system was essential for this change. Andersen said,

> Any system that didn't have the tests [living documentation] would halt the development and it would have been a re-write.

The Talia project team at Pyxis Technologies in Montreal, Quebec, had a similar experience. Talia is a virtual assistant for enterprise systems, a chat robot with complex rules that communicates with employees. From the first day of development, the Talia team used Specification by Example to build a living documentation system. A year later, they had to rewrite the core of the virtual agent engine from scratch—and that's when the investment in living documentation paid off. André Brissette, the Talia product director, commented,

> Without that, any major refactoring would be a suicide.

Their living documentation system made the team confident that the new system would work the same as the old one when the change was complete. It also enabled Brissette to manage and track the project's progress.

The team at Songkick, a London-based consumer website about live music, used a living documentation system to facilitate change when redeveloping activity feeds on their site. They had realized that the feeds were implemented in a way that wouldn't scale to the required capacity; living documentation supported them when they were rebuilding the feeds. Phil Cowans, the CTO of Songkick, estimates that the team saved at least 50% of the time needed to implement change because they had a living documentation system. According to Cowans,

> Because we had such a good coverage and we really trusted the tests [in the living documentation system], we felt very confident making big changes to the infrastructure rapidly. We knew that the functionality wouldn't change, or if it did change, it would be picked up by a test.

The development team at ePlan Services, a pension service provider based in Denver, Colorado, has used Specification by Example since 2003. They build and maintain a financial services application with numerous stakeholders, complex business rules, and complex compliance requirements. Three years after starting the project, a manager with unique knowledge about the legacy parts of the system moved to India. According to Lisa Crispin, a tester working for ePlan Services and author of *Agile Testing: A Practical*

Guide for Testers and Teams (Addison Wesley, 2009), the team worked hard to learn what the manager knew and build it into living documentation. A living documentation system enabled them to capture the specialist's knowledge about their business processes and make it instantly available to all the team members. They eliminated a bottleneck in knowledge transfer, which enabled them to efficiently support and extend the application.

The Central Patient Administration project team at the IHC Group in Oostkamp, Belgium, implemented a living documentation system with similar results. The ongoing project, which started as a rewrite of a legacy mainframe system, began in 2000. Pascal Mestdach, a solution architect on the project, said that the team benefited greatly:

> There were just a few people who knew what some functionality on the legacy system did—that became much clearer now because the team has a growing suite of tests [living documentation] against that functionality and it describes what it does. Also questions can be answered when a specialist is on holiday. It's more clear to other developers what a piece of software is doing. And it is tested.

These examples illustrate how a living documentation system helps delivery teams share knowledge and deal with staff changes. It also enables businesses to react to market changes more efficiently. I explain this in more detail in chapter 3.

Higher product quality

Specification by Example improves collaboration between delivery team members, facilitates better engagement with business users, and provides clear objective targets for delivery—leading to big improvement in product quality.

Two case studies stand out. Wes Williams, an agile coach from Sabre Holdings, and Andrew Jackman, a consultant developer who worked on a project at BNP Paribas, described how projects that had failed several times before succeeded with Specification by Example. The approach described in this book helped their teams conquer the complexity of business domains that were previously unmanageable and ensure high quality of deliveries.

At Sabre Holdings, Wes Williams worked on a two-year airline flight-booking project complicated by global distribution and data-driven processes. The project involved 30 developers working in three teams on two continents. According to Williams, the first two attempts to build the system failed, but the third—which used Specification by Example—succeeded. Williams had this to say:

> ❝ We went live with a large customer [a big airline] with very few issues and had only one severity 1 issue during [business acceptance] testing, related to fail-over. ❞

Williams estimates that Specification by Example was one of the keys to success. In addition to ensuring higher quality, Specification by Example also facilitated trust between developers and testers.

At BNP Paribas, the Sierra project is another great example of how Specification by Example leads to high-quality products. Sierra is a data repository for bonds that consolidates information from several internal systems, rating agencies, and other external sources and distributes it to various systems inside the bank. Various systems and organizations used the same terms with different meanings, which caused a lot of misunderstanding. The first two attempts to implement the system failed, according to Channing Walton, one of the developers on the team that helped make the third attempt a success. The third effort succeeded partially because Specification by Example enabled the team to tackle complexity and ensure a shared understanding. Product quality of the end result was impressive. The project has been live since 2005 "with no major incidents in production," according to Andrew Jackman, a consultant developer on the Sierra project. Most people currently working on the Sierra project were not there when the project started, but the level of quality is still very high.

Similar results were obtained by Bekk Consulting for a branch of a major French bank with a car-leasing system. According to Aslak Hellesøy, a member of the original team and the author of Cucumber, a popular automation tool that supports Specification by Example, they had only five bugs reported in the two years since the system went live, even though the software is now maintained by a completely new team.

Lance Walton worked as a process consultant for a branch of a large Swiss bank in London on a project to develop an order-management system that had failed to start several times before. Walton stated that the project was implemented in an environment where it was assumed that systems required a support team at least as big as the development team. His team used Specification by Example and delivered a system to production nine months after the project started, passed the business acceptance testing in one day, and reported no bugs for six months after that. According to Walton, the new system required no additional support staff, cost less than predicted, and enabled the team to deliver a finished product earlier. In comparison, the team next to them had ten times more people working on support than development. According to Walton,

> ❝ At the moment the team is still releasing every week and the users are always happy with it. From the point of quality, it is superb. ❞

The techniques of Specification by Example work for brownfield as well as greenfield projects. It takes time to build up trusted documentation and clean up legacy systems, but teams see many benefits quickly, including confidence in new deliverables.

A good example is the foreign exchange cash-management system at JP Morgan Chase in London. Martin Jackson, a test automation consultant on the project, said that the business analysts expected the project to be late—instead, it was delivered two weeks early. High product quality enabled them to successfully complete the business-acceptance testing phase in a week instead of four weeks, as originally planned. Jackson said,

> We deployed it and it worked. The business reported back to the board as the best UAT experience they ever had.

Specification by Example also enabled Jackson's team to quickly implement "quite a significant technical change" late in the project development, improving the precision of calculations. Jackson reported:

> All the functionality covered by the FitNesse suite [living documentation] went through the whole of system test, whole of UAT, and live to production without a single defect. There were several errors outside of the core calculation components that were captured during system testing. What made the UAT experience so good for the business was that when calculation errors appeared, we were all pretty certain that the root cause was going to be upstream from the calculation code itself. As a result of the FitNesse suite, it was easier to diagnose the source of defects and hence the cleaner and faster delivery through to production.

The software development team at Weyerhaeuser in Denver, Colorado, writes and maintains several engineering applications and a calculation engine for wooden frames. Before applying Specification by Example, construction engineers were not usually involved in software development, even though the team was dealing with complex scientific calculation formulas and rules. This caused numerous quality issues and delays, and the process was further complicated by the fact that the engine is used by several applications. According to Pierre Veragen, the SQA lead on the project, the hardening phase prior to release would drag on and a release would rarely go out without problems.

After implementing Specification by Example, the team now collaborates on specifications with structural engineers and automates the resulting validations. When a change request comes in, the testers work with structural engineers to capture the expected calculation results and record them as specifications with examples before development begins. The engineer who approves a change later writes the specifications and tests.

Veragen states that the main benefit of the new approach is that they can make changes with confidence. In early 2010, with more than 30,000 checks in their living documentation system, they haven't noticed big bugs in years and have now stopped tracking bugs. According to Veragen:

> We don't need the [bug count] metrics because we know it's not coming back...engineers love the test-first approach and the fact that they have direct access to automated tests.

Lance Walton worked on a credit risk-management application for a branch of a large French bank in London. The project began with external consultants helping the team adopt Extreme Programming (XP) practices, but they did not adopt any of the Specification by Example ideas (although XP includes customer tests, which is closely related to executable specifications). After six months, Walton joined the project and found the quality of the code to be low. Although the team was delivering every two weeks, the code was written in a way that made validation complicated. Developers tested only the most recently implemented features; as the system grew, this approach became inadequate. "When a release happened, people would sit around nervously, making sure that everything was still running and we'd expect a few issues to come up within hours," said Walton. After they implemented Specification by Example, the quality and confidence in the product significantly improved. He added:

> We were pretty confident that we could release without any issues. We got to the point where we would quite happily deploy and go out for lunch without sticking around to see if it was OK.

In contrast, a website-rewrite project at the Trader Media Group in the United Kingdom suffered from quality problems when the team stopped using Specification by Example. Initially, the team was collaborating on specifications and automating the validation. They stopped under management pressure to deliver more functionality earlier and faster. "We noticed that the quality took a nose dive," said Stuart Taylor, the test team leader. "Where before it was quite hard for us [testers] to find defects, later we found that one story could produce four, five defects."

Not only for agile teams

Collaborating on specifications isn't something that only agile teams can benefit from. In *Bridging the Communication Gap*,[†] I suggested that a similar set of practices could be applied to more traditional structured processes. I came across an example of a company that did just that while researching this book.

Matthew Steer, a senior test consultant at the Sopra Group in the UK, helped a major telecommunication company with a third-party offshore software delivery partner implement these practices. The main reason for change was the realization that projects were suffering from poorly defined requirements. Steer compared delivery in the year when ideas were implemented to the costs of delivering software the previous year. Not surprisingly, with a Waterfall approach these projects did not get to a zero-defect level, but the changes "increased upstream defect detection and reduced downstream rework and costs." According to Steer:

> We were able to demonstrate the effectiveness of this approach by catching many more defects earlier in the life cycle that were traditionally found at later phases. The volumes of defects at the end of the life cycle significantly reduced and the pile increased at the early phases of the life cycle.

The end result was a delivery cost savings of over 1.7 million GBP in 2007 alone.

[†] Gojko Adzic, *Bridging the Communication Gap: Specification by Example and Agile Acceptance Testing* (Neuri Limited, 2009).

Less rework

Generally, frequent releases promote quick feedback, enabling development teams to find mistakes and fix them sooner. But iterating quickly doesn't prevent mistakes. Often, teams take three or four stabs at implementing a feature; developers claim this is because customers don't know what they want until they get something to play with. I disagree. With Specification by Example, teams generally hit the target in the first attempt. This saves a lot of time and makes the delivery process more predictable and reliable.

The Sky Network Services (SNS) group at British Sky Broadcasting Corporation in London is responsible for broadband and telephony provisioning software with high business workflow and integration complexity. The group consists of six teams. They have been using Specification by Example for several years. According to Rakesh Patel, a senior agile Java developer there, "We do tend to deliver when we say we do," and the group has a great reputation within Sky. At one time, Patel briefly worked with a different organization; he compared the two teams as follows:

> Every time they [developers in the other organization] give software to testers towards the end of the sprint, testers find something wrong and it always comes back to the developers. But here [at Sky] we don't have that much churn. If we have an issue, we have an issue to make a test go green during development—it either does or it doesn't. We can raise it there and then.

Several other teams noticed a significant reduction of rework, including LeanDog, a group developing an aggregation application for a large insurance provider in the United States. Their application presents a unified user interface on top of a host of mainframe and web-based services and is further complicated by a large number of stakeholders from across the country. Initially, the project suffered from many functional gaps in requirements, according to Rob Park, an agile coach at LeanDog who helped the team with the transition. He said,

> As we started figuring stuff out, we needed clarification, and then we found out that we have to actually do something else.

The team implemented Specification by Example, which resulted in much better specifications and reduced rework. Although developers continue to have questions for business analysts when they start working on a story card, "The questions have dropped considerably, as has the amount of back and forth we have to have and the questions are a lot different," said Park. For him, the most rewarding aspect of Specification by Example is "getting the sense of the story and knowing the extent of the story as you start to build it."

Many teams have also discovered that using Specification by Example to make requirements more precise at the start of a development cycle makes it easier to manage product backlogs. For example, being able to spot stories that are too vague or have too many gaps in required functionality early on prevents problems later. Without Specification by Example, teams often discover problems in the middle of an iteration, which interrupts the flow and requires time-consuming renegotiations—in larger companies, stakeholders who decide on the scope are often not readily available.

Specification by Example helps teams establish a collaborative specification process that reduces the number of problems discovered in the middle of an iteration. Additionally, Specification by Example fits into short iterations and doesn't require months of writing long documents.

Less rework is a major advantage for the Global Talent Management team at Ultimate Software in Weston, Florida. Collaborating on specifications had a significant impact on focusing the development effort. According to Scott Berger, a senior development engineer in test at Ultimate Software:

> Meeting with our product owners to review our test scenarios prior to the team accepting a story readily allows the working group (product owner, developer, tester) to clarify ambiguous or missing requirements. On occasion, the outcome of the meeting has even resulted in the cancellation of stories, for example, when test scenarios reveal hidden complexity or conflicting requirements within the system. After one such discussion, the decision was made to nearly redesign an entire feature! Product owners are afforded the opportunity to rewrite and reslice the specifications, as opposed to having the development effort begin and halt or cancel the story midstream. By holding these meetings, we find ourselves being both more productive and efficient, because waste is reduced and vague and missing specifications are minimized. It also allows the team to come to a common understanding of what is expected.

Most teams have significantly reduced or completely eliminated rework that occurred as a result of misunderstood requirements or neglected customer expectations. The practices described in this book allowed teams to engage better with their business users and ensure a shared understanding of results.

Better work alignment

Another important benefit of Specification by Example is the capacity to align different software development activities into short iterative cycles. From my experience and according to the case studies in this book, one of the most common stumbling points for teams moving to Scrum is the inability to fully complete tasks inside an iteration. Many teams hold onto the "old world" concepts: finish development first, then finish testing, and, finally, polish the product enough for it to be deployable. This fosters the illusion that development is completed in stages, when in fact subsequent testing and fixing are required for completion. One "done" column on the Scrum board means a developer thinks something is finished, a "done-done" column means the tester agrees, and so on (there are even reports of "done-done-done" columns). Work often falls into this pattern, and the results from testing affect the next cycle, causing much variability and making the delivery process less predictable.

Specification by Example resolves this issue. The practices described in this book enable teams to clearly define a target that's universally understood and objectively measured. As a result, many teams find that their analysis, development, and testing activities became better aligned.

A good example of improved alignment occurred at uSwitch, one of the busiest websites in the United Kingdom. uSwitch implemented Specification by Example in 2008 because they had difficulty knowing when a feature was completed. "We'd finish something, give it over to the QA department, and they would immediately say to us that we forgot to test it in a certain scenario. This caused a lot of problems for us," said Stephen Lloyd, a developer who works on the website. By implementing Specification by Example, they overcame that problem. Lloyd said that they're now better integrated as a team and have a better understanding of the needs of the business. The process changes also resulted in improved software quality. Hemal Kuntawala, another developer working on the site, had this comment:

> Our error rates have dropped significantly, across the site. The turnaround of fixing problems is much quicker than it was previously. If a problem does occur on the live site, we can normally get a fix out within a few hours, where previously it took days or weeks to get something fixed.

The team at Beazley, a specialist insurance company, also experienced improved alignment. Their business analysts work from the United States with developers and testers in the United Kingdom. They implemented Specification by Example primarily to ensure that software is finished when an iteration ends. Ian Cooper, a development team leader at Beazley, said:

> We've always done unit testing but the problem was that there was a gap around these tests telling us if the software works, not if it does what the customer wanted. We didn't even use to have testers testing in the same cycle. They were feeding back the information from the previous iteration into the current iteration. That's gone now. We have a much clearer idea of acceptance.

The team working from New Zealand on AdScale.de, a marketplace for online advertising, had similar experiences. Two years after the project started, increasing complexity of the user interface and system integrations made the code base too large to be effectively managed just with unit testing. Developers would think that something was done, move on, and then have to redo the work after the testers' review. Because of the disconnect between testers and developers, it took a long time to find problems. Issues from previous iterations were affecting future ones, disrupting the flow of development. After implementing Specification by Example, development and testing were more closely aligned. Clare McLennan, a developer/tester working on the project, declared:

> It took a lot of pressure from the release process—because the feedback is instantaneous. Previously, developers would be frustrated at us because their features hadn't gone out. At the same time we were frus-

trated at them because they haven't fixed the thing so we couldn't test their features. We were waiting for them and they were waiting for us. That's gone now because it only takes an hour to do all the testing. The features aren't coming back into the next iteration. ❞

Specification by Example allows teams to define expected functionality in a clear, objective, and measurable way. It also speeds up feedback, improving the development flow and preventing interruptions to planned work.

Remember

- Building the product right and building the right product are two different things. You need to do both in order to succeed.

- Specification by Example provides just enough documentation at the right time, helping to build the right product with short iterations or flow-based development processes.

- Specification by Example helps to improve the quality of software products, significantly reduces rework, and enables teams to better align analysis, development, and testing activities.

- In the long term, Specification by Example helps teams create a living documentation system, a relevant and reliable description of the functionality that's automatically updated with the programming language code.

- The practices of Specification by Example work best with short iterative (Scrum, Extreme Programming [XP]) or flow-based (Kanban) development methods. Some ideas are also applicable to structured development (Rational Unified Process, Waterfall) processes, and there have been cases where companies saved millions as a result.

2

Key process patterns

Specification by Example is a set of process patterns that facilitate change in software products to ensure the right product is delivered effectively. The key patterns that are commonly shared by the most successful teams that I interviewed in researching this book, along with their relationships, are shown in figure 2.1. Most of the teams implemented new process ideas by trial and error during their search for ways to build and maintain software more efficiently. By revealing the patterns in their processes, I hope to help others implement these ideas deliberately.

Why patterns?

The process ideas presented in this book make up patterns in the sense that they are recurring elements used by different teams; I am not referring to Christopher Alexander's pattern definitions. Process ideas that I have cited occur in several different contexts and produce similar results. I haven't documented the forces and changes expected in more traditional pattern books. Due in part to the case studies in this book, the Agile Alliance Functional Testing Tools group organized several pattern-writing workshops to document and build a catalog of patterns in a more traditional sense, but this work will take some time to complete. I've decided to leave expanding the patterns into a more traditional format for future editions of this book.

In *Bridging the Communication Gap*, I focused mostly on the tangible outputs of Specification by Example, such as specifications and acceptance tests. I neglected to consider that teams in various contexts might need radically different approaches to produce the same artifacts. In this book, I focus on process patterns, how artifacts are created, and how they contribute to later artifacts in the flow.

Just-in-time

Successful teams don't implement the entire sequence at one time or for all the specifications, as shown in figure 2.1—especially not before development starts. Instead, teams derive the scope from goals once a team is ready for more work, for example, at the beginning of a project phase or a milestone. They proceed with specifications only when the team is ready to start implementing an item, such as at the start of the relevant iteration. Don't mistake the sequence in figure 2.1 for big Waterfall specifications.

Key process patterns of Specification by Example

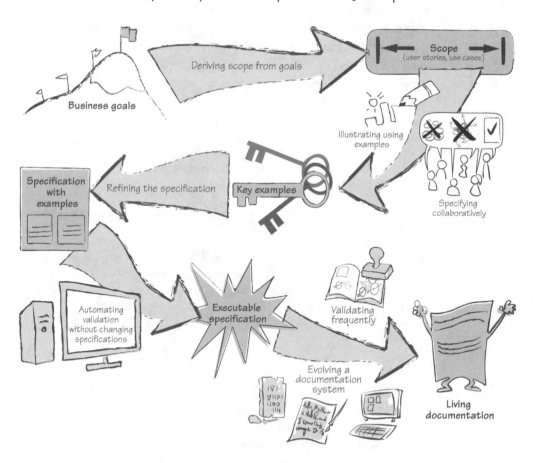

Figure 2.1 The key process patterns of Specification by Example

In this chapter, I present a brief overview of the key process patterns. Then we'll go over the key challenges and ideas for implementing each of these patterns in different contexts in part 2.

Deriving scope from goals

Implementation scope offers a solution to a business problem or a means to reach a business goal. Many teams expect a customer, a product owner, or a business user to decide on the scope of work before the implementation starts (everything that occurs before the implementation is often ignored by the software development team). After business users specify exactly what they want, software delivery teams implement it. This is supposedly what will make the customers happy. In fact, this is when issues with building the right product begin.

By relying on customers to give them a list of user stories, use cases, or other relevant information, software delivery teams are asking their customers to design a solution. But business users aren't software designers. If the customers define the scope, the project doesn't benefit from the knowledge of the people in the delivery team. This results in software that does what the customer asked but not what they really wanted.

Instead of blindly accepting software requirements as a solution to an unknown problem, successful teams *derive scope from goals*. They begin with a customer's business goal. Then they collaborate to define the scope that will achieve that goal. The team works with the business users to determine the solution. The business users focus on communicating the intent of the desired feature and the value they expect to get out of it. This helps everyone understand what's needed. The team can then suggest a solution that's cheaper, faster, and easier to deliver or maintain than what the business users would come up with on their own.[1]

Specifying collaboratively

If developers and testers aren't engaged in designing specifications, those specifications have to be separately communicated to the team. In practice, this leaves many opportunities for misunderstanding; details can get lost in translation. As a consequence, business users have to validate the software after delivery, and teams have to go back and make changes if it fails validation. This is all unnecessary rework.

Instead of relying on a single person to get the specifications right in isolation, successful delivery teams collaborate with the business users to specify the solution. People coming from different backgrounds have different ideas and use their own experienced-based techniques to solve problems. Technical experts know how to make better use

---

[1] For some good examples, see http://gojko.net/2009/12/10/challenging-requirements

of the underlying infrastructure or how emerging technologies can be applied. Testers know where to look for potential issues, and the team should work to prevent those issues. All this information needs to be captured when designing specifications.

Specifying collaboratively enables us to harness the knowledge and experience of the whole team. It also creates a collective ownership of specifications, making everyone more engaged in the delivery process.

Illustrating using examples

Natural language is ambiguous and context dependent. Requirements written in such language alone can't provide a full and unambiguous context for development or testing. Developers and testers have to interpret requirements to produce software and test scripts, and different people might interpret tricky concepts differently.

This is especially problematic when something that seems obvious actually requires domain expertise or knowledge of jargon to be fully understood. Small differences in understanding have a cumulative effect, often leading to problems that require rework after delivery. This causes unnecessary delays.

Instead of waiting for specifications to be expressed precisely for the first time in a programming language during implementation, successful teams *illustrate specifications using examples.* The team works with the business users to identify *key examples* that describe the expected functionality. During this process, developers and testers often suggest additional examples that illustrate edge cases or address areas of the system that are particularly problematic. This flushes out functional gaps and inconsistencies and ensures that everyone involved has a *shared understanding* of what needs to be delivered, avoiding rework that results from misinterpretation and translation.

If the system works correctly for all the key examples, then it meets the specification that everyone agreed on. Key examples effectively define what the software needs to do. They're both the target for development and an objective evaluation criterion to check to see whether the development is done.

If the key examples are easy to understand and communicate, they can be effectively used as unambiguous and detailed requirements.

Refining the specification

An open discussion during collaboration builds a shared understanding of the domain, but resulting examples often feature more detail than is necessary. For example, business users think about the user-interface perspective, so they offer examples of how something should work when clicking links and filling in fields. Such verbose descriptions constrain the system; detailing how something should be done rather than what is required is wasteful. Surplus details make the examples harder to communicate and understand.

Key examples must be concise to be useful. By *refining the specification,* successful teams remove extraneous information and create a concrete and precise context for development and testing. They define the target with the right amount of detail to implement and verify it. They identify what the software is supposed to do, not how it does it.

Refined examples can be used as acceptance criteria for delivery; development isn't done until the system works correctly for all examples. After providing additional information to make key examples easier to understand, teams create specifications with examples, which is a specification of work, an acceptance test, and a future functional regression test.

Automating validation without changing specifications

Once a team agrees on specifications with examples and refines them, the team can use them as a target for implementation and a means to validate the product. The system will be validated many times with these tests during development to ensure that it meets the target. Running these checks manually would introduce unnecessary delays, and the feedback would be slow.

Quick feedback is an essential part of developing software in short iterations or in flow mode, so we need to make the process of validating the system cheap and efficient. An obvious solution is automation. But this automation is conceptually different from the usual developer or tester automation.

If we automate the validation of the key examples using traditional programming (unit) automation tools or traditional functional-test automation tools, we risk introducing problems if details get lost between the business specification and technical automation. Technically automated specifications will become inaccessible to business users. When the requirements change (and that's *when,* not *if*) or when developers or testers need further clarification, we won't be able to use the specification we previously automated. We could keep the key examples both as tests and in a more readable form, such as Word documents or web pages, but as soon as there's more than one version of the truth, we'll have synchronization issues. That's why paper documentation is never ideal.

To get the most out of key examples, successful teams automate validation without changing the information. They literally keep everything in the specification the same during automation—there's no risk of mistranslation. As they *automate validation without changing specifications,* the key examples look nearly the same as they did on a whiteboard: comprehensible and accessible to all team members.

An automated Specification with Examples that is comprehensible and accessible to all team members becomes an *executable specification.* We can use it as a target for development and easily check if the system does what was agreed on, and we can use that same document to get clarification from business users. If we need to change the specification, we have to do so in only one place.

If you've never seen a tool for automating executable specifications, this might seem unbelievable, but look at figure 2.2 and figure 2.3. They show executable specifications fully automated with two popular tools, Concordion and FitNesse.

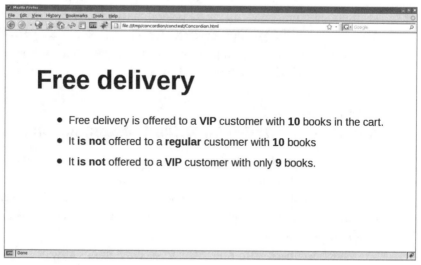

Figure 2.2 An executable specification automated with Concordion

The prize pool is divided among the winners using the following distribution for winning combinations (number of correct hits out of six chosen numbers). Example below is for $2M payout pool.

Prize Distribution for Payout Pool	2,000,000	
Winning Combination	Pool Percentage?	Prize Pool?
6	68	1,360,000
5	10	200,000
4	10	200,000
3	12	240,000

Figure 2.3 An executable specification automated with FitNesse

Many other automation frameworks don't require any translation of key examples. This book focuses on the practices used by successful teams to implement Specification by Example rather than tools. To learn more about the tools, visit http://specificationby example.com, where you will be able to download articles explaining the most popular tools. See also the "Tools" section in the appendix for a list of suggested resources.

Tests are specifications; specifications are tests

When a specification is described with very concrete examples, it can be used to test the system. After such specification is automated, it becomes an executable acceptance test. Because I write about only these types of specifications and tests in this book, I'll use the words *specifications* and *tests* interchangeably; for the purposes of this book, there's no difference between them.

This doesn't mean there aren't other kinds of tests—for example, exploratory tests or usability tests are not specifications. The context-driven testing community tries to distinguish between these classes of tests by using the name checks for deterministic validations that can be automated and tests for non-deterministic validations that require human opinion and expert insight.[†] In the context-driven language, this book addresses only designing and automating checks. With Specification by Example, testers use expert opinion and insight to design good checks in collaboration with other members of the team. Testers don't execute these checks manually, which means they have more time for other kinds of tests.

[†] See www.developsense.com/blog/2009/08/testing-vs-checking

---

Validating frequently

In order to efficiently support a software system, we have to know what it does and why. In many cases, the only way to do this is to drill down into programming code or find someone who can do that for us. Code is often the only thing we can really trust; most written documentation is outdated before the project is delivered. Programmers are oracles of knowledge and bottlenecks of information.

Executable specifications can easily be validated against the system. If this validation is frequent, then we can have as much confidence in the executable specifications as we have in the code.

By checking all executable specifications frequently, teams I talked to quickly discover any differences between the system and the specifications. Because executable specifications are easy to understand, the teams can discuss the changes with their business users and decide how to address the problems. They constantly synchronize their systems and executable specifications.

Evolving a documentation system

The most successful teams aren't satisfied with a set of frequently validated executable specifications. They ensure that specifications are well organized, easy to find and access, and consistent. As their projects evolve, the teams' understanding of the domain changes. Market opportunities also cause changes to the business domain models. The teams that get the most out of Specification by Example update their specifications to reflect those changes, evolving a living documentation system.

Living documentation is a reliable and authoritative source of information on system functionality that anyone can access. It's as reliable as the code but much easier to read and understand. Support staff can use it to find out what the system does and why. Developers can use it as a target for development. Testers can use it for testing. Business analysts can use it as a starting point when analyzing the impact of a requested change of functionality. It also provides free regression testing.

A practical example

In the rest of this book, I'll focus on process patterns rather than artifacts of the process. To put things into perspective and ensure that you understand these terms, I've included an example of artifacts produced during the entire process, from business goals to the living documentation system. The discussion of the example indicates the chapters in which I'll discuss each part of the process.

Business goal

A business goal is the underlying reason for a project or project milestone. It's the guiding vision that got the business stakeholders, internal or external, to decide to invest money in software development. Commercial organizations should be able to clearly see how such goals can either earn, save, or protect money. A good start for a business goal could be "Increase repeat sales to existing customers." Ideally, a goal should be measurable, so it can guide the implementation. The right software scopes for "Increase repeat sales to existing customers by 10% over the next 12 months" and "Increase repeat sales to existing customers by 500% over the next 3 months" are most likely very different. A measurable goal makes it possible to ascertain whether the project succeeded, to track progress, and to prioritize better.

An example of a good business goal

Increase repeat sales to existing customers by 50% over the next 12 months.

Scope

By applying the practices that I'll describe in chapter 5, we derive the implementation scope from the business goals. The implementation team and the business sponsors come up with ideas that can be broken down into deliverable software chunks.

Let's say we identify a theme for a customer loyalty program that can be broken down into basic loyalty system features and more advanced bonus schemes. We decide to focus on building a basic loyalty system first: customers will register for a VIP program, and VIP customers will be eligible for free delivery on certain items. We'll postpone any discussion on advanced bonus schemes for later. Here's the scope for this example:

User stories for a basic loyalty system

- In order to be able to do direct marketing of products to existing customers, as a marketing manager I want customers to register personal details by joining a VIP program.

- In order to entice existing customers to register for the VIP program, as a marketing manager I want the system to offer free delivery on certain items to VIP customers.

- In order to save money, as an existing customer I want to receive information on available special offers.

Key examples

By applying the practices described in chapters 6 and 7, we produce detailed specifications for the appropriate scope once our team starts implementing a particular function. For example, when we start working on the second item of the scope—free delivery— free delivery must be defined. During collaboration, we decide that the system will offer free delivery on books only, to avoid logistical problems related to shipping electronics and large items. Because the business goal is to promote repeat sales, we try to get customers to buy several items; "free delivery" becomes "free delivery for five or more books." We identify key examples, such as a VIP customer buying five books, a VIP customer buying fewer than five books, or a non-VIP customer buying books.

This leads to a discussion about what to do with customers who purchase both books and electronics. Some suggestions relate to expanding the scope: for example, splitting the order in two and offering free delivery for the books only. We decide to postpone this option and implement the simplest thing first. We won't offer free delivery if there is anything other than books in the order. We add another key example to the current set, to be revisited later:

Key Examples: Free delivery

- VIP customer with five books in the cart gets free delivery.
- VIP customer with four books in the cart doesn't get free delivery.
- Regular customer with five books in the cart doesn't get free delivery.
- VIP customer with five washing machines in the cart doesn't get free delivery.
- VIP customer with five books and a washing machine in the cart doesn't get free delivery.

Specification with examples

By applying the practices from chapter 8, we refine the specification from the key examples and create a document that's self-explanatory and formatted in a way that will make it easy to automate the validation later (as shown below):

Free delivery

- Free delivery is offered to VIP customers once they purchase a certain number of books. Free delivery is not offered to regular customers or VIP customers buying anything other than books.
- Given that the minimum number of books to get free delivery is five, then we expect the following:

Examples

Customer type	Cart contents	Delivery
VIP	5 books	Free, Standard
VIP	4 books	Standard
Regular	10 books	Standard
VIP	5 washing machines	Standard
VIP	5 books, 1 washing machine	Standard

This specification—a self-explanatory document—can be used as a target for implementation and as a driver for an automated test so we can objectively measure when the implementation is done. It's stored in a repository of specifications, to become part of the living documentation. An example would be a FitNesse wiki page or a Cucumber feature file.

Executable specification

When our developers start working on the feature described in the specification, the test based on this specification will initially fail because it's not yet automated and the feature isn't yet implemented.

The developers will implement the relevant feature and connect it to the automation framework. They'll use an automation framework which pulls the inputs from the specification and validates the expected outputs without requiring them to actually change the specification document. The ideas and practices in chapter 9 will help automate the specification efficiently. Once the validation is automated, the specification becomes executable.

Living documentation

All the specifications for all implemented features will be validated frequently, most likely by an automated build process. This helps to prevent functional regression issues while ensuring that specifications stay current. The team will use the practices from chapter 10 so that frequent validation goes smoothly.

When the entire user story is implemented, someone will first validate that it's done and then restructure the specifications so that they fit in with the existing specifications for features that were already implemented. They'll use the practices from chapter 11 to evolve a documentation system from the specifications in increments. For example, they might move the specification for free delivery into the hierarchy of features related to delivery, potentially merging them with other free-delivery examples triggered by different factors. In order to make the documentation easier to access, they might set up links between the specification for free delivery and the specifications for other delivery types.

Then the cycle starts again. Once we need to revisit the rules for free delivery—for example, when working on the advanced bonus schemes or in order to extend the functionality to split orders with books from orders with other items—we'll be able to use the living documentation to understand the existing functionality and specify changes. We can use the existing examples to make specifying collaboratively and illustrating using examples more effective. We'll then produce another set of key examples, which will lead to an increment of the specification for free delivery that will ultimately be merged with the rest of the specifications. And the cycle will repeat.

Now that we have had a quick overview of key process patterns, we'll take a closer look at living documentation in chapter 3. In chapter 4, I present ideas on how to start adopting Specification by Example, followed by ideas on implementing individual process patterns in part 2.

Remember

- The key process patterns of Specification by Example are deriving scope from goals, specifying collaboratively, illustrating specifications using examples, refining the specifications, automating validation without changing the specifications, validating the system frequently, and evolving living documentation.

- With Specification by Example, functional requirements, specifications, and acceptance tests are the same thing.

- The result is a living documentation system that explains what the system does and that is as relevant and reliable as the programming language code but much easier to understand.

- Teams in different contexts use different practices to implement process patterns.

3

Living documentation

There are two popular models today for looking at the process and artifacts of Specification by Example: the acceptance-testing-centric model and the system-behavior-specification model.

The acceptance-testing-centric model (often called acceptance test-driven development, ATDD, or A-TDD) focuses on the automated tests that are part of the Specification by Example process. In this model, the key benefits are clearer targets for development and preventing functional regression.

The system-behavior-specification-centric model (often called behavior-driven development or BDD) focuses on the process of specifying scenarios of system behavior. It centers on building shared understanding between stakeholders and delivery teams through collaboration and clarification of specifications. Preventing functional regression through test automation is also considered important.

I don't consider one of these models superior to the other; different models are useful for different purposes. The acceptance-testing-centric model is more useful for initial adoption if a team has many functional quality issues. When things are running smoothly, the behavior-specification-centric model is useful for explaining the activities of short-term and mid-term software delivery.

Preventing functional regression through test automation is the key long-term benefit of Specification by Example in both models. Although regression testing is certainly important, I don't think that's where the long-term benefits come from. First, Specification by Example isn't the only way to prevent functional regression. The team at uSwitch, for example, disables many tests after implementing the related functionality for the first time (more on this in chapter 12); they still maintain a high level of quality. Second, Capers Jones, in *Estimating Software Costs*, points out that the average defect-removal efficiency of regression testing is only 23%.[1] That can't justify the long-term investment made by successful teams to implement Specification by Example.

---

[1] See Capers Jones, *Estimating Software Costs: Bringing Realism to Estimating* (McGraw-Hill Companies, 2007), 509. Also see http://gojko.net/2011/03/03/simulating-your-way-out-of-regression-testing

While researching this book, I had the privilege of interviewing teams that had used Specification by Example for five years or more. Their experiences, especially those in recent years, helped me see things from a different perspective—a documentation-centric one. Many of the teams I interviewed realized that the artifacts of Specification by Example are valuable as documentation over the long term. Most discovered this after years of experimenting with ways to define specifications and tests. One of my main goals as author of this book is to present living documentation as a first-class artifact of Specification by Example. This should help readers implement a living documentation system quickly and deliberately, without years of trial and error.

In this chapter, I'll cover the documentation-centric model and its benefits. This model focuses on business-process documentation and ensures effective long-term maintenance and support of business processes. This model is particularly useful for ensuring the long-term benefits of Specification by Example. It also prevents many common test maintenance implementation problems (more on this later in the chapter).

Why we need authoritative documentation

I've lost count of the number of times someone has given me a lengthy book about a system and included a warning that it's not entirely correct. Like cheap wine, long paper documentation ages rapidly and leaves you with a bad headache if you try to use it a year after it was created. On the other hand, maintaining a system without any documentation also causes headaches.

We need to know what a system does to be able to analyze the impacts of suggested changes, support it, and troubleshoot. Often, the only way to find out what the system does is to look at the programming language source code and reverse-engineer the business functionality. When I interviewed Christian Hassa, owner of TechTalk, for this book, he called the process of digging out functionality from the code "system archeology." He explains a situation that will no doubt be familiar to most readers:

> We had a project where we needed to replace a legacy system. None of the stakeholders knew how certain calculations/reports were created. The users just consumed the result and trusted the old system blindly. It was horrible to reverse-engineer the requirements from the old application, and of course it turned out that some things the old system did were wrong.

Even when the undocumented code is correct, reverse engineering is an impossible task for business users, testers, support engineers, and, on most projects, even the average developer. Clearly this approach doesn't work. We need something better.

Good documentation is useful for more than software development. Many companies could benefit greatly from having good documentation about their business processes, especially as more and more businesses are becoming technology-driven. Business-process documentation is as hard to write and as costly to maintain as any kind of system documentation.

The ideal solution would be a documentation system that's easy and cheap to maintain, so that it can be kept consistent with the system functionality even if the underlying programming language code is changed frequently. The problem with any kind of comprehensive documentation is, in fact, costly maintenance. From my experience, changing the parts that are outdated doesn't contribute significantly to cost. Often, cost is the result of time spent on finding what needs to be changed.

Tests can be good documentation

Automated tests suffer from the opposite problem. It's easy to find all the places that need to be updated; automated tests can be frequently executed, and any tests that fail are obviously no longer in sync with the underlying code. But unless the tests are designed so they're easy to modify, updating them after a system change can take a lot of time. One of the pitfalls of the acceptance-test-centric approach is that it neglects this effect.

Teams that focus on tests and testing often neglect to write tests that will be easy to maintain. Over time, problems lead these teams to look for ways to specify and automate tests so they will be easier to update. Once the tests become easy to maintain, the teams start seeing many other long-term benefits from Specification by Example. Adam Knight's team at RainStor, a UK-based provider of online data-retention solutions, realized that if tests reveal the underlying purpose, they can be easily maintained. He says:

> As you develop a harness of automated tests, those can become your documentation if you set them up properly to reveal the purpose behind them. We produced HTML reports that listed tests that were run and their purpose. Investigation of any regression failures was much easier. You could resolve conflicts more easily because you could understand the purpose without going back to other documentation.

For me, the most important point is in the last sentence: they don't have to use any other kind of documentation once the tests are clear.

Lisa Crispin of ePlan Services said that one of the biggest ah-ha moments for her was when she understood how valuable the tests were as documentation:

> We get this loan payment and the amount of interest we applied isn't correct. We think there is a bug. I can look at the FitNesse test and put in the values. Maybe the requirements were wrong, but here's what the code is doing. That saves so much time.

Andrew Jackman said that the Sierra team uses test results as a knowledge base for support:

> Business analysts see the advantage of this all the time. When someone asks where some data in Sierra comes from, they often just send the link to a test result—and it is reasonable documentation. We don't have specifications in Word documents.

I mentioned that the team at the Iowa Student Loan Liquidity Corporation used their tests to estimate the impact of a business model change and guide the implementation. The team at SongKick used their tests to guide the implementation of a system change and saved an estimated 50% of the time required as a result. I heard similar stories from many other teams.

When a team uses a piece of information to guide development, support the system, or estimate the impact of business changes, it's misleading to call that information a "test." Tests aren't used to support and evolve our systems; documentation is.

Creating documentation from executable specifications

When a software system is continuously validated against a set of executable specifications, a team can be certain that the system will do what the specifications say—or, to put it differently, that the specifications will continue to describe what the system does. Those specifications live with the system, and they're always consistent. Because we find out about any differences between specifications and the underlying system functionality right away, they can be kept consistent—at a low cost. Tim Andersen of Iowa Student Loan said that he trusts only this kind of documentation:

> If I cannot have the documentation in an automated fashion, I don't trust it. It's not exercised.

Executable specifications create a body of documentation, an authoritative source of information on the functionality of a system that doesn't suffer from the "not entirely correct" problem and that's relatively cheap to maintain. If specifications with examples were pages, the living documentation system would be the book.

A living documentation replaces all the artifacts that teams need for delivering the right product; it can even support the production of external user manuals (although probably not replace them). It does that in a way that fits nicely with short iterative or flow processes. Because we can define the specifications as we grow the underlying software system, the resulting documentation will be incremental and cheap to write. We can build business-process documentation at the same time as the supporting systems and use that documentation to evolve the software and help run the business. The world doesn't have to stop for six months while someone is compiling 500 pages of material. André Brissette from Pyxis says this is one of the least-understood parts of agile development:

> Beginners think that there is no documentation in agile, which is not true. It's about choosing the types of documentation that are useful. For people who are afraid that there is no documentation, this kind of test is a good opportunity to secure themselves and see that there is still documentation in an agile process, and that's not a two-feet-high pile of paper. This is something lighter, but bound to the real code. When you ask, "does your system have this feature?" you don't have a Word document that claims that something is done; you have something executable that proves that the system really does what you want. That's real documentation.

Most automation tools used for Specification by Example already support managing specifications over websites or exporting test results in HTML or PDF form, which is a good start for creating a documentation system. I expect there will be a lot of innovation in the tools over the next several years to assist with building up documentation from specifications with examples. One interesting project is Relish,[2] which imports specifications with examples from several automation tools and formats them to create a documentation system that's easy to use. See figure 3.1.

---

[2] See www.relishapp.com

Figure 3.1 Relish builds documentation websites from executable specifications.

Benefits of the documentation-centric model

The documentation-centric model of Specification by Example should help teams avoid the most common issues with long-term maintenance of executable specifications. It should also help teams create useful documentation that will facilitate software evolution over time and help to avoid maintenance problems caused by a lack of shared knowledge.

Many teams I interviewed replaced the heart of their system or rewrote large parts of it while keeping specifications with examples and using them to guide the whole effort. This is where the investment in living documentation really pays off. Instead of spending months on system archeology and verifications, a living documentation system already provides requirements for technical updates and changes.

I think teams should consider living documentation as a separate artifact that's as important as the system they're delivering. The idea that the documentation is a key deliverable is at the core of the documentation-centric model. I expect this model resolves most of the common problems that, over time, cause teams to fail with Specification by Example. Although it hasn't been proven by any of the case studies in this book, I consider this premise important for the future. I hope that the readers of this book will be able to get great results easier and faster because of looking at the process from this different perspective.

For example, understanding that living documentation is an important artifact instantly determines whether to put the acceptance tests in a version-control system. A focus on business-process documentation avoids overly technical specifications and keeps the specifications focused on what the system is supposed to do from a business perspective, not on test scripting. Cleaning up test code no longer requires a separate explanation. Enhancing the structure or clarity of tests is no longer something to put on the technical debt list: It's part of the standard list of tasks for delivery. The flaw in delegating the work on acceptance tests to junior developers and testers suddenly becomes obvious. The fact that useful documentation has to be well organized should prevent teams from piling up thousands of incomprehensible tests in a single directory.

By considering the living documentation a separate artifact of the delivery process, teams can also avoid overinvesting in it. They can discuss up front how much time they want to spend building the living documentation system and avoid falling into the trap of gold-plating the tests at the expense of the primary product.

I suspect that keeping specifications too abstract might be a potential pitfall of the documentation model. I expect this model to work better for software systems that are built to automate complex business processes. User-interface centric projects where the complexity isn't in the underlying processes might not benefit as much.

Remember

- There are several models of looking at Specification by Example. Different models are useful for different purposes.

- Specification by Example allows you to build up a good documentation system incrementally.

- Living documentation is an important artifact of the delivery process, as vital as code.

- Focusing on creating a business-process documentation system should help you avoid the most common long-term maintenance problems with specifications and tests.

4

Initiating the changes

Many ideas central to Specification by Example have been around for decades. In the late 80s, Gerald Weinberg and Donald Gause wrote about communication problems with software requirements in *Exploring Requirements: Quality Before Design.*[1] The authors suggested that the best way to check for completeness and consistency of requirements is to design black-box tests against them—effectively suggesting the duality of specifications and tests in Specification by Example. In 1986, the German army used what later became the V Model to describe ways to build acceptance tests before implementation for validation. Today, we use the same method but refer to acceptance tests as specifications with examples. Ward Cunningham applied the practices of illustrating using examples and automating validation without changing specifications on the WyCASH+ project in 1989.[2]

Unfortunately, these ideas didn't catch on at the time. Long development phases made them impractical to execute. People spent months trying to write abstract requirements for projects that would last years. Detailing everything upfront with examples would delay that even longer.

Agile development changed the way the industry thinks about software delivery phases—and shortened these phases significantly. This made Specification by Example feasible. Iteration and flow-based projects can benefit greatly from Specification by Example. With so little time to complete a delivery phase, we need to eliminate as much unnecessary work as possible. Common problems that require fixing are rework, duplicated tasks caused by miscommunication, time wasted working back from code in order to understand the system, and time spent repeatedly executing the same tests manually.

---

[1] Gerald M. Weinberg and Donald C. Gause, *Exploring Requirements: Quality Before Design* (Dorset House Publishing Company, 1989).
[2] http://fit.c2.com/wiki.cgi?FrameworkHistory

Effective delivery with short iterations or in constant flow requires removing as many expected obstacles as possible so that unexpected issues can be addressed. Adam Geras puts this more eloquently: "Quality is about being prepared for the usual so you have time to tackle the unusual."

Specification by Example is the solution: a means for dealing with the usual so that we have more time to deal with the unusual within the few days or weeks of a software delivery cycle.

In this chapter, we'll look at how to begin changing process and team culture so you can implement Specification by Example. We'll review three team case studies that represent different ways to integrate collaboration on specifications into iterations and flow development. Finally, I present useful ideas for fitting this process into development environments that require sign-off and traceability on requirements.

How to begin changing the process

Starting a process change is never easy, especially if you're trying to fundamentally change how team members collaborate. To get over the initial resistance and build a case for further changes, most teams started by implementing a practice that improved product quality or saved time over the short term. The most common starting points were these:

- If there's already a process change going on, use it to implement key ideas of Specification by Example.

- Use the ideas of Specification by Example as inspiration for improving product quality.

- Implement functional test automation, for teams that don't have automated functional tests.

- Introduce automated executable specifications, for teams that have test automation separate from development.

- Use test-driven development (TDD) as a stepping-stone, for teams that practice it.

All of these starting points will produce benefits in the short term and lead to further improvements.

Implement Specification by Example as part of a wider process change
When: On greenfield projects

Four teams I interviewed implemented the core ideas of Specification by Example when moving to an agile software development process. There was no need to fight resistance to process changes or obtain management support.

 Implementing Scrum, XP, or any other agile process is a shock therapy anyway, so if you can, you might as well try to implement Specification by Example at the same time.

Teams that were able to do this reported fewer problems and implemented the process more quickly than teams that started from a dysfunctional Scrum environment. This is most likely because all four of these teams had significant support as part of their agile migration (three had consultants on site, and the fourth had a team member with prior exposure to Specification by Example).

Focus on improving quality

Instead of focusing on a particular target process, the team at uSwitch (see chapter 12) decided to focus on improving product quality. They asked all members to present suggestions for improvement and used these as inspiration. They ended up implementing most of the process patterns of Specification by Example with little resistance.

From a management perspective, this is a particularly good approach if individuals on the team are likely to resist a process change. People might complain against Scrum, agile, Specification by Example, Kanban, or anything else that's process related. An open initiative to improve quality is less likely to cause complaints. David Anderson advocates focusing on quality in Kanban[3] as the first step of his recipe for success.

 Start by identifying the biggest obstacle to delivering high-quality software; then solve it.

If developers and testers aren't working closely together and have a difference of opinion about whether something is of acceptable quality, it might be useful to visualize activities

---

[3] David Anderson, *Kanban: Successful Evolutionary Change for Your Technology Business* (Blue Hole Press, 2010).

related to releasing a product. At LMAX, an electronic trading exchange, Jodie Parker made all the release activities visible by creating a release candidate board, which showed a high-level view of the three teams' progress. It featured the status of all the planned deliverables, the main focus of the release, a set of tasks that would have to be done before a release, and critical issues that would have to be addressed before a release. All the teams could see this information and then come up with suggestions for improving delivery flow.

Start with functional test automation
When: Applying to an existing project

The majority of teams I interviewed adopted Specification by Example by starting with functional test automation and then gradually moving from testing after development to using executable specifications to guide development. That seems to be the path of least resistance for projects that already have a lot of code and that require testers to run their verifications manually.

Several teams sought to solve the problem of bottlenecks at the testing phase, a result of testers having to constantly catch up with development. With short delivery cycles (weeks or even days), extensive manual testing is impossible. Testing then piles up at the end of one iteration and spills over into the next, disrupting flow. Functional test automation removes the bottleneck and engages testers with developers, motivating them to participate in the process change. Markus Gärtner says:

> For a tester who comes from "testing is the bottleneck" and continuous fighting against development changes, it was very, very, very appealing to provide valuable feedback even before a bug was fixed with automated tests. This is a motivating vision to work toward.

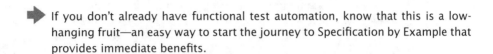

If you don't already have functional test automation, know that this is a low-hanging fruit—an easy way to start the journey to Specification by Example that provides immediate benefits.

Automating functional tests works well as a first phase of adoption of Specification by Example, for several reasons:

- It brings immediate benefit. With automated tests, the length of the testing phase is significantly reduced, as is the number of issues escaping to production.
- Effective test automation requires a collaboration of developers and testers and starts to break down the divide between these two groups.

- Legacy products rarely have a design that supports easy testing. Starting with functional test automation forces the team to address this and make the architecture more testable, as well as sort out any issues around test reliability and test environments. This prepares the ground for automating executable specifications later.

- When most testing is manual and the team works in short cycles, testers are often a bottleneck in the process. This makes it virtually impossible for them to engage in anything else. Test automation gives them time to participate in specification workshops and start looking at other activities, such as exploratory testing.

- Initial test automation enables the team to run more tests, and run them more frequently, than manual testing. This often flushes out bugs and inconsistencies, and the sudden increase in visibility helps business stakeholders see the value of test automation.

- Writing and initially automating functional tests often requires involvement of business users, who have to decide whether an inconsistency is a bug or the way the system should work. This leads to collaboration among testers, developers, and business users. It also requires the team to find ways to automate tests so business users can understand them, preparing the way for executable specifications.

- Faster feedback helps developers see the value of test automation.

- Automating functional tests helps team members understand the tools required to automate executable specifications.

Isn't this just shifting work?

A common objection to freeing up testers by getting programmers to collaborate on test automation is that programmers will have more work and this will slow down delivery of functionality. In fact, the general trend in the industry is for teams to have more programmers than testers, so moving work from testers to developers is not necessarily bad—it might remove a bottleneck in your process.

Automating functional tests will get the team to work closer and prepare the system for executable specifications. To get the most out of this approach, automate functional tests using a tool for executable specifications and design them well, using the ideas from chapter 9 and chapter 11. Automating tests using traditional tester record-and-replay testing tools won't give you the benefits you need.

Start by automating high-risk parts of the system

Working to cover all of a legacy system with automated tests is a futile effort. If you use functional test automation as a step to Specification by Example, develop enough tests to show the value of test automation and get used to the tools. After that, start implementing executable specifications for changes as they come and build up test coverage gradually.

To get the most out of initial functional test automation, focus on automating the parts of the system that are risky; these are the areas where problems can cost you a lot of money. Preventing issues there will demonstrate immediate value. Good functional test coverage will give your team more confidence. The benefits from automating parts with less risk are probably not as noteworthy.[†]

_____
[†] See http://gojko.net/2011/02/08/test-automation-strategy-for-legacy-systems

Introduce a tool for executable specifications
When: Testers own test automation

On projects that already have functional test automation fully owned by testers, a key challenge is to break the imaginary wall between testers and developers. There's no need to prove the value of test automation or to flush out issues around test environments, but the mindset of the team has to become more collaborative.

This problem is mostly cultural (more on that soon), but sometimes it's also financial. With an expensive test automation framework such as QTP, licensed per seat, developers and business analysts are intentionally kept far from the tests. Once the attitude toward collaboration changes, a team can work together on specifications and automate the validation without changing them.

Several teams got pushed in this direction when they had a problem that couldn't be appropriately tested with their existing automation toolkit. They used this situation as a good excuse to start using one of the automation tools for executable specifications. (See the "Tools" section in the appendix for examples or additional articles on tools at http:// specificationbyexample.com)

 Teams discovered that using an automation tool for executable specifications got developers more engaged in test automation and provided business users with a greater understanding of the tests.

Developers then became more engaged in test automation and began running tests on their machines; they were able to see the value of quick feedback from functional tests. Business users could understand automated tests using a tool for executable specifications and participate in specifying related acceptance criteria. After that, changing the process to design executable specifications and tests up front was relatively simple.

When working with a large insurance provider, Rob Park's team used a proof of insurance PDF as an excuse to introduce a tool for automating executable specifications and move functional testing to an earlier stage in the development cycle. Park says:

> QTP wasn't able to test it—it could verify that the window would pop up without an error message, but that's it. I wanted to be able to have the developers run tests in the first place on their machines, which was one of the limitations of QTP [due to cost per seat]. I went with JBehave. We kind of threw it all in all at once, and it really just took off in a week. We can now let these acceptance tests themselves drive the design of the underlying controller.

At Weyerhaeuser, Pierre Veragen and the team worked with a custom test automation tool that recorded tests through the user interface. The cost of maintenance was high. After a change that broke many tests, he was able to justify moving to FitNesse after estimating that rewriting existing tests in the new tool would take less time than re-recording all the broken tests. Moving to FitNesse allowed the team to work more closely with engineers on executable specifications and sparked the move to Specification by Example.

Use test-driven development as a stepping stone
When: Developers have a good understanding of TDD

➡ Another common strategy for adopting Specification by Example is to grow the process from (unit) test-driven development, especially when working on a greenfield project.

Test-driven development practices are much better documented and understood in the community than Specification by Example. If a team already has good TDD practices in place, there's probably no need to demonstrate the value of automated tests or change the design to make their software more testable. Executable specifications can be seen as an extension of test-driven development to business rules. (The term *acceptance-test-driven development* is a popular synonym for Specification by Example.)

At ePlan Services, Lisa Crispin used this approach when they were first implementing Specification by Example:

> ❝ I couldn't get people interested in acceptance tests. On Mike Cohn's suggestion, I just picked a story, went to the developer working on a story, and asked, "Could we pair up writing a test on this story?" Developers would see how easy it is. In the next sprint I picked a different story and a different person. We right away found a bug, where he didn't really understand the requirement. So the developers immediately saw the value. ❞

When a team has a good understanding of TDD, making the case for executable specifications is easy: Explain them as tests for business functionality.

How to begin changing the team culture

For the most part, implementing Specification by Example involves a cultural change—getting people to think about collaborating on requirements and changing the way business people, developers, and testers contribute to specifications. Here are some helpful ideas for changing your team culture.

Avoid "agile" terminology
When: Working in an environment that's resistant to change

Agile software development methods are plagued with terminology and buzzwords. *Scrums, stand-ups, user stories, backlogs, masters, pair programming*, and other terms like these are easily misunderstood and cause confusion. To some, they can even be overwhelming and scary. Anxiety caused by jargon is one of the biggest reasons why people push back and resist any change to their process—or passively wait for it to fail. In my experience, many business users find it hard to understand technical terms used by the development team, making it hard for them to grasp ideas related to process improvement and engage with the team.

> ➡ It's entirely possible to implement Specification by Example without using technical terminology. If you work in an environment that's resistant to change, avoid jargon when you start out.

Don't refer to user stories, acceptance tests, or executable specifications—implement Specification by Example without offering definitions. This will provide people who want to oppose you with less ammunition. Explain Specification by Example as the process of gathering examples to clarify requirements, deriving tests, and automating them.

Adam Knight implemented most of the key elements of Specification by Example at RainStor without making a big deal about it. The process grew without up-front plan-ning, and Knight says that nobody else in the company knows about Specification by Example. "People aren't really aware of anything specific," he said. For his team, it's just a process they created themselves.

Pierre Veragen used a similar approach to improve one team's software process at Weyerhaeuser. The team maintains a legacy application with over a million lines of code. They were resistant to implementing anything with the name agile. With-out using any big words, Veragen suggested automating tests below the user interface to make testing more efficient. When the team got their heads around that, he then suggested that developers start running tests on their machines to get faster feedback and align testing and development. With some hand holding and monitoring, Veragen ultimately got the team members to stop thinking about testing as something that comes after development. This took about six months, mostly because the automated test suite had to become big enough for developers to start seeing test failures when they introduced problems into the code. Veragen commented:

> People working in engineering realized that failing tests on their ma-chine were actually pointing to problems in their code. When this hap-pened to a developer, he got the idea and stopped questioning why he had to run the tests.

To implement a process change without technical terminology, make the problems visible and gently push people in the right direction to solve them. When the team comes up with a solution to a problem, even with some help, they'll have a sense of ownership and commit to following through on process changes.

 ## Ensure you have management support

Most teams significantly changed the way they worked while implementing Specifica-tion by Example. For many, this meant changing the way they approached specifica-tions, development, and testing—and learning how to collaborate better within a team and with external stakeholders.

Many people got confused when roles started changing. Testers had to get much more involved in analysis. Developers had to get more involved in testing. Analysts had to change the way they collected and communicated requirements. Business users had to take a much more active role in preparing specifications. Such big changes require man-agement support; otherwise, they're destined to fail. Clare McLennan had this to say:

> You need to get the management support for the project, especially if you have an existing system already, because it's going to take quite a bit of time to get to a point where you actually have a good, stable test system. You've got to go through all the iterations, see where it's not stable or where it gives you strange answers, fix that, and repeat again. If you spend time over a year or so, you'll get an invaluable system. If you don't, or if you think it's a quick fix to get UI tests with click, click, click, then you'll get something unmaintainable and with little value.

At the beginning, automation of executable specifications was a challenge for many teams, because it's conceptually different from what both testers and developers were used to when automating tests (more on this in chapter 9). Teams had to learn how to use a new tool, find a good way to design executable specifications, and structure their living documentation. For the first several months, the productivity of the development team drops before it increases. This requires management understanding, approval, and support.

 Without management buy-in and support, the chances of success with a process change are slim.

If management responds with pressure rather than support, people will fall back into their old ways of doing things and start protecting their position rather than collaborating. Sharing the success stories and benefits outlined in chapter 1 should help with getting that support, but if that fails, it's better to look at less-ambitious ways to improve the process or take smaller steps.

Sell Specification by Example as a better way to do acceptance testing

Several teams, including the ones working in strictly regulated environments, got to the point where user acceptance testing as a phase in software delivery was no longer needed. (Some companies call this phase customer acceptance testing or business acceptance testing.) This doesn't mean that they weren't testing for user acceptance. Specifying and checking the acceptance criteria is different from user acceptance testing as a software delivery phase. It's so important that it shouldn't be left to the end. Executable specifications and frequent validation make development teams check for user acceptance continuously. The product doesn't get delivered to the users unless all their acceptance tests pass.

Once the executable specifications are comprehensive enough and validated frequently, the trust between a development team and its customers increases to the level that verifying software manually after delivery becomes unnecessary. (This doesn't mean that testers shouldn't perform exploratory testing before delivery.)

 I expect that most teams will be able to justify the cost of implementing Specification by Example on the basis of avoiding late acceptance testing. Changing the process so that a team can get there faster should have measurable financial benefits, which can then justify an investment in process change.

Short iterations or flow-based development significantly increase the frequency of potential releases. Let's say that you want to have 12 releases over the next 12 months (most of the teams I interviewed would do twice that figure), and that the user acceptance testing takes in average 3 days. This means that over the next year you'll spend 36 days in user acceptance testing, assuming the best-case scenario: You never catch any problems and software is always accepted (in which case, why test it for 3 days?). More realistically, acceptance testing at the end, rework, and retesting will take at least 2 months over a 12-month period.

If you begin by collaborating to specify the acceptance criteria and automate the validation, you won't have to waste time with manual testing and rework. There's a cost to pay for the automation, but Specification by Example can reduce time-to-market significantly.

Specification by Example has many other benefits, but this is the easiest one to present to business stakeholders and the easiest to quantify. If you need to sell this process change to your business stakeholders, try selling it as a way to get to the market two months earlier every year.

Don't make test automation the end goal

One of the most common early mistakes made by the teams I interviewed was setting functional test automation as the end goal of the process change. Business users generally think of functional test automation as something to do with testing and hence something they don't need to get involved in. Unless developers understand that automated tests need to be human readable to improve communication, they'll automate them in a way that minimizes development effort.

When teams focused only on test automation, they didn't get better collaboration.

This approach often leads to tests that are too technical and that are scripts rather than specifications, a common failure pattern (see "Scripts aren't specifications" in chapter 8). In the long term, tests automated in this way became an impediment to change, not a facilitator.

If you use functional test automation as a step toward Specification by Example, make sure that everyone on the team is aware of the end goal. When functional test automation takes hold, it's time to move on.

 ## Don't focus on a tool

Three people I interviewed started the journey by selecting a tool they wanted to use. Developers had heard about FitNesse or Cucumber and decided to try it out on their project. I've been guilty of that myself as well; this approach has a small chance of success.

 Specification by Example isn't programmer centric, and programmers using a tool in isolation aren't going to get far.

This approach often ends up with programmers using a nontechnical tool, intended for executable specifications, to manage technical, developer-oriented tests. This is a waste of time.

Of the three cases where developers focused on using a particular tool, only Ian Cooper's team at Beazley succeeded in creating a good process. They pushed hard to involve testers and business analysts and then adjusted the way they wrote and organized tests to support that. They were also critical of the benefits they were getting from the tool and looked for easier ways to get those benefits.

In the other two cases, teams focused on a tool, not on high-level collaboration and process changes. They ended up wasting a lot of time and effort building a suite of technical tests that business users and testers weren't able to use. They paid a big price in terms of effort and time spent on test maintenance without any of the benefits of Specification by Example.

Keep one person on legacy scripts during migration
When: Introducing functional automation to legacy systems

Rewriting functional tests and automating them using a new tool takes time. Until the new validation system grows, any existing tests might need to be maintained and kept up-to-date. A good way to address this issue is to delegate that work to a single person and write off that person's time while planning for the immediate future.

James Shore and Shane Warden describe a pattern for process change on legacy projects called "the Batman" in *The Art of Agile Development*.[4] The Batman is a dedicated person who jumps in to solve urgent issues and resolve important bugs, while the rest of the team keeps on working on new functionality. Markus Gärtner used this approach to gradually move a set of tests to an automation tool for executable specifications. He detailed his experience:

> When we transitioned our tests from shell-based scripts to tests based on FitNesse, we started with two members working on the new stuff, while three team members maintained the old legacy test scripts. Over time, we got more and more testers involved in the new approach. First three, then another one, and finally we were able to throw the old scripts away completely.
>
> The underlying idea was the Batman, who dove in to solve problems. I remember that some of my colleagues even bought a toy car from Hot Wheels—the Batmobile—and gave that to our Batman at that time. Initially, I had the idea to rotate the Batman but never applied this, since my colleagues were knowledge silos at that time. We changed that with the new approach, and I try to rotate the Batman role so that everyone gets to deal with the old stuff and the new stuff during the transition. Getting everyone's buy-in is crucial.

➡ By delegating the work required to update legacy items to a single person, teams are able to move more quickly toward the goal of migrating to a new process.

This idea is similar to Alistair Cockburn's "Sacrifice One Person" strategy,[5] where one person is assigned to handle distracting tasks and the rest of the team moves forward at full speed.

---

[4] James Shore and Shane Warden, *The Art of Agile Development* (O'Reilly Media, 2007).
[5] http://alistair.cockburn.us/Sacrifice+one+person+strategy

Track who is running—and not running—automated checks
When: Developers are reluctant to participate

In cases where developers came from a more structured process background—where programmers write code and testers test it—teams had problems getting programmers to participate in the process. This has to change for Specification by Example to work.

Pierre Veragen had a unique solution to get programmers involved in the process. He created a simple centralized reporting system that told him when and where the executable specifications were checked:

> In the fixture code I put a little thing that told me when people were running tests on their machines. That group was pretty shy. I used this to find out when people aren't running the tests to go and talk to them and see what's wrong and whether they had any problems. The idea was to get a more objective feedback than "Yes, it worked fine."

By tracking who isn't running tests before committing, he was able to focus his efforts on the team members who had issues or required assistance. Veragen says that all the programmers knew about the process from the start, so that instead of monitoring the actual test results, he tracked only whether someone executed tests.

➡ Monitor when tests are being run, so programmers will run automated checks.

This is an interesting approach for larger teams, where a coach cannot work with all the members all the time. I expect the effects to be similar to publishing the locations of speed cameras on highways—programmers will know that someone is looking, and they'll take more care to run the checks.

How teams integrated collaboration into flows and iterations

Understanding how to fit collaboration into a delivery cycle is one of the biggest challenges when teams start implementing Specification by Example.

Differences between Specification by Example and Waterfall analysis

Many people I meet at conferences think that incrementally building up a documentation system means going back to the Waterfall ideas of big up-front analysis. During his presentation "How to Sell BDD to the business"[†] in November 2009, Dan North said that BDD is effectively V-Model compressed into two weeks. This isn't an entirely accurate description, but it's a good start.

There are a few crucial differences between the Waterfall analysis approach and what Specification by Example is trying to achieve. It's important to understand these underlying principles because that will help you fit the practices into your process, whatever it is. These are the key factors differentiating Specification by Example from more established analysis:

- Provide fast feedback and focus through quick turnaround; get small chunks of software done efficiently, instead of trying to handle large chunks at once.

- Emphasize effective, efficient communication instead of long, boring documents.

- Establish shared ownership so specifications aren't handed over or thrown over imaginary walls to become code or tests.

- Integrate cross-functional teams where testers, analysts, and developers work together to build the right specification of the system instead of working alone.

[†] http://skillsmatter.com/podcast/agile-testing/how-to-sell-bdd-to-the-business

There's no universal solution for a process change, and each team will need to decide how best to extend their way of delivering software. Following are some nice representative examples that will help you get started. I've chosen three good case studies, one for each popular process. The Global Talent Management team works according to a flow-based Kanban framework. The Sierra team delivers software using an Extreme Programming iteration-based process. The Sky Network Services group runs iterations based on Scrum.

Global Talent Management team at Ultimate Software

The Global Talent Management team at Ultimate Software is one of 16 teams working on their human resources management system. The team consists of a product owner, a user experience expert, four testers, and ten developers. When I interviewed Scott Berger and Maykel Suarez, who were part of this team, their project had been under way for eight months. The team uses a Kanban flow process.

Because the product analyst (a combination of an analyst and a product owner) is busy, the team tries to use his time efficiently when collaborating on specifications. The product analyst explains a story at a high level with "story points" (in their case, story points aren't estimates of complexity but bullet-list items that explain stories). They avoid technology-specific language as much as possible when writing story points. The story is then added to the Kanban board as part of the backlog.

In a daily meeting, limited to 30 minutes, the lead engineers meet with the product analyst and anyone else on the team who is interested in the backlog. They quickly run through the stories in the backlog, checking that each story is sliced correctly, that it makes sense, and that it's implementable in four days or less—as a team, they imposed this deadline for each story. During the meeting, they also clarify any open questions and look at story dependencies.

The story then goes into a queue for writing specifications with examples, which are used as acceptance tests. A team member who will work on implementing the story pairs up with someone who will focus on the testing to write the outlines of these specifications. (They don't have formal tester or developer roles in the team, but I'll use those roles to refer to this pair of people in this section to make it clearer.) Berger explained:

> By leveraging this pair, we're able to cut down on the necessary tests required for this story, because a developer has more intimate knowledge of the code. This has proven quite successful, because these pairs generally root out any inconsistencies and design flaws that exist and aren't caught in the initial story review.

After they define an outline, the tester usually completes the scenarios in a Given-When-Then format. The pair and the product analyst meet and review the scenarios in an in-depth Story Knowledge and Information Transfer (SKIT) session. This addresses the risk that a programmer and a tester won't be able to come up with good specifications without an analyst. When the product analyst approves the scenarios, the team regards them as the requirements. Other than minor text alterations, no further changes are allowed to these requirements until the story is delivered.

The developer will then automate the scenarios, usually prior to implementing production code. This allows the tester to spend more time completing exploratory testing. The tester might also work on automation, but that's no longer his focus. Berger said that this collaboration allows them to work productively:

> Developers who intimately know the code are much quicker in terms of automating, and actually write code that allows them to query their objects (instead of automating through the user interface), and derive a greater benefit while developing, since many more error conditions and combinations are explicitly described. Since we are now testing under the GUI, our test execution is much quicker and more stable. Testers are free to spend more time exercising the code and providing feedback.

All the executable specifications have to pass for the development stage to finish. All the tests are executed again during the run-tests phase, this time integrated with the work of other teams. While waiting for approval phase, the team does a quick product demo for the product analyst and obtains a sign-off.

According to Berger, this process leads to results that are of exceptionally high quality:

> By working closely with our product analysts, and using our tests as a basis for requirements, we are able to achieve an exceptionally high level of quality. The business has collected metrics, and one specifically that I think adequately provides an insight into our efforts in terms of our commitment to quality is Defect Detection Efficiency (DDE). Upon measuring the Global Talent Management team, it was determined that our DDE is 99% [for Q1-Q3 2010]!

Sierra team at BNP Paribas

The Sierra team at BNP Paribas builds a back-office reference data management and distribution system. The team consists of eight developers, two business analysts, and a project manager. Because there are no dedicated testers, everyone on the team is responsible for testing. Their stakeholders are off-site business users. Change requests typically require a lot of analysis and work with the stakeholders.

The project has been under way for about five years, so it's reasonably mature, and business analysts have many existing executable specifications to use as examples. Andrew Jackman, who was a member of this team when I interviewed him, says this is one of the rare examples in the financial services industry where Extreme Programming is applied almost by the book.

Their development process starts with the project manager, who selects the stories for an iteration in advance. The business analysts work with remote stakeholders to prepare the acceptance criteria in detail before an iteration starts. They use examples of existing specifications to drive structure of the new ones. If the new specifications are significantly different from any existing ones, a pair of developers will review the tests to provide early feedback and ensure the tests can be automated.

Their iterations start every second Wednesday. When an iteration starts, the whole team gets together for a planning meeting and reviews the upcoming stories in the order of priority. The goal is to ensure that all the developers understand what the story is about, to estimate the stories, and to check for technical dependencies that would make a different order of delivery better. They'll also break down the story into tasks for development. By the time a story is reviewed in a planning meeting, the acceptance criteria for that story are generally already well specified.

The team occasionally discovers that a story wasn't well understood. When they were running weeklong iterations, such stories could disrupt the flow, but two-week iterations allow them to handle such cases without much interruption to the overall process.

The stories are then implemented by pairs of developers. After a pair of developers implements a story and all the related tests pass, a business analyst will spend some time doing exploratory testing. If the analyst discovers unexpected behavior, or realizes that the team has not understood all the effects of a story on the existing system, he will extend the specification with relevant examples and send the story back to the developers.

Sky Network Services

The Sky Network Services (SNS) group at the British Sky Broadcasting Company maintains a system for broadband provisioning. The group consists of six teams, and each team has five to six developers and one or two testers. The entire group shares six business analysts. Because the teams maintain separate functional components that differ in terms of maturity, each team has a slightly different process.

The entire group runs a process based on Scrum in two-week sprints. One week before a sprint officially starts, they organize a preplanning coordination meeting attended by two or three people from each team. The goal of that meeting is to prioritize the stories. By the time they meet, the business analysts have already collected and specified some high-level acceptance criteria for each story. After the meeting, testers will start writing the specifications with examples, typically collaborating with a business analyst. Before the sprint officially starts, each team will have at least one or two stories with detailed specifications with examples ready for automation.

The iterations start every second Wednesday, with a cross-team planning meeting to inform everyone about overall progress and the business goals of the upcoming iteration. The teams then go into individual planning meetings. Some teams spend 15 minutes going through the stories briefly; others spend a few hours going over the details. Rakesh Patel, a developer who works on the project, says that this is mostly driven by the maturity of the underlying component:

> At the moment we're working on a component that's been there for a long time and adding more messages to it. There is not really much need for the whole team to know what that involves; we can wait until we pick up the story card. Some other teams are building a new GUI, completely new functionality, and then it might be more appropriate for the whole team to sit down and discuss this in depth and try to work out what needs to be done. At that point we might also discuss nonfunctional requirements, architecture, etc.

After the planning meeting, the developers start working on the stories that already have specifications with examples. Business analysts and testers work on completing the acceptance criteria for all the stories planned for the iteration. Once they finish the specifications for a story, they'll meet with a developer designated to be the "story champion" (see the sidebar) and go through the tests. If everyone thinks they have enough information to complete a story, the story card gets a blue sticker, which means that it's ready for development.

Once development is completed, the business analysts will review the specifications again and put a red sticker on the card. Testers will then run additional tests on the story and add a green sticker when the tests pass. Some stories will involve their support team, database administrators, or system administrators, who review the story after the testers. Database administrators put a gold star on the story card, and system administrators add a silver star when they've reviewed the results. Stickers ensure that everyone who needs to be involved in a story knows about it.

Instead of big specification meetings, the teams at SNS organize a flow process. They still have a two-phase specification process, with business analysts and testers preparing all the examples upfront and then reviewing them with a developer later. This gives developers more time to focus on development work. Instead of involving all the developers in the review to ensure they understand a story, the story champion is effectively responsible for transferring the information while pairing with other developers.

The previous three examples show how teams can fit collaboration into short iterations and even flow-based processes, demonstrating that there's no generic and universally applicable approach to structuring the process. All the teams successfully integrated collaboration into their short release cycles but used different approaches depending on the team structure, availability of their business users, and complexity of changes coming into the delivery pipeline. For some nice ideas on designing a process to fit your team, see "Choosing a collaboration model" in chapter 6. For more examples, see the case studies in part 3.

Story champion

SNS teams use story champions to ensure an efficient transfer of knowledge while switching pairs of developers who work on a story. Kumaran Sivapathasuntharam, a business analyst working on the project, explains this idea:

> The story is assigned to a particular developer who stays with the story until it's completed. This ensures that there's one point of contact for a story—so if you have an issue with a story, you can talk to the story champion. One person can stay on the story from start to finish so an entire pair doesn't get stuck on it, and they can keep changing the pairs but still having the continuity throughout.

The Global Talent Management team at Ultimate Software has a similar role, called story sponsor. According to Maykel Suarez, the sponsor is responsible for communication with other teams, tracking the progress on the Kanban board, checking status at stand-up meetings, and eliminating roadblocks.

Dealing with sign-off and traceability

For some teams, a big problem with little or no documentation on agile projects is the lack of requirements. This makes sign-offs on requirements or deliverables difficult. As a whole, the software development industry is much less concerned with sign-offs than it was 10 years ago. In some cases, sign-offs are still required because of regulatory constraints or commercial arrangements.

Specification by Example provides artifacts around requirements—living documentation—that can be used for traceability. This enables agile processes to be applied to regulated industries. Bas Vodde and Craig Larman wrote about the first agile development project in the U.S. nuclear industry[6] in *Practices for Scaling Lean and Agile.*[7] The team working on that project used executable specifications to ensure full traceability of requirements, which is critical in nuclear and other safety-critical domains. On the other hand, because of a highly dynamic, iterative, and collaborative approach to building these artifacts, up-front sign-off is practically impossible. Here are some ideas on how to deal with sign-off and traceability constraints.

Keep executable specifications in a version control system

 Several people I interviewed said that keeping executable specifications in the same version control system as the product source code is one of the most important practices for a successful process implementation.

Many automation tools work with executable specifications in plain-text files, so they work nicely with version control systems. This allows you to easily tag and branch the specifications along with the source code. It gives you a current and correct version of tests that can be used to validate any version of your product.

Version control systems are great for traceability because they allow you to find who changed any file, when, and why in an instant. If you store your executable specifications in a version control system, you'll get traceability on requirements and specifications for free. With Specification by Example, the executable specifications will be directly linked to the programming language code (through the automation layer), which means that it will be relatively straightforward to prove code traceability as well.

Executable specifications in a version control system are also less likely to disappear than those stored in a separate requirements or test tool.

Get sign-off on exported living documentation
When: Signing off iteration by iteration

Specification by Example should help build trust between project sponsors and the delivery team and remove the need for sign-off. If you do need to get requirements signed off for commercial or political reasons, you can use the living documentation system for that.

---

[6] I would have loved to include that case study in this book as well, but unfortunately I couldn't get in touch with anyone willing to talk about it.

[7] Craig Larman and Bas Vodde, *Practices for Scaling Lean and Agile Development: Large, Multi-site, and Offshore Product Development with Large-Scale Scrum* (Pearson Education, 2010).

> If you need to get sign-off on specifications before starting to implement func-
> tionality, and it's possible to organize this for each iteration, then you can create
> a Word or a PDF document from the executable specifications planned for the
> next iteration and get sign-off on that.

Some automation tools, such as Cucumber, support exporting to PDF directly, and this
might help you with the process.

Get sign-off on scope, not specifications
When: Signing off longer milestones

> If you need to get sign-off on batches of software larger than what a single itera-
> tion can deliver, try to get sign-off on scope and not on detailed specifications.
> For example, obtain sign-off on user stories or use cases.

Rob Park applied this approach when working with a large U.S. insurance provider. His
team kept a Waterfall approval process for sign-off but significantly cut down on the
material that required it. Park explained:

> There is kind of a bigger process outside of everything we have under
> our control. The business analysts work on Word documents using a tem-
> plate, but they cut the template down from eight pages to two. There is a
> story card approval process where the people who pay for the project actu-
> ally sign off on these story cards before anyone except the business analyst
> actually sees them. So they have this Waterfall process in the company at
> a high level, but once it gets into the team it becomes different.

Word documents are used in this case purely because contractual obligations dictate that
there be paperwork before a story makes it into development. The team uses executable
specifications as their only source of requirements after the scope is approved.

Get sign-off on "slimmed down use cases"
When: Regulatory sign-off requires details

Getting sign-off on scope might not work in a heavily regulated environment. Mike
Vogel of Knowledgent Group worked on a project for the pharmaceutical industry
using a process based on Scrum and extended to satisfy regulatory requirements. His
team used use cases, because the standards of a regulated system can't be met with user
stories alone.

The team used slimmed-down use cases (they called them "structured stories") so that initial capture and ongoing evolution wasn't a big problem. Those use cases would avoid most details about data and decisions (these were extracted into separate data sections). Vogel explained that approach:

> In a use case you would have a nickname for a piece of data, something that the customer understands as part of the domain language. The data section describing that gives the structure and the rules describing the data—not examples. Examples are in the [acceptance] tests/requirements-by-example where we walk the use case building examples that cover and show variations of all our named chunks of data. You vary your examples of the chunks of data that they have factored out.

➡ Get sign-off on "lighter" use cases—without examples.

Vogel's team built a requirements document with those lightweight use cases but without any examples. The result was a document less than 100 pages long for a large project "with all the regulatory required boilerplate," according to Vogel. Throughout the project, they collaborated with the customer to specify the use cases and examples:

> We sit with the customer in the team room and try to work out one use case at a time along with the examples. Discussions are about detailed examples. We end up putting in some details after that and the customer reviews it.

This approach allows the team to get a sign-off on something that closely resembles traditional specifications without overprescribing them. Details come from an iterative and collaborative process; the backlog the customer works with is based on the high-level use cases and the details come later.

Introduce use case realizations
When: All details are required for sign-off

Matthew Steer worked on several projects based on a structured process (Rational Unified Process). The process required full sign-off on all the details, and specifications were captured as use cases. In addition use cases, Steer and his team introduced use case realizations that effectively illustrated use cases with examples. This allowed them to use Specification by Example in a structured process. Steer says:

> The requirements were captured as use cases and supplementary specifications for nonfunctional requirements—quite traditional, by-the-book capture. With use cases we produced use case realizations, examples and scenarios that use cases would fulfill. We created tables with lots of parameters and hooked up data from there and then had flows to show how the use case would be realized. Use case realization was a working version of what that meant to the business, using real scenarios.

> Adding details such as use case realizations is a good idea to get Specification by Example into a formal process—under the radar of the methodology police. It can also help to implement the ideas of Specification by Example when commercial contracts require sign-off on requirements but still allow for later variability in detail.

Steer's team, as well as others mentioned in the previous section, used examples—even if disguised as use-case realizations—instead of only using use cases or tests made against more generic requirements. This made their delivery process more effective.

Technically, a living documentation system instantly provides traceability in requirements changes, because teams use version control systems to store their executable specifications. Iterative development is generally at odds with up-front sign-offs, but you can use the tips from this section to deal with that while the process changes and the delivery team gains trust from the business users. The visibility that a living documentation system provides, along with collaboration on specifications, should help to eliminate the need for sign-offs.

Warning signs

You can track your progress to check if you're implementing Specification by Example properly. As with any metrics, make sure that metrics themselves don't become a goal; otherwise, you'll locally optimize a process to get the numbers right but hurt the long-term results. Use these as measurements to check if the process needs adjustment.

Watch out for tests that change frequently

At XPDay 2009, Mark Striebeck talked about what Google is doing to advance its testing practices.[8] One of the ideas that impressed me was how they measure whether a (unit) test is good or not. When a test breaks, they track changes in the source code until the test starts passing again. If the underlying code was changed, they consider the test to be a good one. If the test changed and the code did not change, they consider it to be bad. By collecting these statistics, they hope to analyze unit test patterns and identify what makes a test good or bad.

I believe that the same criteria can be applied to executable specifications. If a validation fails and you change the code, that means you found and fixed a problem. If a validation fails and you have to change the specification, that means it wasn't written properly.

Business rules should be much more stable than the technology that implements them. Watch out for executable specifications that change frequently. Look for ways to write them better.

You can also measure the time your team spends on changing specifications and related automation code in order to keep it under control. If you spend a significant portion of your iteration doing this, look for better ways to automate tests (see chapter 9 for some good tips).

Watch out for boomerangs

Another good metric to check if you're doing something wrong is looking for the presence of boomerangs. A *boomerang* is a story or a product backlog item that comes back into the process less than a month after it was released. The team thought it was done, but it needs rework. But it's not a boomerang when the business later extends existing requirements to incorporate innovation as the product evolves.

Once you implement Specification by Example, the number of boomerangs should be reduced significantly until they're a rare occurrence. Collaboration on specifications and better alignment of testing and development should eliminate wasteful rework caused by misunderstanding. Reviewing your boomerang trends over several months will show you how much you've improved. If the rate doesn't drop, it means that there's something wrong with the way you implemented the process.

Tracking boomerangs doesn't take a lot of time, usually a few minutes every iteration, but it can help a lot when the time comes to challenge or prove that Specification by Example is working. In larger companies, it can also provide compelling evidence that it's worth doing with other teams. For more complex statistics, you can also track

---

[8] http://gojko.net/2009/12/07/improving-testing-practices-at-google

the time spent on boomerangs, because this figure directly translates into wasted development/testing time and money. If people complain about the time spent on automating executable specifications as unnecessary overhead, compare that to the time they spent working on boomerangs several months earlier. This should be more than enough to build a business case for Specification by Example.

Once the number of boomerangs goes down and they occur relatively rarely, you can stop tracking them. If a boomerang occurs, try to understand where it's coming from. One of my clients had many boomerangs coming from their financial department. This pointed to a communication problem with that particular part of the company; as a result, they looked for better ways to engage the department.

Tracking boomerangs is also a good way to build a business case for introducing Specification by Example. It can help a team pinpoint the waste caused by vague requirements and functional gaps in specifications.

Watch out for organizational misalignment

Many teams started implementing Specification by Example as a way to better align their activities with iterations. After you become familiar with executable specifications and the automation code becomes stable, you should be able to implement a story and completely finish testing it (including manual exploratory testing) inside the same iteration. If your testers are lagging behind development, you're doing something wrong. A similar warning sign is misaligned analysis. Some teams start analysis ahead of the relevant iteration, but they still have regular intervals and flow. Analyzing too much up front, analyzing things that won't be implemented immediately, or being late with analysis when details are needed are signs that the process is wrong.

Watch out for just-in-case code

In *Lean Software Development*[9] Mary and Tom Poppendieck wrote that the biggest source of waste in software development is just-in-case code—software that was written without being needed. I'm not sure whether it's the biggest source of waste, but I've certainly seen lots of money, time, and effort wasted on things that nobody needed or asked for. Specification by Example significantly reduces this problem because it helps us build a shared understanding of what we need to deliver. Jodie Parker says that the conversations and collaboration on specifications helped her team achieve just that:

---

[9] Mary Poppendieck and Tom Poppendieck, *Lean Software Development: An Agile Toolkit* (Addison-Wesley Professional, 2003).

> ❝ When the developers got a story card, they'd very much want to deliver everything within it, to make it technically as fabulous as possible, even though the steer was "do the minimal thing possible to get the value given." It's got to be efficient, but we can always bring in the stories later to refine it. This was addressed using conversations and continually working out if we're able to draw the business model that we're trying to achieve. By domain modeling you can very easily break down this into tasks. Those tasks are then the only thing you can do. Because the tasks are small, you can go off on one of them, but if you do it's very easily spotted by the rest of the team and the team would speak up. When someone's been on a task for several days, we'd have that conversation in the standup. ❞

Watch out for people who implement more than what was agreed on and specified with examples. Another good way to avoid just-in-case code is by discussing not only what you want to deliver but also what's out of scope.

Watch out for shotgun surgery

Shotgun surgery is a classic programming antipattern (also called *code smell*) that occurs when a small change to one class requires cascading changes in several related classes. This telling sign can be applied to living documentation; if a single change in production code requires you to change many executable specifications, you're doing something wrong. Organize your living documentation so that one small change in code leads to one small change in tests (see "Listen to your living documentation" in chapter 11 for some good tips on how to do so). This is one of the key steps to reducing maintenance costs of automation over the long term.

Remember

- Specification by Example is a good way to provide development teams with just-in-time specifications, so it's a key factor for success with short iterations or flow-based development.
- Handle small chunks of software efficiently to enforce quick turnaround time and feedback.
- Emphasize effective, efficient communication instead of long, boring documents.
- Integrate cross-functional teams where testers, analysts, and developers work together to build the right specification of the system.
- Plan for automation overhead upfront.

PART 2

Key process patterns

5

Deriving scope from goals

The F-16 Fighting Falcon is arguably the most successful jet fighter ever de-signed. This is all the more remarkable because it succeeded against all odds. In the 70s, when the F-16 was designed, jet fighters had to be built for speed; range, weaponry, and maneuverability were of little importance to get a production contract.[1] Yet it was the range and maneuverability of the F-16 that made it ideal for its role in combat and ensured its success.

In *97 Things Every Architect Should Know*,[2] Einar Landre quotes Harry Hillaker, the lead designer of the F-16, saying that the original requirement for the aircraft was that it reach speeds of Mach 2-2.5. When Hillaker asked the U.S. Air Force why that was important, they responded that the jet had to "to be able to escape from combat." Although Hillaker's design never got above Mach 2, it allowed pilots to escape from combat with superior agility. It featured many innovations, including a frameless bubble canopy for better visibility, a reclined seat to reduce the effect of g-forces on the pilot, a display that projects combat information in front of the pilot without obstructing his view, and side-mounted control sticks to improve maneuverability at high speed. With these features, the F-16 was superior to alternative designs—and less expensive to pro-duce. It won the design competition. More than 30 years later, it's still in production. With more than 4,400 aircraft sold to 25 countries,[3] the model is a great commercial success. It's also one of the most popular fighter jets and is often featured in action films, such as *X2* and *Transformers: Revenge of the Fallen*.

The F-16 was successful because the design provided a better and cheaper solution than what the customer asked for. The original requirements, including the demand for Mach 2.5 speed, formed one possible solution to a problem—but this problem wasn't

---

[1] See Kev Darling's book *F-16 Fighting Falcon (Combat Legend)* (Crowood Press, 2005).
[2] Richard Monson-Haefel, *97 Things Every Software Architect Should Know* (O'Reilly Media, 2009).
[3] See http://www.lockheedmartin.com/products/f16

65

effectively communicated. Instead of implementing the requirements, the designers sought a greater understanding of the problem. Once they had it, they could pinpoint the real goals and derive their design from those, rather than from suggested solutions or arbitrary expectations about functionality. That's the essence of successful product design, and it's just as important in software design as in aircraft development.

Most of the business users and customers I work with are inclined to present requirements as solutions; rarely do they discuss goals they want to achieve or the specific nature of problems that need solutions. I've seen far too many teams suffer from the hazardous misconception that the customers are always right and that what they ask for is set in stone; this leads teams to blindly accept suggested solutions and then struggle to implement them. Successful teams don't do this.

Like the F-16 designers, successful teams push back for more information about the real problem and then collaborate to design the solution. They do this even for scope. Scope implies a solution. Instead of passing the responsibility for defining scope onto someone else, successful teams are proactive and collaborate to determine good scope with the business users, so that their goals are met. This is the essence of deriving scope from goals.

Collaborating on deriving scope from goals is undoubtedly the most controversial topic in this book. In the last five years, the surge in popularity of value chains in software development has increased awareness of the idea of collaborating on scope and deriving it from business goals. On the other hand, most teams I work with still think that project scope isn't under their control and expect customers or business users to fully define it. In the course of my research for this book, I found a pattern of teams deriving their project scope from goals collaboratively—but this practice is much less common than other key patterns.

I originally thought about leaving this chapter out. I decided to include it for three reasons:

- Defining scope plays an important role in the process of building the right software. If you get the scope wrong, the rest is just painting the corpse.

- In the future, this will be one of most important software development topics, and I want to raise awareness about it.

- Defining scope fits nicely into designing processes from value chains, which are becoming increasingly popular because of lean software development.

In the following two sections I present techniques for influencing scope for teams that have direct control over it and for teams that don't. Teams that have high-level control of their project scope can be proactive and begin to build the right scope immediately. Unfortunately, many teams in several of the large organizations I work with don't have that kind of control—but this doesn't mean they can't influence scope.

Building the right scope

Use cases, user stories, or backlog items provide a broad definition of a project's scope. Many teams consider such artifacts to be the responsibility of the business users, product owners, or customers. Asking business users to provide the scope is, in effect, relying on individuals who have no experience with designing software to give us a high-level solution. Designing a solution is one of the most challenging and most vital steps. Now is the time for a mandatory Fred Brooks quote: In *The Mythical Man-Month*[4] he wrote, "The hardest single part of building a software system is deciding precisely what to build." Albert Einstein said that "the formulation of a problem is often more essential than its solution."

Currently, user stories are the most popular way to define the scope for agile and lean projects. User stories did a fantastic job of raising awareness of business value in software projects. Instead of asking business users to choose between developing an integration platform and building transaction CRUD (Create Update Delete) screens, user stories allowed us to finally start talking to them about things that they could understand and reasonably prioritize. It's important to note that each story should have a clearly associated business value. Unfortunately, teams often choose that value statement arbitrarily (and it's usually the tip of the iceberg). But when we know what a story is supposed to deliver, we can investigate that further and suggest an alternative solution. Christian Hassa of TechTalk explains:

> People tell you what they think they need, and by asking them "Why" you can identify new implicit goals they have. Many organizations aren't able to specify their business goals explicitly. However, once you derived the goals, you should again reverse and derive scope from the identified goals, potentially discarding the originally assumed scope.

This is the essence of a practice I call *challenging requirements* in *Bridging the Communication Gap*. I still think that challenging requirements is an important practice, but doing so is reactive. Although that's definitely better than passive—which best describes the way most teams I've seen work with scope—there are emerging techniques and practices that allow teams to be much more proactive in achieving business goals. Instead of reacting to wrong stories, we can work together with our business users on coming up with the right stories in the first place. The key idea is to start not with user stories but with business goals and derive scope from there collaboratively.

---

[4] Fred Brooks, *The Mythical Man-Month: Essays on Software Engineering* (Addison-Wesley, 1975).

Understand the "why" and "who"

User stories generally have three parts: "As a __ I want __ in order to __ ." Alternative formats exist, but all have these three components.

> Understanding why something is needed and who needs it is crucial to evaluating a suggested solution.

The same analysis can be applied to project scope on a much higher level. In fact, analysing those three aspects at a higher level can push a project into a completely different direction.

Peter Janssens from iLean in Belgium worked on a project where he was on the other end—he was the person giving requirements in the form of solutions. He was responsible for an application that stored local traffic sign information. It started as a simple Access database for Belgium but quickly grew to cover most of the countries in the world. Data collectors for different countries were using local databases, and merging them occasionally.

To make the work more efficient and prevent merging problems, they decided to take the database online and make a web application to maintain it. They spent four months contacting suppliers and comparing bids before finally selecting one offer. The estimated cost for this application was 100,000 euros. But the project took a completely different turn once they thought about who needed to use the application and why. Janssens says:

> The day before the go/no a guy from engineering asked again for the problem, to understand it better. I said, "We need a web solution for the central database." He said, "No, no, let's not jump to conclusions. Don't elaborate immediately which solution you want, please explain it to me." I explained again. And then he said, "So, your problem is actually that you need a single source to work on because you are losing time on merging." "Yes," I said, "correct."
>
> He had a second question: "Who is working on it?" I said, "Look, at this moment we have 10 groups of countries, so 10 people." We had a look at the databases and understood that this type of traffic information doesn't change that often, maybe once or twice a year per country. He said, "Look Peter, your problem will be solved by tomorrow." By tomorrow he added the database to their Citrix (remote desktop) server.

The application had to support ten users in total, and they were using it only to update traffic sign information, which changed infrequently. The Access application could cope with the volume of data; the only real problem they had was merging. Once a technical engineer understood the underlying problem, he could offer a much cheaper solution than the one originally suggested. Janssens explains:

> What I learned is that this was a real confrontation situation—it's always important to understand the core problem that leads to a request. So understanding "why" is important. Eventually, the Citrix solution came to him when we talked about the "who" question. On average there was one user a month working on it.

Even at a scope level, the solution is already implied. Without going into the possible user stories or use cases and discussing specifications for tasks, the fact that someone suggested a web application implies a solution. Instead of spending months to deliver the project, they solved the problem with a quick fix that cost nothing. This is an extreme case, but it demonstrates that understanding why someone needs a particular application and how they'll use it often leads to better solutions.

Understand where the value is coming from

In addition to helping us design a better solution, understanding where the value comes from is immensely helpful when it comes to prioritization. Rob Park's team at a large U.S. insurance provider looks at prioritization only from a higher feature level, which keeps them from going through the same process on the lower story level and saves a lot of time. Park says:

> We keep things at a high level, describe the business value and what's really core to the feature. We break the feature down into stories, which we try to make as small as possible. An example of a feature would be: Deliver proof of insurance as PDF for 14 states. The big thing I've been trying to push, especially from the business side, is "how much is this worth, put the dollar value behind it." In that particular case we were able to get one of the senior guys to say, "Well, 50% of the calls were for this and 50% of those calls were for the proof of insurance cards, so 25% of the calls were dealing with that." They know how many calls they have and how much they would be able to save by generating this PDF instead of having to do all the copy and paste stuff that they were doing before, so they were actually able to put some numbers behind this, which was really cool.

> Raising the discussion to the level of the goals allows teams to deal with scope and priorities more efficiently than just doing so at the story level.

One good example of an area where this helps is effort estimation. Rob Park's team found that discussing goals enabled them to stop wasting time on estimating effort for individual stories:

> " We don't really want to bother with estimating stories. If you start estimating stories, with Fibonacci numbers for example, you soon realize that anything eight or higher is too big to deliver in an iteration, so we'll make it one, two, three, and five. Then you go to the next level and say five is really big. Now that everything is one, two, and three, they're now really the same thing. We can just break that down into stories of that size and forget about that part of estimating, and then just measure the cycle time to when it is actually delivered. "

In *Software by Numbers*,[5] Mark Denne and Jane Cleland-Huang describe a formal method for prioritization that's driven by business value by dividing scope into Minimum Marketable Features. From my experience, predicting how much money something is going to earn is as difficult and prone to error as predicting how long it's going to take to implement that feature. But if your domain allows you to put numbers on features, this will help get the business users involved. Asking them to prioritize features or even business goals works better than asking them to prioritize low-level stories or tasks.

Understand what outputs the business users expect

When goals are hard to pin down, a useful place to start is the expected outputs of the system: Investigate why they're needed and how the software can provide them. Once you nail down expected outputs, you can focus your work on fulfilling the requirements that come with them. Analyzing why those outputs are required leads to formulating the goals of the project.

> Instead of trying to collaborate with business users on specifying how to put things into the system, we should start with examples of outputs. This helps engage business users in the discussion and gives them a clear picture of what they'll get out of the system.

---

[5] Mark Denne and Jane Cleland-Huang, *Software by Numbers: Low-Risk, High-Return Development* (Prentice Hall, 2003).

Wes Williams worked on a project at Sabre where a delay in building the user interface caused a lot of rework:

> The acceptance tests were written against a domain [application layer], before our customer could see the GUI. The UI was delayed for about four months. The customer thought completely differently about the application when they saw the UI. When we started writing tests for the UI they had much more in them than the ones written for the domain [layer]. So the domain code had to be changed, but the customer assumed that that part was done. They had their test there, they drove it and it was passing, and they assumed it was done.

Expected outputs of a system help us discover the goals and determine exactly what needs to be built to support them. Adam Geras used this idea to focus on building the right thing even before agile projects:

> We've used something that we call "report-first" on many of our projects, but it is at the epic story level and our experience with it is mostly in the ERP implementation space. Not agile projects. It has served us extremely well because the rework required to find that one data element that was missing on a report can be extensive. We've been able to avoid that rework by thinking about the outputs first.

Starting with the outputs of a system to derive scope is an idea from the BDD community. This idea has been getting a lot of attention recently because it eliminates a common problem. On many of my early projects, we focused on process flow and putting the data into the system initially. We left the end results of processes, such as reports, for later. The problem with this approach is that the business users can become engaged only when they see results at the visible output stage, which often causes rework. Working from the outputs ensures that the business users can always provide feedback.

Have developers provide the "I want" part of user stories
When: Business users trust the development team

User Stories		
	Business Users	Developers
As a	X	
I want		X
So that	X	

The team at uSwitch collaborates with their business users to define user stories. The business users specify the parts of the story that name a stakeholder and an expected benefit, and the development team specifies the part that implies a solution. In the standard user story format, this would mean that the business users provide direction for the "as a __" and "in order to __" statements, whereas the developers provide content for the "I want __" statement.

➡ A great way to obtain the right scope for a goal is to firmly place the responsibility for a solution on the development team.

If you are fortunate enough to have high-level control of project scope, make sure to involve developers and testers in the discussions about it and focus the suggested solutions on fulfilling clearly defined business goals. This eliminates a lot of unnecessary work later on and sets the stage for better collaboration on specifications.

Parts of a user story

A *user story* describes how a user will get a specific value out of a system. User stories are commonly used by teams to plan and prioritize the scope of short-term work. They're often defined in three parts:

- As a *stakeholder*

- In order to *achieve something valuable*

- I want *some system function*

For example, "As a marketing manager, so that I can market products directly to customers, I want the system to request and record personal information when customers register for a loyalty program."

Different authors suggest different ordering and phrasing of these three parts, but all agree that those three need to be captured. For the purposes of this book, variations in ordering or naming in parts of a user story are irrelevant.

Collaborating on scope without high-level control

For most teams I work with, especially those in big companies, scope is something passed to them from a higher instance. Many teams think that it's impossible to argue about business goals when they maintain only a piece of a large system. Even in those situations, understanding what the business users are trying to achieve can help you focus the project on things that really matter.

Here are some tips for effectively collaborating on project scope when you don't have a high-level control of the project.

Ask how something would be useful

Stuart Ervine worked on a back-office application for a large bank that allowed business users to manage their counterparty relationships in a tree-like hierarchy—a perfect example of a small piece of a large system. Even then, they were able to push back on tasks and get to the real requirements.

Ervine's team was tasked with improving the performance of the hierarchy, which sounds like a genuine business requirement with a clear benefit. But the team could not replicate any performance issues on their part, so any serious improvements would require infrastructural changes.

They asked the users to tell them how improved performance would be useful. It turned out that the business users had been manually performing a complex calculation by going through the hierarchy and adding account balances. They had to open and close tree branches in the user interface for a large number of counterparties and add account balances—a slow and error-prone calculation process.

Instead of improving the performance of the hierarchy, the team automated that calculation for the business users. This made the calculation almost instantaneous and significantly reduced the possibility of errors. This solution delivered better results and was cheaper than the one originally requested.

 Instead of a technical feature specification, we should ask for a high-level example of how a feature would be useful. This will point us towards the real problem.

In *Bridging the Communication Gap,* I advise asking why and repeating the question until the answer starts mentioning money. I now think that asking for an example of how a feature will be useful is a much better way to get to the same result. Asking why something is needed can sound like a challenge and might put the other person in a defensive position, especially in larger organizations. Asking how something would be useful starts a discussion without challenging anyone's authority.

Ask for an alternative solution

In addition to asking for an example of how something would be useful, Christian Hassa advises discussing an alternative solution to get to the real business goals. Hassa explains:

> Sometimes people still struggle with explaining what the value of a given feature would be (even when asking them for an example). As a further step, I ask them to give an example and say what they would need to do differently (work around) if the system would not provide this feature. Usually this helps them then to express the value of a given feature.

➡ A good strategy for discovering additional options from a business perspective is to ask for an alternative solution.

Asking for alternative solutions can make whoever is asking for a feature think twice about whether the proposed solution is the best one. It should also start a discussion about alternatives with the delivery team.

Don't look only at the lowest level

Many teams, influenced by the need to slim down delivery items so that they can fit into an iteration, now break down backlog items to a low level. Although this helps streamline process flow, it might cause the team to lose sight of the big picture.

➡ As a process, Specification by Example works both for high-level and lower-level stories. Once we have a high-level example of how something would be useful, we can capture that as a high-level specification. Such high-level examples allow us to objectively measure whether we've delivered a feature.

Ismo Aro worked on a project at Nokia Siemens Networks where his team experienced setbacks because they didn't have higher-level specifications. He says:

> User stories have to fit into the sprint. When there is a bunch of those that are done, they're tested in isolation. The larger user story isn't actually tested. When the user stories are small grained you can't really tell from the backlog whether things are really done.

Splitting larger user stories into smaller ones that can be delivered individually is good practice. Looking at higher-level stories is still required in order to know when we're done. Instead of a flat, linear backlog, we need a hierarchical backlog to look at both levels.

Lower-level specifications and tests will tell us that we've delivered the correct logic in parts; a higher-level acceptance test will tell us that all those parts work together as expected.

Make sure teams deliver complete features
When: Large multisite projects

Wes Williams blamed the division of work for the problem described in the section "Understand what outputs the business users expect." Teams delivered components of the system (in this case the domain layer and the user interface), which made it hard to divide the work so that they could discuss the expected output for each team with their customers. So they reorganized work into teams that could deliver complete features. Williams commented:

> It took us about six months to put it to feature teams. This made a big difference especially in the sense that it removed some duplication, a lot of repeating, and a lot of rework. Fortunately, we already had a lot of tests that helped us do this. We did have to go back and add features but it was mostly adding—not changing.

When teams deliver features end-to-end, they can get more thoroughly engaged with business users in designing scope and determining what needs to be built, simply because they can discuss full features with the users. For more information on feature teams, see the *Feature Team Primer*.[6]

Even without high-level control of project scope, teams can still influence what gets built by:

- Actively challenging requirements
- Understanding the real business goals
- Understanding who needs what functionality and why

The result will not be as effective as it would be if the right scope had been derived from business goals from the start. But this approach prevents unnecessary rework later in the process and ensures that the business users get what they need.

Further information

At the moment there's a lot of innovation in this field. True to the nature of this book, I've only written about techniques utilized by the teams I interviewed.

---

[6] http://www.featureteams.org

Emerging techniques deserve to be written about, but that's material for another book. To learn more about cutting-edge techniques for deriving scope from goals and mapping out the relationship between them, look for resources on these topics:

- *Feature injection*—A technique to iteratively derive scope from goals through high-level examples

- *Effect mapping*—A visualization technique for project scope through hierarchical analysis of goals, stakeholders, and features

- *User story mapping*—A hierarchical mapping technique for user stories that provides a "big picture" view

Unfortunately, there's little published material on any of the emerging practices. As far as I know, the only published work about feature injection is a comic[7] and the next best thing is a set of scans from Chris Matts's notebook on Picasa.[8] The only published material on effect maps is a book in Swedish with a poor English translation called *Effect Managing IT*[9] and a whitepaper I published online.[10] Jeff Patton features a lot of great material about passive and reactive scoping problems on his blog,[11] and he's been writing a book on agile product design, which I hope will offer more coverage of this field.

Remember

- When you're given requirements as tasks, push back: Get the information you need to understand the real problem; then collaboratively design the solution.

- If you can't avoid getting tasks, ask for high-level examples of how they would be useful—this will help you understand who needs them and why, so you can then design the solution.

- To derive the appropriate scope, think about the business goal of a milestone and the stakeholders who can contribute or be affected by that milestone.

- Start with the outputs of a system to get the business users more engaged.

- Reorganize component teams into teams that can deliver complete features.

- Investigate emerging techniques, including feature injection, user story mapping, and effect mapping to derive scope from goals effectively.

---

[7] See www.lulu.com/product/file-download/real-options-at-agile-2009/5949486 to download a free copy.
[8] http://picasaweb.google.co.uk/chris.matts/FeatureInjection#
[9] Mijo Balic and Ingrid Ottersten, *Effect Managing IT* (Copenhagen Business School Press, 2007).
[10] http://gojko.net/effect-map
[11] www.agileproductdesign.com

6

Specifying collaboratively

Specification by Example is conceptually different from traditional specification or testing processes, especially in the way it relies on collaboration. Specification by Example won't work if we write documents in isolation, even if we implement all the other patterns described in this book.

In *Bridging the Communication Gap*, I focused on large, all-team specification workshops as the primary tool for collaborating on specifications. Probably the biggest lesson I've learned in working on this book is that the situation is a lot more complicated. Different teams in different contexts have their own way of collaborating on specifications, to the extent that even teams from the same group approach collaboration differently.

In this chapter, I present the most common models for collaboration on specifications, including big workshops, smaller workshops, and the most popular alternatives to workshops. This will help you understand the benefits and downsides of various approaches to collaborative specifications. I also present good practices for preparing for collaboration and ideas that will help you choose the right collaboration model for your team.

In order to properly present an example of a collaboration on specifications, we also need to review a related practice: illustrating using examples. You'll read an example of how a specification workshop would play out in chapter 7, in the section "Illustrating using examples: an example."

Let's first deal with the question of whether collaboration is required at all.

Why do we need to collaborate on specifications?

Specifying collaboratively is a great way to build a shared understanding of what needs to be done and to ensure that different aspects of a system are covered by the specifications. Collaboration also helps teams produce specifications that are easy to understand and tests that are easy to maintain.

According to Jodie Parker, failure to collaborate on specifications was one of the biggest problems when they started implementing Specification by Example at LMAX. She says:

> ❝ People just don't realize how valuable a conversation could have been. Developers initially thought that testers aren't interested in the conversations because they were technical, but testers could learn about how to interrogate the code base or they could advise on the potential impact on other tests or changes to the language. Testers also thought that they were too busy. You can only see how valuable this [collaborating on specifications] is by doing it. ❞

Even with perfect understanding of the business domain covered by a software system (and I've never seen a team with that), it's still worth collaborating on specifications. Analysts and testers may know what they want to specify and test but not necessarily how to organize that information to make it easy to automate and drive development—programmers will. Marta Gonzalez Ferrero worked on a project where the testers initially wrote all the acceptance tests themselves, without thinking of them as specifications. She says that, frequently, the developers couldn't use such tests:

> ❝ At the very beginning, testers were working on FitNesse tables and handed them over to developers. This caused problems because developers were coming back saying that pages weren't easy to understand or easy to automate. After that, they started working together. ❞

A failure to collaborate on defining specifications and writing acceptance tests is guaranteed to lead to tests that are costly to maintain. This was one of the most important lessons about test design for Lisa Crispin. She explained:

> ❝ Whenever we had to make a change, we had too many tests [executable specifications] that we had to change. It's hard to refactor when you have many tests. I should have paired with developers to help me design the tests. I could easily formulate the questions; I see what's wrong. Testers knew basic concepts as Don't Repeat Yourself but didn't have a good understanding of the tools. ❞

Because Crispin didn't collaborate with developers on writing and automating executable specifications, she wrote too many specifications and they weren't automated in a way that made long-term maintenance easy.

Many teams I interviewed made similar mistakes early on. When developers wrote specifications in isolation, those documents ended up being too closely tied to the software design and hard to understand. If testers wrote them in isolation, the documents were organized in a way that was hard to maintain. In contrast, successful teams quickly moved on to more collaborative work models.

The most popular collaborative models

Although all the teams I interviewed collaborated on specifications, the ways they approached that collaboration varied greatly, from large all-hands workshops to smaller workshops, and even to informal conversations. Here are some of the most common models for collaboration along with the benefits the teams obtained.

Try big, all-team workshops
When: Starting out with Specification by Example

Specification workshops are intensive, hands-on domain and scope exploration exercises that ensure that the implementation team, business stakeholders, and domain experts build a consistent, shared understanding of what the system should do. I explain them in detail in *Bridging the Communication Gap*. The workshops ensure that developers and testers have enough information to complete their work for the current iteration.

 Big specification workshops that involve the entire team are one of the most effective ways to build a shared understanding and produce a set of examples that illustrate a feature.

During these workshops, programmers and testers can learn about the business domain. Business users will start understanding the technical constraints of the system. Because the entire team is involved, the workshops efficiently use business stakeholders' time and remove the need for knowledge transfer later on.

Initially, the team at uSwitch used specification workshops to facilitate the adoption of Specification by Example. Jon Neale describes the effects:

> It particularly helped the business guys think about some of the more obscure routes that people would take. For example, if someone tried to apply for a loan below a certain amount, that's a whole other scenario [than applying for a loan in general]. There's a whole other raft of business rules that they wouldn't have mentioned until the last minute.

Specification workshops helped them think about those scenarios up front and helped us go faster. It also helped the development team to interact with the other guys. Having that upfront discussion helped drive the whole process—there was a lot more communication straight away. 99

Implementing Specification workshops into PBR workshops

Product Backlog Refinement (PBR) workshops are one of the key elements of well-implemented Scrum processes. At the same time, I've found that most teams that claim to run Scrum actually don't have PBR workshops. PBR workshops normally involve the entire team and consist of splitting large items on the top of the backlog, detailed analysis of backlog items, and re-estimation. In *Practices for Scaling Lean and Agile*,[†] Bas Vodde and Craig Larman suggest that PBR workshops should take between 5 and 10 percent of each iteration.

Illustrating requirements using examples during a Product Backlog Refinement workshop is an easy way to start implementing Specification by Example in a mature Scrum team. This requires no additional meetings and no special scheduling. It's a matter of approaching the middle portion of the PBR workshop differently.

The Talia team at Pyxis Technologies runs their workshops like this. André Brissette explains this process:

66 This usually happens when the product owner and the Scrum master see that the top story on the backlog is not detailed enough. For example, if the story is estimated at 20 story points, they schedule a maintenance workshop during the sprint. We think that it's a good habit to have this kind of a session every week or every two weeks in order to be certain that the top of the backlog is easy to work with. We look at the story; there is an exchange between the product owner and the developers on the feasibility of it. We draw some examples on the whiteboard, identify technical risk and usability risks, and developers will have to make an evaluation or appraisal of the scope. At this time we do planning poker. If everyone agrees on the scope of the feature and the effort that it will take, then that's it. If we see that it is a challenge to have a common agreement, then we try to split the story until we have items that are pretty clear and the effort is evaluated and agreed to. 99

[†] Craig Larman and Bas Vodde, *Practices for Scaling Lean & Agile Development: Large, Multisite, and Offshore Product Development with Large-Scale Scrum* (Pearson Education, 2010).

Large workshops can be a logistical nightmare. If you fail to set dates on a calendar up front, people might plan other meetings or not be readily available for discussions. Regularly scheduled meetings solve this issue. This practice is especially helpful with senior stakeholders who want to contribute but are often too busy. (Hint: call their secretary to schedule the workshops.)

If you have a problem getting enough time from business users or stakeholders, try to fit into their schedule or work on specifications during product demos when they're in the room. This is also effective if the business users and delivery team don't work from the same location.

Large workshops are an effective way to transfer knowledge and build a shared understanding of the requirements by the entire team, so I highly recommend them for teams that are starting out with Specification by Example. On the other hand, they cost a lot in terms of people's time. Once the process matures and the team builds up domain knowledge, you can move on to one of the alternatives.

Try smaller workshops ("Three Amigos")
When: Domain requires frequent clarification

Having a single person responsible for writing tests, even with reviews, isn't a good approach if the domain is complex and testers and programmers frequently need clarification.

 Run smaller workshops that involve one developer, one tester, and one business analyst.

A popular name for such meetings is Three Amigos. Janet Gregory and Lisa Crispin suggest a similar model for collaboration in *Agile Testing,*[1] under the name The Power of Three. (I used to call such workshops Acceptance Testing Threesomes until people started complaining about the innuendo.)

A Three Amigos meeting is often sufficient to get good feedback from different perspectives. Compared to larger specification workshops, it doesn't ensure a shared understanding across the entire team, but it's easier to organize than larger meetings and doesn't need to be scheduled up front. Smaller meetings also give the participants more flexibility in the way they work. Organizing a big workshop around a single small monitor is pointless, but three people can sit comfortably and easily view a large screen.

---

[1] Lisa Crispin and Janet Gregory, *Agile Testing: A Practical Guide for Testers and Agile Teams* (Addison-Wesley Professional, 2009).

To run a Three Amigos meeting efficiently, all three participants have to share a similar understanding of the domain. If they don't, consider allowing people to prepare for the meeting instead of running it on demand. Ian Cooper explains this:

> The problem with organizing just a three-way is that if you have an imbalance of domain knowledge in the team, the conversation will be led by the people with more domain expertise. This is similar to the issues you get with pairing [pair programming]. The people knowledgeable about the domain tend to dominate the conversation. The people with less domain expertise will sometimes ask questions that could have quite a lot of interesting insight. Giving them an option to prepare beforehand allows them to do that.

A common trick to avoid losing the information from a workshop is to produce something that closely resembles the format of the final specification. With smaller groups, such as the Three Amigos, you can work with a monitor and a keyboard and produce a file. Rob Park worked on a team at a large U.S. insurance provider that collaborated using Three Amigos. Park says:

> The output of the Three Amigos meeting is the actual feature file—Given-When-Then. We don't worry about the fixtures or any other layer beneath it, but the acceptance criteria is the output. Sometimes it is not precise—for example, we know we'd like to have a realistic policy number so we would put in a note or a placeholder so we know we're going to have a little bit of cleanup after the fact. But the main requirement is that we're going to have all these tests in what we all agree is complete, at least in terms of content, before we start to code the feature.

Stuart Taylor's team at TraderMedia has informal conversations for each story and produces tests from that. A developer and a tester work on this together. Taylor explains the process:

> When a story was about to be played, a developer would call a QA and say, "I'm about to start on this story," and then they would have a conversation on how to test it. The developer would talk about how he is going to develop it using TDD. For example, "For the telephone field, I'll use an integer." Straightaway the QA would say, "Well, what if I put ++, or brackets, or leading zeros, etc."

The QA would start writing [acceptance] tests based on the business acceptance criteria and using the testing mindset, thinking about the edge cases. These tests would be seen by the BA and the developer. During showcasing we'd see them execute.

Producing a semiformal test collaboratively ensures that the information won't get distorted during automation later on. It also helps to share knowledge about how to write good specifications with examples; this is only feasible if the entire group can sit around a single monitor and a keyboard. Don't try to draft semiformal documents in an all-hands workshop, because it won't encourage everyone to get involved.

Teams that work on mature products and already have a good knowledge of the target domain don't necessarily have to run meetings or have separate conversations to discuss the acceptance criteria for a story. Developers and testers might not necessarily need to provide as much input up front into the specifications, and they can resolve small functional gaps and during implementation. Such teams can collaborate with informal conversations or reviews.

Pair-writing
When: Mature products

Even in cases where the developers knew enough to work without big workshops, teams found it useful to collaborate on writing specifications with examples.

> Analysts can provide the correct behavior but developers know the best way to write a test so that it's easy to automate later and fits into the rest of the living documentation system.

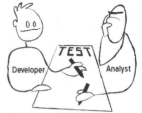

Andrew Jackman's team at BNP Paribas works on a relatively mature product. They have experimented with different models of writing tests and concluded that they need to get both business analysts and developers involved in writing the tests. He says:

> When developers were writing the tests, it was easy to misunderstand what the story is about. If you don't have the interaction with the business analysts, it's only the developers' view of a thing. We moved to BAs writing the tests and that made a big difference. The challenge is when they write a story, that story might influence a number of existing tests, but

they can't foresee that. The BAs like to write a test that shows a workflow for a single story. Generally that leads to a lot of duplication because a lot of the workflows are the same. So we move bits of the workflow into their own test.

Some teams—particularly those in which the business analysts cause a bottleneck or don't exist at all—get testers to pair with programmers on writing tests. This gives the testers a good overview of what will be covered by executable specifications and helps them understand what they need to check separately The team at Songkick is a good example. Phil Cowans explains their process:

> QA doesn't write [acceptance] tests for developers; they work together. The QA person owns the specification, which is expressed through the test plan, and continues to own that until we ship the feature. Developers write the feature files [specifications] with the QA involved to advise what should be covered. QA finds the holes in the feature files, points out things that are not covered, and also produces test scripts for manual testing.

Pairing to write specifications is a cheap and efficient way to get several different perspectives on a test and avoid tunnel vision. It also enables testers to learn about the best ways to write specifications so that they're easy to automate, and it allows developers to learn about risky functional areas that need special attention.

Have developers frequently review tests before an iteration
When: Analysts writing tests

The business users that work with Bekk Consulting on the Norwegian Dairy Herd Recording System don't work with developers when writing acceptance tests, but they frequently involve developers in reviewing the tests. According to Mikael Vik, a senior developer at Bekk Consulting, this approach gives them similar results:

> We're always working closely with them [business users] on defining Cucumber tests. When they take their user stories and start writing Cucumber tests, they always come and ask us if it looks OK. We give them hints on how to write the steps and also come up with suggestions on how our Cucumber domain language can be expanded to effectively express the intention of the tests.

If developers aren't involved in writing the specifications, they can spend more time implementing features. Note that this increases the risk that specifications won't contain all the information required for implementation or that they may be more difficult to automate.

Try informal conversations
When: Business stakeholders are readily available

Teams that had the luxury of business users and stakeholders sitting close by (and readily available to answer questions) had great results with informal ad hoc conversations. Instead of having big scheduled workshops, anyone who had a stake in a story would briefly meet before starting to implement it.

> Informal conversations involving only the people who will work on a task are enough to establish a clear definition of what needs to be done.

"Anyone who has a stake" includes the following:

- The analysts who investigate a story
- The programmers who will work on implementing it
- The testers who will run manual exploratory tests on it
- The business stakeholders and users who will ultimately benefit from the result and use the software

The goal of such informal conversations is to ensure that everyone involved has the same understanding of what a story is about. At LMAX, such conversations happened in the first few days of a sprint. Jodie Parker explains:

> Conversations would be done on demand. You've got the idea and your drawings, and you really understand how it is going to be implemented. If you've not already written down the acceptance tests, a developer and a tester can pair on this. If the conversations didn't happen, things would end up being built but not being built right.

Some teams, such as the one at uSwitch.com, don't try to flush out all the acceptance criteria at this point. They establish a common baseline and give testers and developers enough information to start working. Because they sit close to the business users, they can have short conversations as needed (see chapter 12 for more information).

Some teams decide whether to have an informal discussion or a larger specification workshop based on the type of the change introduced by a story. Ismo Aro at Nokia Siemens Networks used this approach:

> We have an agreement to have ATDD test cases [specifications], not necessarily a meeting. If the team feels it's coming naturally, then it's OK not to do the meeting. If it seems harder and they need input from another stakeholder, then they organize an ATDD meeting [Specification workshop]. This might be due to the team knowing a lot about the domain. When you are adding a small increment to the old functionality, it's easier to figure out the test cases.

Preparing for collaboration

Collaborating on specifications is a great way to ensure shared understanding and flush out intricate details that people would never think about in isolation. If the topic of discussion requires a lot of up-front analysis or the team members don't have the same level of knowledge, starting from scratch in the discussions can be inefficient and frustrating. To address this, many teams introduced a preparatory phase, shown in figure 6.1, to ensure that the features are described in enough detail to facilitate a fruitful discussion.

Start of work on examples

two weeks ahead	few days ahead	iteration kick-off	inside iteration
enough for detailed analysis	collect & answer key open questions	renegotiate items that blow up	risk of severe flow interruption

Figure 6.1 Teams generally fall into four groups depending on when they start working on examples. Those who need more time for analysis and chasing open questions start earlier.

This preparation involves working with stakeholders upstream to prepare some initial examples and initial analysis. Depending on the availability of team members, it can be done by either a single person—often in an analyst role—or a small group of senior people.

Hold introductory meetings
When: Project has many stakeholders

Teams with many stakeholders (for example, when the software is used by many departments inside a company or has several external customers driving requirements) in general run an introductory meeting several days before the start of an iteration. Some teams call this meeting pre-planning.

 The purpose of an introductory meeting is to gather some initial feedback on upcoming stories and filter the ones that are too vague to be accepted into planning.

The introductory meeting isn't supposed to deliver perfectly refined specifications but to give the team enough time to gather external feedback on key issues that could be quickly identified. This isn't the iteration planning or Scrum planning meeting. Running the introductory meeting several days before the start of a sprint gives the team an opportunity to discuss open questions with remote stakeholders before the real specification refinement or planning meeting.

Many teams define high-level acceptance criteria in this introductory meeting, with bullet points rather than detailed examples. This helps focus the later work by specifying the basic cases they will test.

With smaller teams, such as the team at ePlan Services, developers, stakeholders, the project manager, and the product owner participate in this introductory meeting. With larger teams or groups of teams, only a few people participate. At Sky Network Services, which has six teams, each team sends two or three people to this meeting.

Involve stakeholders

A collaborative specification process works because it taps into the collective brain of business users and development team members and ensures that they all understand the specifications in the same way.

Many teams involved their business analysts or product owners, but not the customer stakeholders, in the discussions. In those cases, the teams consistently delivered products that met the business analysts' or product owners' expectations. But these expectations often weren't what the end users wanted. As far as I'm concerned, business analysts are part of the delivery team, not customer representatives.

➡️ To get the best results, actual stakeholders have to be involved in the collaboration on specifications. They are the ones who can really make decisions.

When a project has many interested parties, all the requirements are often funneled through a single person, typically called a product owner. This works well for scope and prioritization but not specifications. Lisa Crispin's team at ePlan Services ran into this problem. She says:

> The product owner wanted to own everything but at the same time he can't get everything right. He is doing the job of three or four people. Nobody has the bandwidth to do everything. Sometimes we need an answer to complete a story, but he can't provide that answer. He didn't understand the accounting requirements, for example. We still had to go and talk to stakeholders directly to understand that.
>
> He felt that we were going around him, so we had to really find the balance of keeping the product owner in the loop and still getting the information from the people who are going to be using that functionality. If there was a difference, we had to get them in the room to discuss it.

A single person can't possibly know everything about everything. Having a single decision maker on board to determine priorities is a must, but once the top-priority story gets selected, the team must try to collaborate with the relevant stakeholders on specifications for particular stories. In *Practices for Scaling Lean and Agile*, Larman and Vodde make the distinction between clarification and prioritization. They argue that prioritization must always be done by one person but that clarification can be done by the team itself.

It's important to involve the end stakeholders even if the team thinks they know the domain well enough to build good specifications by themselves. Mike Vogel worked on a technical data management project where the developers understood parts of the domain and its technical constraints better than the end users. To meet the project schedule, they were frequently forced to limit or exclude the stakeholders from collaboration on specifications—which Vogel thinks was one of their biggest mistakes. He says:

> We started doing too much of the test creation and definition of the acceptance criteria ourselves. So we could set up the meta programming that drove the system faster than them and we were under heavy schedule pressure. But there would be subtleties that neither we nor the customer understood, and they weren't able to pick that up from the tests.

If possible, include the actual stakeholders in the collaboration on specifications. This will ensure that you get the right information from an authoritative or dependable source and reduce the need for up-front analysis.

In larger organizations this might require some persuasion and politics, but it will be worth it. If your team has one, work with the product owner on finding a way to get in touch with stakeholders directly without interfering with the product owner's stakeholder management responsibilities.

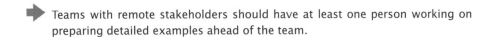

Undertake detailed preparation and review up front
When: Remote stakeholders

➤ Teams with remote stakeholders should have at least one person working on preparing detailed examples ahead of the team.

In the teams I interviewed, the person who worked ahead of the team was typically a business analyst or a tester. They worked with the stakeholders to analyze the requirements, agree on the structure of the examples, and capture the values for the most important cases. Teams working with vague requirements that needed a lot of analysis and clarification also had one person working ahead of the team.

In most teams, a developer also reviewed the initial examples early to provide technical feedback. This guaranteed that the team detected most functional gaps and questions early on. Stakeholders could then answer these questions up front, so the team wouldn't get stuck when collaboratively reviewing a story.

Many teams failed to implement this step when they started out, especially if they based their process on time-bound iterations. It seems logical that everything related to a particular story should be done within a single sprint or a single iteration. If the domain is complex, time-boxing both the specification and the development effort to a single iteration can cause developers to get stuck frequently.

The Sierra team at BNP Paribas tried to time-box everything in the same iteration, but they found this approach didn't allow them to work efficiently. Instead, their business analyst started working one step ahead of the rest of the team. Andrew Jackman says:

> ❝ Our project manager who's effectively the product owner will have prepared in advance the stories that he wants us to play. He and the business analyst already had them for the next iteration up on the board, and the business analyst went though preparing the acceptance tests. We used to not do this, but when developers tried to write a [acceptance] test we suddenly asked questions and found out that we were missing analysis. ❞

Putting the initial examples together ahead of an iteration also enables the team members to be better prepared for the collaborative discussion. Ian Cooper's team at Beazley uses this approach. Their business analysts and stakeholders are based in the United States, but the development team is in the UK. He says:

> Given the nature of the product and the fact that we're serving U.S. customers, time zones became an issue and there is no real easy access to the customer. Business analysts are proxies and they often took questions to answer later. Developers knew a lot about the domain, so analysts and developers were running the show. Testers didn't really participate.
>
> We found it easier to get the analyst to do the first pass through what was required and then come to the meeting. Testers will quite often run through all possible scenarios and ask about edge cases. Testers are given more time to read through stuff and understand it, to think about what the issues might be. This enables them to participate much better.

If stakeholders can't participate in the collaboration for specifications, then the risk that the delivery team will misunderstand their goals increases substantially. To reduce risk, teams with remote users performed more analysis up front than the teams who had direct access to their business users.

If you decide to start analysis before the iteration, be sure that this responsibility is assigned to a dedicated team member to avoid dragging the entire team into it; this defeats the point of iteration scope. When an analyst works upstream with the business users and stakeholders, other team members may need to take over some of the analyst's downstream tasks.

Have team members review stories early
When: Analysts/domain experts are a bottleneck

If analysts or subject matter experts cause a bottleneck in the process, they won't be able to conduct much analysis before the relevant iteration. This might not be a problem if the stakeholders are readily available to answer questions or if the product is mature; functional gaps won't appear late in development.

On the other hand, if the team finds that they don't have enough information to write the executable specifications, someone has to provide analysis earlier. That someone doesn't necessarily have to be a business analyst or a subject matter expert. It could be a tester or a developer.

> Developers and testers can help to take the load off domain experts (when they're causing a bottleneck) and do a first-pass review to spot the common problems. This increases the overall throughput of the team and also helps to build cross-functional teams.

Clare McLennan worked on a web advertising project where the stakeholders were in Germany and the team was in New Zealand—almost 12 hours apart. The testers played the role of local analysts. They couldn't make decisions for the customers, so they worked ahead of the team. McLennan says:

> To avoid the time zone problems we had to make sure that we have a handle on a story. If the testers read through it and it makes sense to them, they interrupt a programmer to make sure that it makes sense to them as well.

For the Global Talent Management team at Ultimate Software, the product owner is busy so the rest of the team helps with analysis work. A "cell" consisting of two developers and a tester reviews each story early on to prepare for the meeting with the product owner, identifying any open questions. Maykel Suarez says that this approach helped them use everyone's time more efficiently:

> The bigger team, around 17 people, put a lot of pressure on decision-making. The solution was to create cells. Now a cell (one tester, two developers) is able to make decisions more quickly. The flow process allowed working on those preparation meetings in chunks smaller than two-week iterations, usually just two-three stories. So, having three people in a meeting for 15–30 minutes every 3–5 days didn't seem like a waste of time or resources.

Prepare only initial examples
When: Stakeholders are readily available

The teams with stakeholders who are readily available to answer questions didn't spend too much time preparing detailed examples up front. They still found it useful to identify some initial examples, to get the basic structure in place before the discussion.

> Identifying initial examples gets the basic structure in place and helps discussions run more efficiently.

André Brissette often uses examples provided by the external customers to start the work on specifications for the Talia project at Pyxis Technologies. He's the business stakeholder for the development team and also works with external customers. When the customers propose new functionality, they send examples of how the system would work; those examples become part of the future specification.

The team at uSwitch works in the same location as their stakeholders, so they don't need a lot of up-front preparation. Anyone on the team can suggest a new story during a stand-up meeting; the person who makes the suggestion often prepares basic examples beforehand.

Having initial examples ready from the beginning helps run the discussion more efficiently because the team doesn't have to experiment with the best structure of examples to illustrate a requirement or identify key attributes. They can instead focus on understanding the initial examples and extending them.

 ## Don't hinder discussion by overpreparing

A preparatory phase shouldn't replace collaboration. It should just make the collaboration more effective. Some teams prepared too much information up front because testers approached the executable specifications from the perspective of combinatorial functional regression checking. They specified every possible combination of input arguments in the tests.

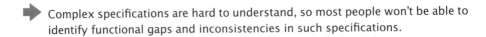 Complex specifications are hard to understand, so most people won't be able to identify functional gaps and inconsistencies in such specifications.

With complex specifications, the effect of up-front analysis will be similar to what occurs when traditional requirements are handed down from analysts to developers. Instead of collaborating to build a shared understanding, developers just take the requirements, leading to misunderstanding and a higher probability that functional gaps won't be identified until late in the process.

Jodie Parker's team at LMAX took preparation too far and ended up with examples that seemed complete. This made them skip the discussions—and resulted in functional gaps in specifications. Parker advises preparing "just enough" examples up front:

> Because we were all very new to the process, at first our developers said that it's not enough information to work on. Then the business analysts completely prescribed very much everything and our hands were tied. When the time came to do any development on the cards, there was no creativity, no way to do a simpler solution, because it was too prescribed.

> If you read a card and say, "OK, I completely understand that," you just go off and work, and you could have made a million and one assumptions. If you read a card and there is enough of "I'm not quite sure," it pushes you to have a conversation, drawing it out at the start of an iteration, and then talking about different implementations and their effects. The testers would then consider how this impacts tests. BAs could think about what's also coming up soon and see how that fits in. "Just enough" means that your developer, BA, and QA are standing against a board and really discussing how this needs to work.

Whether you decide to have someone work one week ahead to prepare initial examples or hold an introductory meeting to identify open questions, remember that the goal is to prepare for the discussion later, not replace it.

Choosing a collaboration model

I don't think there's a one-size-fits-all heuristic that will help you choose the best model for your team, including the balance between individual up-front work and more hands-on collaboration. After comparing the teams who had similar processes, I suggest basing your decision on the following criteria:

- How mature is the product?
- How much domain knowledge is there in the team?
- How much analysis do typical changes require?
- How close are the business users to the development team? Are they readily available to discuss and verify examples?
- Where's the bottleneck in the process?

Immature products require big workshops and lots of up-front analysis. With immature products, it's important to get testers and developers to contribute to specifications more actively, because the underlying system is changing frequently and they have insights that the business users won't have.

Mature products might allow for less analysis up front and other models of collaboration. A mature product probably means that there will be few surprises. Business analysts and product owners most likely have a good idea of what the technology can give them, and they can do a good job of preparing examples up front.

If the team is relatively new or if testers and developers don't have a solid understanding of the business domain, it's worth running big workshops. All-hands workshops are a great way to efficiently transfer the knowledge about the business domain to the entire team. Once the team understands the business domain better, smaller and more focused discussions might be sufficient.

If typical changes require a lot of analysis, then someone in an analyst role should work ahead of the team to prepare detailed examples with stakeholders. Otherwise, any discussion during the workshops will end quickly and with too many open questions. If relatively small and well-understood features normally come into development, preparing some basic examples up front to make the discussion run more smoothly might be sufficient.

Teams with remote business users typically have to do more work up front than those with business users who are readily available to answer open questions. If the business users aren't available for specification workshops at all, most questions and functional gaps have to be identified and addressed up front.

Finally, there's no point in overloading team members who are already a bottleneck in the process. The teams where testing is a bottleneck should get developers and business analysts much more engaged in up-front work. Likewise, the teams where business analysts or subject matter experts are the bottleneck should get testers to help with up-front analysis.

Remember

- Specification by Example relies heavily on collaboration between business users and delivery team members.

- Everyone on the delivery team shares the responsibility for the right specifications. Programmers and testers have to offer input about the technical implementation and the validation aspects.

- Most teams collaborate on specifications in two phases: Someone works up front to prepare initial examples for a feature, and then those who have a stake in the feature discuss it, adding examples to clarify or complete the specification.

- The balance between the work done in preparation and the work done during collaboration depends on several factors: the maturity of the product, the level of domain knowledge in the delivery team, typical change request complexity, process bottlenecks, and availability of business users.

7
Illustrating using examples

Examples are a good way to avoid ambiguities and communicate with precision. We use examples in everyday conversation and in writing without even thinking about it—when I searched online for the phrase "for example," Google returned more than 210 million pages that use this term.

With traditional specifications, examples appear and disappear several times in the software development process. Business analysts often get examples of existing orders, invoices, and reports from business users, which they translate into abstract requirements. Developers invent examples to explain edge cases and clarify them with business users or analysts and then translate the cases to code, without recording the examples. Testers design test cases that are examples of how the system is expected to work; they keep these examples to themselves and don't communicate them to programmers or analysts.

Everyone invents their own examples, but there's nothing to ensure that these examples are even consistent, let alone complete. In software development, this is why the end result is often different from what was expected at the beginning. To avoid this, we have to prevent misinterpretation between different roles and maintain one source of truth.

Examples are a good tool for avoiding communication problems. We can avoid playing the telephone game by ensuring that we capture all the examples—from start to finish—and use them consistently in analysis, development, and testing.

Marta Gonzalez Ferrero was working as a test lead at Beazley when they introduced Specification by Example. According to her, the development team was committing to more work than they could produce, and they often realized they needed a lot more information than they were getting at the start of the implementation. The situation was further complicated by the fact that they were running six-week iterations, and the development team and the business analysts were on different continents. The acceptance criteria that the programmers were receiving from the business analysts was relatively abstract (for example, "make sure that for this business unit all correct products are displayed"). Finding out that something important was missing halfway through an iteration would seriously disrupt the output. One iteration ended with customers saying that the team delivered something completely different from what was expected. The last week of each iteration was reserved for the model office: effectively, an iteration demonstration. Ferrero traveled to the United States for one model office and worked with business analysts on illustrating requirements with examples for two days. As a result, the team committed to 20% less work for the next iteration and delivered what they promised.

"The feeling in the team was also much better," said Ferrero. "Before that, they [the developers] were working with a feeling that they were making it up as they go, and had to wait for feedback from business analysts." According to Ferrero, the amount of rework dropped significantly after they started illustrating requirements using examples.

Ferrero's wasn't the only team to experience results like these. Almost all the teams profiled in this book confirmed that illustrating requirements using examples is a much more effective technique than specifying with abstract statements. Because examples are concrete and unambiguous, they're an ideal tool for making requirements precise—this is why we use them to clarify meaning in everyday communication.

In *Exploring Requirements*,[1] Gerald Weinberg and Donald Gause write that one of the best ways to check if requirements are complete is to try designing black-box test cases against them. If we don't have enough information to design good test cases, we definitely don't have enough information to build the system. Illustrating requirements using examples is a way to specify how we expect the system to work with enough detail that we can check that assertion. Examples used to illustrate requirements are good black-box tests.

From my experience, it takes far less time to illustrate requirements with examples than to implement them. Concluding that we don't have enough information to illustrate something with examples takes far less time than coming to the same realization after trying to implement the software. Instead of starting to develop an incomplete story only to see it blow up in the middle of an iteration, we can flush such problems out during the collaboration on specifications while we can still address them—and when the business users are still available.

In May 2009 I ran a three-hour workshop on Specification by Example[2] during the Progressive .NET tutorials. Around 50 people, mostly software developers and testers, participated in this workshop. We simulated a common situation: A customer directs the team to a competitor site and asks them to copy some functionality.

---

[1] Gerald M. Weinberg and Donald C. Gause, *Exploring Requirements: Quality Before Design* (New York, Dorset House, 1989).
[2] See http://gojko.net/2009/05/12/examples-make-it-easy-to-spot-inconsistencies

I copied the rules of a blackjack game from a popular website and asked the participants to illustrate those rules using examples. Although the requirements were taken from a real website and fit on a single sheet of paper, they were ambiguous, redundant, and incomplete. In my experience, this is often the case when requirements are captured as Word documents.

The participants were divided into seven teams, and each team had only one person with knowledge of blackjack. After the workshop, all the participants agreed that discussing realistic examples helped flush out inconsistencies and functional gaps. By running a feedback exercise (see sidebar), I measured the level of shared understanding. Six out of seven teams came up with the same answers to difficult edge cases, even though most people on the team had no previous exposure to the target domain. Illustrating requirements with examples is a very effective way to communicate domain knowledge and ensure a shared understanding. I've seen this effect on real software projects, as have many teams that I interviewed for this book.

Feedback exercises

Feedback exercises are a good way to check whether a group of people has a shared understanding of a specification. When someone suggests a special case after a story has been discussed, the person running the workshop should ask the participants to write down how they think the system should work. The entire group then compares the answers. If they all match, everyone understands the specification in the same way. If the answers don't match, then it's useful to organize the results into clusters and get one person from each cluster to explain their answers. The discussion will reveal the source of misunderstanding.

Illustrating requirements using examples is a simple idea, but it's far from easy to implement. Finding the right set of examples to illustrate a requirement turns out to be quite a challenge.

In this chapter, I begin by putting things in perspective using an example of the process. Then, I present good ideas for identifying the right set of examples to illustrate a business function. Finally, I cover ideas for illustrating cross-cutting functionality and concepts that aren't easy to capture with precise values.

Illustrating using examples: an example

To clarify how illustrating a requirement using examples works, let's take a look at an example involving a fictional company, ACME OnlineShop. This is the only fictional company in the book, but I had to invent one to keep the example simple. Acme is a small web store whose development team started a Specification workshop. Barbara, a business analyst, spent some time the week before with Owen, the company owner, to get some initial examples. She's facilitating the workshop and introduces the first story:

> BARBARA: The next thing on the list is free delivery. We have arranged deal with Manning to offer free delivery on their books. The basic example is this: If a user purchases a Manning book, say *Specification by Example*, the shopping cart will offer free delivery. Any questions?

> DAVID, a developer, spots a potential functional gap. He asks: Is this free delivery to anywhere? What if a customer lives on an island off South America? That free delivery will cost us much more than we earn from the books.

> BARBARA: No, this isn't worldwide, just domestic.

> TESSA, a tester, asks for another example. She says: The first thing I'd check when this comes for testing is that we don't offer free delivery for all books. Can we add one more case to show that the free delivery is offered only for Manning books?

> BARBARA: Sure. For example, *Agile Testing* was published by Addison-Wesley. If a user buys that, then the shopping cart won't offer free delivery. I think this is relatively simple; there isn't a lot more to it. Can anyone think of any other examples? Can we play around with the data to make it invalid?

> DAVID: There aren't any numerical boundary conditions, but we could play with the list in the shopping cart. For example, what happens if I buy both *Agile Testing* and *Specification by Example*?

> BARBARA: You get free delivery for both books. As long as a Manning book is in the shopping cart, you get free delivery.

> DAVID: I see. But what if I buy *Specification by Example* and a fridge? That delivery would be much more expensive than our earnings from the book.

> BARBARA: That might be a problem. I didn't talk about that with Owen. I'll have to get back to you on this. Any other concerns?

> DAVID: Not apart from that.

> BARBARA: OK. Do we have enough information to start working, apart from the fridge problem?

> DAVID AND TESSA: Yes.

> BARBARA: Great. I'll get back to you on that fridge problem early next week.

In this example, the team quickly clarified a vague requirement from both the testing and the development perspective. They also illustrated the requirement with examples to capture their shared understanding.

Examples should be precise

Good examples help us avoid ambiguities. In order to do that, there must be no room for misunderstanding. Each example should clearly define the context and how the system should work in a given case and, ideally, describe something we can easily check.

Don't have yes/no answers in your examples
When: The underlying concept isn't separately defined

When describing processes, many teams I interviewed oversimplified examples by using yes/no answers. This can be misleading and give people the false sense that they have shared understanding when they don't.

For example, TechTalk had this issue when illustrating the requirements for email alerts in a web-based refund system. They had examples of conditions about when to send emails, but they didn't discuss the email contents. "The customer expected us to include the failing case and the resolution, and we didn't capture that," said Gaspar Nagy, a developer who worked on this system.

I ran a specification workshop for a major investment bank. The team was discussing how payments are routed to different systems. They started by listing examples in a table with conditions on the left and different subsystems on the right, marking the columns yes or no depending on whether the destination receives a transaction or not. Instead of yes/no, I asked them to write down the key attributes of the messages sent to each of the systems. At that point, several interesting cases came up that most of the developers misunderstood. For example, instead of a transaction update, one of the systems was expecting two messages: one to cancel an existing transaction and one to book a new one.

 Watch out for examples that have yes/no answers and try to rewrite them to be more precise.

You can still leave yes/no in examples as long as the underlying concept is illustrated separately. For example, one set of examples can tell you whether an email is sent or not, while another set of examples illustrates the email's contents.

Avoid using abstract classes of equivalence
When: You can specify a concrete example

Classes of equivalence (such as "less than 10") or variables can create an illusion of shared understanding. Without choosing a concrete example, different people might, for example, understand differently whether negative values are included or left out.

When equivalence classes are used as input parameters, expected outputs have to be specified as formulas with variables representing the input values. This effectively replicates the description of the functionality. It doesn't provide a concrete example to verify it; the value of illustrating using examples is lost.

Classes of values have to be translated into something concrete for automation, which means that whoever automates the validations will have to translate the specifications into automation code. This means more opportunities for misunderstanding and misinterpretation.

From my experience, the things that seem obvious in requirements can trick us the most. Confusing concepts are discussed and explored. But the ones that seem clear— with different people understanding them differently—will go undetected and cause problems.

 Instead of classes of equivalence, always use a representative concrete example. Concrete examples allow us to automate the validation of specifications without changing them and ensure that all team members have a shared understanding.

You can safely use equivalence classes as expected outputs, particularly when the process you're trying to describe isn't deterministic. For example, stating that the result of an operation should be between 0.1 and 0.2 still makes a specification testable. A concrete value makes it more precise if the process is deterministic; try to use concrete values, even for outputs.

Examples should be complete

We should have enough examples to describe the entire scope of a feature. Expected behavior in primary business cases and simple examples are a good start, but they're rarely the sum of what needs to be implemented. Here are some ideas on how to extend an initial set of examples to provide a full picture of functionality.

Experiment with data

 Once you have a set of examples that you think is complete, look at the structure of the examples and try to come up with valid combinations of inputs that could violate the rule. This helps reveal what you might have missed, making the specification more complete and stronger.

If the examples include numerical values, try to use large and small numbers around different boundary conditions. Try to use a zero or negative numbers. If the examples include entities, consider whether you can use more than one object, whether an example without that entity is still valid, and what happens if the same entity is specified twice.

When collaborating on specifications, I expect testers in particular to help with finding examples like these. They should have techniques and further heuristics to identify potential problematic cases.

Many of the technical edge cases you identify won't represent valid examples; that's fine. Don't cover them in detail unless you're demonstrating error messages for invalid arguments (in which case these are valid examples for that business function). Thinking about these different cases might flush out inconsistencies and edge cases you might not have thought about earlier.

One risk of experimenting with data is that the output will have too many examples with insignificant differences. This is why the next step, refining the specification (described in the next chapter), is important.

Ask for an alternative way to check the functionality
When: Complex/legacy infrastructures

In complex IT systems, it's easy to forget about all the places where you should send a piece of information.

 To test whether you have a good set of examples specifying a story, ask the business users to think of an alternative way to verify the implementation.

"How else would you be able to test this?" is a good question to kick off that discussion. Bas Vodde also suggests asking, "Is there anything else that would happen?" When I asked this question

Initial test   Alternative test

in the same specification workshop discussed in "Don't have yes/no answers in your examples," we discovered a legacy data warehouse that some people thought should receive the transaction and that others thought should be ignored. This discovery prompted us to have a discussion and close this functional gap.

Pascal Mestdach had similar experiences on the Central Patient Administration project at IHC. They often had problems when customers presumed data stored in a new application would also be sent to the legacy application during the migration period, but the team didn't understand these requirements. Asking the customers for an alternative way to test the feature would have revealed their expectation that they see the information in the legacy system as well.

Asking for an alternative way to check functionality is also a useful way to help the team discuss the best place to automate the validation.

Examples should be realistic

Ambiguities and inconsistencies are flushed out when we illustrate a feature with examples, because examples focus the discussion on real cases instead of abstract rules. For this to work, the examples have to be realistic. Invented, simplified, or abstracted examples won't have enough detail or exhibit enough variation for this. Watch out for abstract entities, such as "customer A." Find a real customer who has the characteristic you want to illustrate, or, even better, focus on the characteristic and not the customer.

Avoid making up your own data
When: Data-driven projects

⮕ Using real data is important on data-driven projects, when a great deal can depend on slight variations and inconsistencies.

Mike Vogel from Knowledgent Group worked on a greenfield project using metadata-driven ETL to populate a data repository for pharmaceutical research. They used Specification by Example, but both the team and the customer invented examples to illustrate the functionality instead of looking at real data samples. He says the approach didn't help them avoid inconsistencies:

> ❝They [customer representatives] were making up examples; they didn't deal with real variations. They assumed they could do certain things and left it out of examples. When the data from real systems came in, there were always too many surprises.❞

This is an even greater problem with projects that involve legacy systems, because legacy data often defies expected consistency rules (and rules of logic in general).

Jonas Bandi worked at TechTalk on rewriting a legacy application for school data management where significant complexity resulted from understanding existing legacy data structures and relationships. They expected that Specification by Example would protect them from boomerangs (see "Watch out for boomerangs" in chapter 4) and bugs, but this didn't happen. They were inventing examples based on their understanding of the domain. The real legacy data often had exceptions that surprised them. Bandi says:

> Even when the scenarios [test results] were green and everything looked good, we still had a lot of bugs because of the data from the legacy application.

To reduce the risk of legacy data surprising the team late in the iteration, try to use realistic data from the existing legacy system in the examples instead of specifying completely new cases.

Using existing data might require some automated obfuscation of sensitive information, and it has an impact on data management strategies for automation. For some good solutions to this problem, see "Test data management" in chapter 9.

Get basic examples directly from customers
When: Working with enterprise customers

Teams that sell enterprise software to several customers rarely have the luxury of involving customer representatives in collaborative specification workshops. Product managers collect requirements from different customers and decide on release plans. This introduces the possibility of ambiguity and misunderstanding. We can have perfectly precise and clear examples that don't capture what the customers want.

> Ensure that the examples used to illustrate the specifications are realistic. Realistic examples contain data that comes from the clients.

We can apply the same trick used to ensure shared understanding inside the team when we work with external stakeholders. André Brissette uses customer emails as a starting point for the discussion about automated dialogs in the Talia system:

> They would write an email such as, "It would be easier if I could ask this to Talia, and she would tell me this, and then I would be able to do that." In this case, the user provides the first draft of the dialog.

Brissette records emails like these and uses them as the initial examples to illustrate the required features. This ensures that the external stakeholders' requests are satisfied. See figure 7.1 for an example of the resulting specification. Note that this example should ideally be further refined later. See the section "Scripts are not specifications" in chapter 8.

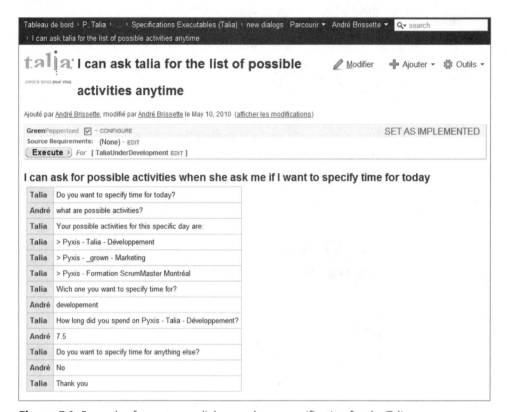

Figure 7.1 Example of a customer dialog used as a specification for the Talia system

Adam Knight's team at RainStor uses this approach to develop an archiving system for structured data. They work with customers to get realistic data sets and expected targets for representative queries. When the customer can't give them a specific use case, they push back and ask for examples, sometimes organizing workshops with the customers. A common example when customers can't give them a specific use case is when a reseller who doesn't yet have a buyer wants the system to support something because they suspect it will make it easier to sell. One example is a request to mirror functionality available in email archiving systems. Knight says:

> ❝They looked at an email archiving system and said we need to be able to work in the same way. An email archiving system would have thousands of emails, but in our system you could have billions of records. Do you want the same level of granularity? What about logging? That is the most difficult kind of requirement. Generally we try to push back and get examples. We arrange demos to prototype functionality and walk through that.❞

To avoid ambiguities and misunderstanding between what the product manager thinks the customers need and what they ask for, insist on examples when communicating with customers. These examples can then be used to kick-start the discussion during specification workshops. They should be included in the final executable specifications to ensure that the customers' expectations are met.

Examples should be easy to understand

A common mistake teams make when starting out with Specification by Example is to illustrate requirements using complex and convoluted examples. They focus on capturing realistic examples in precise detail and create huge, confusing tables with dozens of columns and rows. Examples like these make it hard to evaluate consistency and completeness of specifications.

One of the main reasons I prefer examples over abstract statements as requirements is that they allow me to think about functional gaps and inconsistencies. Making things precise makes it easier to spot missing cases. This requires an understanding of the entire set of examples for a particular feature. If the examples aren't easy to understand, we won't be able to evaluate their completeness and consistency. Here are some ideas on how to avoid that problem and still keep the examples precise and realistic.

 ### Avoid the temptation to explore every combinatorial possibility

When teams start illustrating their requirements using examples, testers often misunderstand the purpose of that process and insist on covering every possible combination of arguments. There isn't much point in going through examples that illustrate existing cases; that doesn't improve understanding.

➡️ When illustrating using examples, look for examples that move the discussion forward and improve understanding.

I strongly advise against discarding any examples suggested as edge cases without discussion. If someone suggests an edge case example that the others consider to have been covered already, there might be two possible reasons: Either the person making the suggestion doesn't understand the existing examples, or they have genuinely found something that breaks the existing description that the others don't see. In both cases, it's worth discussing the example to ensure that everyone in the room has the same level of examples suggested as edge casesunderstanding.

Look for implied concepts

When you use too many examples to illustrate a single function or the examples are complex, this often means that the examples should be described at a higher level of abstraction.

 Look at the examples and try to identify concepts that are hidden and implied. Make those concepts explicit and define them separately. Restructuring examples like this will make the specifications easier to understand and will lead to better software design.

Looking for missing and implied concepts and making them explicit in system design is one of the core ideas of domain-driven design.[3]

 I facilitated a workshop for a team that was rewriting an accounting subsystem and gradually migrating trades from the legacy system to the new product. The workshop was focused on a requirement to migrate Dutch trades to the new system. We started writing examples on a whiteboard and quickly filled all the available space. Looking at the examples, we discovered that we were explaining three things: how to decide which trades are Dutch, how to decide which trades are migrated, and what happens to a trade once it's migrated.

Because we were illustrating all these things at the same time, we had a combinatorial explosion of relevant cases to deal with. When trying to summarize the examples, we identified two implied concepts: a trade location and a migration status. We then broke this requirement into three parts and used a separate, focused set of examples to illustrate each part. We had a specification of how to decide whether a trade is Dutch or not (how to calculate the location of a trade). Another focused set of examples illustrated how the location of a trade affects its migration status. In that set, we used Netherlands only once, without having to go through all the cases that constitute a Dutch trade. The third set of examples illustrated the difference in processing between migrated and non-migrated trades.

---

[3] Eric Evans, *Domain-Driven Design: Tackling Complexity in the Heart of Software* (Boston, Addison-Wesley Professional, 2003).

Splitting the specification this way allowed the team to significantly improve the design of the system—because three different sets of examples clearly pointed to modular concepts. The next time they had a requirement to migrate a set of trades, they could focus only on changing the definition of a migrated trade. What happens to the trade after it's migrated stays the same. Likewise, the way a trade location is determined doesn't change.

Separating the concepts also facilitated a much more meaningful discussion about trade locations because we were dealing with a small and focused set of examples. We discovered that some people thought the registered location of the company whose stock is being traded determines the location, whereas others thought that only the stock exchange where the company is listed was relevant.

Looking for missing concepts and raising the level of abstraction is no different than what happens in daily communication. Try to give a simple instruction such as "If you come by car, book parking in advance" without using the word *car*; instead, focus on its properties. One way to specify a car is as a transport vehicle with four wheels, four doors, four seats, and a diesel engine. But we also have two-door cars, other types of engines, different numbers of seats, and so on. Listing all those examples would make the instructions ridiculously complicated; instead, we create a higher-level concept to improve communication. How a car is made is irrelevant to parking instructions; what's important is whether the person will arrive by car or not.

Whenever you see too many examples or complicated examples in a specification, try to raise the level of abstraction for those descriptions and then specify the underlying concepts separately.

By illustrating requirements using precise realistic examples and structuring them to be easy to understand, we can capture the essence of required functionality. We also ensure that we've explored the requirements in enough detail for developers and testers to have enough information to start working. These examples can replace abstract requirements in the delivery process and serve as a specification, a target for development, and a verification for acceptance acceptance testing.

Illustrating "nonfunctional requirements"

Illustrating isolated functional requirements with examples is relatively intuitive, but many teams struggle to do this with functionality that's cross-cutting or difficult to describe with discrete answers. At most of my workshops on Specification by Example, there's usually at least one person who claims that this is possible for "functional" requirements but there's no way that this could work for "nonfunctional" requirements because they aren't that precise.

> ## What are nonfunctional requirements?
>
> Characteristics such as performance, usability, or response times are often called nonfunctional because they aren't related to isolated functionality. I generally disagree with the practice of categorizing requirements as functional or nonfunctional, but that's probably a topic for another book. Many features commonly termed nonfunctional imply functionality. For example, performance requirements might imply a caching function, persistence constraints, and so on. From my experience, what most people think of when they say *nonfunctional* are functional requirements that are cross-cutting (for example, security) or not discrete but measurable on a sliding scale (for example, performance). Dan North points out[†] that requirements listed as nonfunctional usually imply that there's a stakeholder whom the team hasn't yet explicitly identified.
>
> ———————————
> † In private communication

So far, I haven't seen a single nonfunctional requirement that couldn't be illustrated using examples. Even usability, perhaps the vaguest and most subjective concept in software development, can be illustrated. Ask your usability expert to show you a website that she likes; that's a good, realistic example. The validation of such examples might not be automatable, but the example is realistic and precise enough to spark a good discussion. Here are some ideas that will help you capture "nonfunctional requirements" with examples.

Get precise performance requirements
When: Performance is a key feature

Performance tests often require a separate environment similar to the production one. Developers working on performance-critical systems often can't run those tests on their machines. This doesn't mean that teams should skip a discussion about performance requirements.

➤ Having the performance criteria clearly specified and illustrated using examples will help build shared understanding and provide the development team with a clear target for implementation.

At RainStor, performance is critical for their data-archiving tools, so they make sure to express the performance requirements in detail. Performance requirements are collected in the form "The system has to import X records within Y minutes on Z CPUs." Developers then either get access to dedicated testing hardware or have the testers run tests for them and provide feedback.

➡ Remember that "faster than the current system" isn't a good performance requirement. Tell people exactly how much faster and in what way.

Use low-fi prototypes for UI

User interface layouts and usability can't be specified easily with examples fitting into truth tables or automated tests. This doesn't mean that we can't discuss examples.

I often create paper prototypes that are glued together from cutouts of user interface elements and website prints. Going through one or two examples is a good way to ensure that we have all the information a customer needs on a screen.

Business users often find it hard to think beyond the user interface, because that's what they work with. This is why boomerangs often happen when a client looks at the software on a screen.

➡ Instead of discussing backend processing, we can sometimes get more concrete information up front by working through a user interface example.

Several teams I interviewed use Balsamiq Mockups,[4] a web/desktop application for low-fi user interface prototyping. I find paper prototypes easier to work with because we can use cutouts and write notes, but a software system works better when we want to share our work.

At RainStor, Adam Knight took this approach even further by creating an interactive prototype to explore vague requirements with clients. He says:

> Rather than a paper prototype we put together some example command line prototype interfaces using shell scripts and then walked these through with the customer, asking them to give us details on how they'd use the new functionality in our system.

This interactive workshop provided functional examples that the development team later used to illustrate requirements. Teams can use this approach to identify scope as well. (See "Don't look only at the lowest level" in chapter 5.)

---

[4] www.balsamiq.com/products/mockups

Try the QUPER model
When: Sliding scale requirements

When requirements don't lead to discrete, precise results, they're hard to argue about. When was the last time you had a meaningful discussion about why web pages should load in less than two seconds, rather than three seconds or one second? Most of the time, requirements like these are accepted without discussion or understanding.

At the Oresund Developer conference in 2009, Björn Regnell presented QUPER,[5] an interesting model for illustrating requirements that aren't discrete but that work on a sliding scale (for example, startup time or response times). I haven't tried this on a project yet, but because it provides some interesting food for thought, I decided to include it in the book.

QUPER visualizes sliding-scale requirements along the axes of cost and quality. The idea of the model is to estimate cost-benefit breakpoints and barriers on the sliding scale and expose them for discussion.

The QUPER model assumes that such requirements produce benefits on the S curve and that there are three important points on the curve (called breakpoints). *Utility* is the point where a product moves from unusable to usable. For example, the utility point for startup time of a mobile phone is one minute. *Differentiation* describes when the feature starts to develop a competitive advantage that will influence marketing. For example, the differentiation point for mobile phone startup is five seconds. *Saturation* is where the increase in quality becomes overkill. It makes no difference to the user if a phone takes half a second or one second to start, making one second a possible saturation point for mobile phone startup. Regnell argued that going beyond the saturation point means that we're investing resources in the wrong area.

Another assumption of the model is that increases in quality don't lead to linear cost increases. At some point, cost becomes steep. The product might have to be rewritten using a different technology or there will be a significant impact on architecture. These points are called cost barriers in the model.

 Defining barriers and breakpoints for sliding scale requirements allows us to have a more meaningful discussion on where the product fits in the market and where we want it to be.

We can use breakpoints and barriers to define relevant targets for different phases of the project and make sliding scale requirements measurable. Regnell suggested setting these as intervals rather than discrete points because this works better with the continuous

---

[5] See http://oredev.org/videos/supporting-roadmapping-of-quality-requirements and the IEEE Software journal, Mar/Apr 2008.

nature of quality requirements. For example, the target for a feature that just needs to work as well as in competing software should most likely be close to the utility point, definitely not going over the differentiation point. The target for unique selling points of a product should be between the differentiation and saturation points. Visualizing cost barriers on the same curve will help the stakeholders understand how far they can push the targets without having to invest significantly more than ethan expected.

Use a checklist for discussions
When: Cross-cutting concerns

Often, the customers feel safer when they impose a global generic requirement. I've participated in many projects where performance requirements were defined globally; for example, "All web pages will load in less than a second." In most cases, implementing that requirement (and other global requirements like it) is a waste of money. Most often, only the home page and some key functions had to load in less than a second; many other pages could load more slowly. In the QUPER model language, only the loading time of a small number of key pages needs to be close to the differentiation point. Other pages might load in a period of time closer to the utility point.

The problem is that these requirements are defined close to the start of a project, when we still don't know what the product is going to look like.

Rather than taking such requirements at face value, Christian Hassa suggests using these cross-cutting requirements as a checklist for discussions. Hassa says:

> It's easy to specify "The system should respond in 10 milliseconds" globally for the whole system, but you don't necessarily need that level of response time for every feature. What exactly does the system have to do in 10 milliseconds? Does it need to send an email, record the action, or reply? We create acceptance criteria for each feature with this nonfunctional criteria in mind.

A checklist for discussions will ensure that you begin to consider all the important questions when reviewing a story. You can use it to decide which of the cross-cutting concerns apply to a particular story and then focus on illustrating those aspects.

Build a reference example
When: Requirements are impossible to quantify

Because it's subjective and depends on many factors, usability is hard to quantify. But that doesn't mean that it can't be specified by example. In fact, it can only be specified that way.

Usability and similar nonquantifiable features, such as playability and fun, are key for video games. These qualities can't be easily specified with documents that detail traditional requirements. Supermassive Games, a video game studio based in the UK, applies an agile process to game development. The teams at Supermassive use checklists to ensure that different aspects of quality are covered in detail, but that isn't enough to deal with the uncertainty and subjectivity of those features.

Harvey Wheaton, studio director at Supermassive, said that these features have "elusive quality" during his presentation at SPA2010 conference.[6] According to Wheaton, they typically focus on getting one feature finished to the final level of quality early on; then, the team can use that as an example what "done" means:

> We build what we call a "vertical slice" as early on in the process as we can, typically at the end of our pre-production phase. This vertical slice is a small section of the game (e.g., one level, part of a level, the game introduction) and is to final (shippable) quality. This is usually supplemented by a "horizontal slice," i.e., a broad slice of the whole game but blocked out and in low fidelity, to give an idea of the scale and breadth of the game.
>
> You can get a lot of use out of reference or concept art to illustrate the visual look and fidelity of the final product and employ people specifically for this, to produce high quality artwork that shows how the game will look.

Instead of trying to quantify features that have an elusive quality, Supermassive Games builds a reference example against which team members can compare their work.

▶ Building a reference example is an effective way to illustrate nonquantifiable features using examples.

---

[6] http://gojko.net/2010/05/19/agile-in-a-start-up-games-development-studio

In summary, instead of using the categorization "nonfunctional requirements" to avoid a difficult conversation, teams should ensure they have a shared understanding of what their business users expect out of a system, including cross-cutting concerns. Even if the resulting examples aren't easy to automate later on, having an up front discussion and using examples to make expectations explicit and precise will ensure that the delivery team focuses on building the right product.

Remember

- Using a single set of examples consistently from specification through development to testing ensures that everyone has the same understanding of what needs to be delivered.

- Examples used for illustrating features should be precise, complete, realistic, and easy to understand.

- Realistic examples help spot inconsistencies and functional gaps faster than implementation.

- Once you have an initial set of examples, experiment with data and look for alternative ways to test a feature to complete the specification.

- When examples are complex and there are too many examples or too many factors present, look for missing concepts and try to explain the examples at a higher level of abstraction. Use a set of focused examples to illustrate the new concepts separately.

8

Refining the specification

> In its rough form, a diamond is a lusterless, translucent crystal that resembles a chip of broken glass. For it to be transformed into a jewel, it must be cut into a particular gem shape and then polished, facet by facet.
>
> —Edward Jay Epstein, *The Diamond Invention*[1]

Collaborative discussion is a great way to build a shared understanding, but that isn't enough to drive any but the simplest of projects. Unless the team is very small and the project is very short, we need to record this knowledge in a way that doesn't depend on peoples' short-term memory.

Taking a photo of the whiteboard after a discussion on key examples is a simple way to capture this knowledge, but the examples are just raw material. Raw examples are like uncut diamonds—very valuable but not nearly as much as in a processed form. Separating real diamonds from rock, polishing them, and breaking them into sizes that are easy to sell increases the value significantly. The same can be said for the key examples we use to illustrate a requirement. They're a great starting point, but in order to get the most value out of them we have to refine them, polish them to show the key points clearly, and create specifications that teams can use both now and in the future.

One of the most common reasons for failing with Specification by Example is not taking the time to process these raw examples. Discussion about specifications often leads to experimentation. We discover new insights and restructure examples to look at them from a higher level of abstraction. This results in some great examples but also a lot of dead ends and rejected ideas. We don't necessarily need to capture all these intermediary examples or record how we got to the result.

---

[1] http://www.edwardjayepstein.com/diamond/chap11.htm

On the other hand, just recording the key examples we want to keep without any explanation won't allow us to communicate the specification effectively to anyone who hasn't participated in the discussions.

Successful teams don't use raw examples; they *refine the specification* from them. They extract the essence from the key examples and turn it into a clear and unambiguous definition of what makes the implementation complete, without any extraneous detail. This acceptance criterion is then recorded and described so that anyone can pick up the resulting specification and understand it at any time. This specification with examples captures the conditions of satisfaction, the expected output of a feature, and its acceptance test.

> ### Specifications with examples are acceptance tests
>
> A good specification, with examples, is effectively an acceptance test for the described functionality.

Ideally, a specification with examples should unambiguously define the required functionality from a business perspective but not how the system is supposed to implement it. This gives the development team the freedom to find the best possible solution that meets the requirements. To be effective in these goals, a specification should be

- Precise and testable
- A true specification, not a script
- About business functionality, not about software design

Once the functionality is implemented, the specification that describes it will serve a different purpose. It will document what the system does and alert us about functional regression. To be useful as long-term functional documentation, the specification has to be written so that others can pick it up months or even years after it was created and easily understand what it does, why it's there, and what it describes. To be effective in these goals, a specification should be

- Self explanatory
- Focused
- In domain language

This chapter focuses on how to refine specifications to achieve all these goals. But first, to put things into a more concrete perspective, I show examples of good and bad specifications. At the end of this chapter, we'll refine the bad specification by applying the advice given in this chapter.

An example of a good specification

An example of a very good specification with examples is shown here.

Free delivery

- Free delivery is offered to VIP customers once they purchase a certain number of books. Free delivery is not offered to regular customers or VIP customers buying anything else than books.

- Given that the minimum number of books to get free delivery is five, then we expect the following:

Examples

Customer type	Cart contents	Delivery
VIP	5 books	Free, Standard
VIP	4 books	Standard
Regular	10 books	Standard
VIP	5 washing machines	Standard
VIP	5 books, 1 washing machine	Standard

This specification is self-explanatory. I often show this example to people at conferences and workshops, and I've never had to say a single word to explain it. The title and the introductory paragraph explain the structure of the examples so that readers don't need to work back from the data to understand the specified rule. Realistic examples are also there, to make the specification testable and explain the behavior in edge cases, for example, what happens when someone buys exactly 5 books.

This is a specification, not a script for how someone might test the examples. It doesn't say anything about application workflow or session constraints. It doesn't explain how the books are purchased, just what the available delivery mechanism is. It doesn't try to talk about any implementation specifics. That's all left to the developers to work out in the best way possible.

This specification is focused on a particular rule for free delivery. It includes only the attributes relevant for that rule.

An example of a bad specification

Compare the previous specification to the example shown in figure 8.1. This is a great example of a very bad specification.[2]

Simple Acceptance Test for Payroll

First we add a few employees

Employees			
id	name	address	salary
1	Jeff Languid	10 Adamant St; Laurel MD 20707	1005.00
2	Kelp Holland	128 Baker St; Cottonmouth, IL 60066	2000.00

Next we pay them.

Pay day	
pay day	check number
1/31/2001	1000

We make sure their paychecks are correct. The blank cellls will be filled in by the Paycheckinspector fixture. The cells with data in them already will be checked.

Paycheck inspector				
id	amount	number	name	date
1	1005			
2	2000			

Finally we make sure that the output contained two, and only two paychecks, and that they had the right check numbers.

Paycheck inspector
number
1000
1001

Figure 8.1 A confusing specification

Although it has a title and some text around the tables, seemingly to explain what's going on, the effect of that is marginal. Why is this document called "simple"? It's payroll related, obviously, but what exactly is it specifying?

It's not really clear what this document is specifying. We need to work backwards from the test data to understand the rules. It seems to verify that the checks are printed with unique numbers, starting from a number that's given as a parameter. It also seems to validate the data printed on each check. It also explains in words that one check is printed per employee.

---

[2] This example is from a real project and was previously included with FitNesse. We used it in a workshop on refining the specifications in June 2010 in London. As a result, the example was changed in the FitNesse distribution.

This document has a lot of seemingly incidental complexity—names and addresses aren't really used anywhere in the document apart from the setup. Database identifiers appear in the tables, but they're irrelevant for the business rules. The database identifiers are used in this example to match employees with the Paycheck Inspector, introducing technical software concepts into the specification.

The Paycheck Inspector was obviously invented just for testing. When I read this for the first time, I imagined Peter Sellers in a Clouseau outfit inspecting checks as they go out. I'm sure that this isn't a business concept.

Another interesting issue is the presence of blank cells in the assertion part of this specification, and the two Paycheck Inspector tables seem unrelated. This example is from FitNesse, and blank cells in that tool print test results for troubleshooting without checking anything. That effectively makes this specification an automated test that a human has to look over—pretty much defeating the purpose of automation. Blank cells in FitNesse are typically a sign of instability in tests, and they're a signal that something is missing. Either the automated test is hooking into the system in the wrong place, or an implicit rule is hidden there that makes the test results unrepeatable and unreliable.

The language used in the specification is inconsistent, which makes it hard to make a connection between inputs and outputs. What is the 1001 value in the table at the bottom? The column header tells us that it's a number, which is a technically correct but completely useless piece of information. The second box has a check number, but what kind of a number is that? What's the relationship between these two things?

Presuming that the addresses are there because checks are printed as part of a statement with an address for automated envelope packaging, the test based on this specification fails to verify at least one very important thing: that the right people got paid the right amount. If the first person got both checks, this test would happily pass. If they both got each other's salaries, this test would pass. If a date far in the future was printed on the checks, our employees might not be able to cash them, but the test would still pass.

Now we come to the real reason for the blank cells. Printing order of checks is not specified. This is a functional gap that makes the system hard to test in a repeatable way. The author of this FitNesse page decided to work around that technical difficulty in the specification, not in the automation layer, and created a test that gives false positives.

Without more context information it's hard to tell whether this test is verifying one thing only. If the check printing system is used for anything else, I'd prefer to pull out the fact that check numbers are unique and start from a configured value in a separate page. If we only print salary checks, it's probably part of salary check printing.

We'll refine this horrible document later in this chapter. But first, let's go over what makes a good specification.

What to focus on when refining specifications

In the introduction to this chapter I laid out some goals for good specifications. Here are some good ideas on how to achieve those goals.

Examples should be precise and testable

A specification needs to be an objective measure of success, something that will unambiguously tell us when we're finished with development. It has to include verifiable information—combinations of parameters and expected outputs that can be checked against the system.

In order to satisfy these criteria, a specification has to be based on precise realistic examples. See the "Examples should be precise" section in chapter 7 for some good techniques on how to ensure that the examples are precise.

Scripts are not specifications

Business users will often think about performing an action through the user interface or through several steps, explaining how they'd use the system to achieve something instead of what the system is supposed to do. Such examples are scripts, not specifications.

A *script* explains how something can be tested. It describes business functionality through lower-level interactions with a system. A script requires the reader to work back from the actions and understand what's really important and what exactly is being illustrated. Scripts also bake the test into workflow and session constraints, which might change in the future even when the underlying business rules don't change.

A *specification* explains what the system does. It focuses on the business functionality in the most direct way possible. Specifications are shorter because they describe the business concepts directly. That makes them easier to read and understand than scripts. Specifications are also a lot more stable than scripts, because they won't be affected by changes in workflow and session constraints.

Here's an example of a script:

1 Log on as user *Tom*.

2 Navigate to the *home page*.

3 Search for *Specification by Example*.

4 Add *first* result to shopping cart.

5 Search for *Beautiful Testing*.

6 Add *second* result to shopping cart.

7 Verify that number of items in cart is *2*.

This script tells us *how* something is done but doesn't directly explain *what* we're specifying. Take a piece of paper and try to write down what exactly this example is specifying before continuing to read the next paragraph. Were you able to write down anything at all? If so, do you think that's the only thing that the example could possibly describe?

There are so many possibilities for what this example describes. One option is that multiple items can be added to the shopping cart. An equally possible option is that the shopping cart is empty after a user logs on. A third option is that the first search result for Specification by Example and second search result for Beautiful Testing can be added to the shopping cart.

This is a very precise and testable example; we can execute it and confirm whether the system gives us the expected result or not. The problem with this script is that it doesn't contain any information on what functionality it actually represents. The people who wrote it might know exactly what it's supposed to do when they implement the functionality for the first time. Six months later, that will no longer be obvious.

This script isn't a good communication tool. We can't really tell what this is about or know which part of the system is wrong. If the test based on this script suddenly starts failing, someone will have to spend a lot of time analyzing many different areas of code.

The step in which Tom logs on at the start is most likely required because of workflow constraints of the website. Unless this example illustrates a business rule related to this user in particular, the fact that Tom is the person who logs on is irrelevant. If his user account is disabled for any reason, this test will start failing, but the system might not necessarily have a problem. Someone will have to waste a lot of time to discover that.

Capturing acceptance criteria with scripts instead of specifications costs a lot of time in the long term, and we can save this time if we take a few minutes to restructure the examples up front. For an example of how to refine such scripts to more useful specifications, see the "Refining in practice" section at the end of this chapter. Rick Mugridge and Ward Cunningham have a lot of good advice on restructuring scripts to be better specifications in *Fit for Developing Software* (Prentice Hall, 2005).

Don't create flow-like descriptions

Watch out for descriptions of flows (first do this, then do that, ...). Unless you are specifying a genuine process flow, this is often a sign that a business rule is illustrated using a script. Such scripts will cause a lot of long-term maintenance problems.

Watch out for descriptions of *how* the system should work. Think about *what* the system should do.

Ian Cooper's team at Beazley realized that about six months after they started implementing Specification by Example. During a team retrospective, they started arguing that their acceptance tests are too costly to maintain. Looking for ways to reduce the cost, they restructured scripts into specifications. Cooper said:

> 66 Models we had for doing tests were the same as manual tests, translated into scripts. Our early tests were following a scripting approach; the test was a sequence of things with some checks at the end. Once we changed over to "what should it do," it became a lot easier. 99

Describing acceptance tests as scripts instead of specifications is one of the most common mistakes teams make early on. Scripts work relatively well as a development target with short iterations, because people still remember what the script describes when they implement it for the first time. But they're hard to maintain and understand later. It can take several months for this problem to show up, but when it does, it will hurt badly.

Specifications should be about business functionality, not software design

Ideally, a specification should not imply software design. It should explain the business functionality without prescribing how it's going to be implemented in software. This serves two purposes:

- It allows developers to find the best possible solution now.
- It allows developers to improve the design in the future.

Specifications that focus on business functionality, without describing the implementation, enable the implementation to change more easily. A specification that doesn't say anything about software design won't need to change when the design improves. Such specifications facilitate future change by acting as an invariant. We can run the tests unmodified based on those specifications after we improve the software design, to ensure that all the previous functionality is still there.

 ## Avoid writing specifications that are tightly coupled with code

▶ Specifications that are tightly coupled with code and closely reflect the software implementation result in tests that are brittle.

Changes in software design break such tests, even when the business functionality described by the test doesn't change. Specifications with examples that produce brittle tests introduce additional maintenance costs instead of facilitating change. Aslak Hellesøy points this out as one of the key lessons he learned about Specification by Example:

> We wrote too many acceptance tests, and sometimes they were too tightly coupled with our code. Not quite as coupled as unit tests would have been, but still coupled. In the worst case it would take up to eight hours after a big refactoring to update the test scripts. So we learned a lot about striking a good balance between how many tests you have and how you write them.

> Watch out for names and concepts in specifications that come from software implementations and do not exist in the business domain. Examples are database identifiers, technical service names, or object class names that aren't first-order domain concepts, and concepts invented purely for automation purposes. Rewrite the specifications to avoid these concepts, and they'll be much easier to understand and maintain long term.

Technical tests are important, and I'm not arguing against having such tests that are closely coupled with the software design. But such tests should not be mixed with executable specifications. A common mistake for teams starting with Specification by Example is to drop all technical tests, such as the ones at the unit or integration level, and expect that executable specifications will cover all aspects of the system. Executable specifications guide us in delivering the right business functionality. Technical tests validate low-level technical quality aspects of the system. We need both, but we shouldn't mix them. Technical test automation tools are much better suited for technical tests than the tools we use to automate executable specifications. They'll enable the team to maintain such tests much easier.

Resist the temptation to work around technical difficulties in specifications
When: Working on a legacy system

Legacy systems often have lots of technical quirks, and they're hard to change. Users have to work around these technical difficulties, and it becomes difficult to distinguish the real business process from workarounds.

Some teams fell into a trap by including these process workarounds in their specifications. This binds the specifications not only to the implementation but also to those technical issues. Such specifications are ineffective as a facilitator of change in legacy systems. They quickly become expensive to maintain. One small change in code might require hours of updating executable specifications.

Johannes Link worked on a project where about 200 different objects had to be constructed to run the basic test scenarios. Those dependencies were described in the executable specifications, not in the automation layer. A year later, test maintenance became so costly that the team was pushing back on changes. Link says:

> Changing one feature broke a lot of tests. They couldn't afford to implement some new requirements, because this would have been too costly in terms of the tests, and they knew they needed the tests to keep the bug rate low.

Most automation tools[3] for executable specifications separate the specification from the automation process (more on this in the "How does this work?" tip at the beginning of chapter 9). The specification is in human-readable form, and the automation process is captured using a separate automation layer of programming language code.

➡ Solve technical difficulties in the automation layer. Don't try to solve them in the test specifications.

This will allow you to change and improve the system more easily. Solving technical difficulties in an automation layer allows you to benefit from programming language features and tools when describing and maintaining technical validation processes. Programmers can apply techniques and tools to reduce duplication, create maintainable code, and easily change it. If the technical workarounds are contained in the automation layer, the specifications will be unaffected when you improve the technical design and the workarounds are no longer required.

Pushing technical workflows into the automation layer also makes specifications shorter and easier to understand. The resulting specification will explain the business concepts at a higher level of abstraction, focusing on the aspects that are important for a particular set of examples (more on this in the "Specifications should be focused" section later in this chapter).

---

[3] See http://specificationbyexample.com for more information on tools that support automation.

Don't get trapped in user interface details
When: Web projects

 When starting out with Specification by Example, many teams wasted a lot of time by describing irrelevant examples of minor user interface details. They were following the process of Specifying by Example for the sake of the process, not to extend their understanding of the specification.

The user interface is visual, so it's easy to think about. I've seen projects where teams and customers spent hours describing navigation menu links. But that part of the user interface carried virtually no risk, and that time could have been spent discussing much more important functions.

Phil Cowans had a similar experience at Songkick when they started implementing Specification by Example, and he thinks about that as one of the key early mistakes.

> Early on we spent too long testing trivial bits of user interface, because that was easy to do. We didn't spend enough time digging into edge cases and alternative paths through the application. It's quite easy to test what you can see, but ultimately you need to have a deep understanding of what the software does rather than what the user interface looks like. Thinking in terms of user stories and paths through the application really helps.

Instead of dwelling on user interface details, it's more useful to think about user journeys through the website. When specifying collaboratively, invest time in parts of the specifications in proportion to their importance to the business. Items that are important and risky should be explored in detail. Those that aren't that important might not need to be specified so precisely.

Specifications should be self-explanatory

When an executable specification test fails because of a functional regression, someone has to look at it, understand what went wrong, and find out how to fix it. This can happen years after the specification was originally written, when the people who wrote it are no longer working on the same project. That's why it's important for specifications to be self-explanatory.

Of course, ensuring that a specification is self-explanatory also helps to avoid any misunderstanding when we develop the specified functionality for the first time. Here are a few tips to ensure that specifications are self-explanatory.

Use a descriptive title and explain the goal using a short paragraph

> Just a few words at the start of a specification can make a big difference and save a lot of time later.

If a specification contains only inputs and expected outputs, anyone who reads that document will have to reconstruct the business rule from the examples.

It's crucial to choose a descriptive title for a specification. The title should summarize the intent. Think about what you'd type into Google's search box to look for a specification if it were somewhere on the web, and use that as the title. This will make it easy for readers to discover the appropriate specification when searching for an explanation of a piece of functionality.

FINDER
The other, other search engine.

My specification's title

SEARCH

A reader also needs to understand the structure of the specification and its context. Explain the goal of the specification and the structure of examples in a few words—no more than a short paragraph—and put it in a header. A good trick for writing the description is to write only the examples first and then try to explain them to someone else. Capture what you said while explaining the examples, and put that in the header of the specification.

Show and keep quiet
When: Someone is working on specifications alone
In order to: Check whether a specification is self-explanatory

> To check if a specification is self-explanatory, get someone else to look at the document and try to understand it, without you saying a word about it.

To ensure that a specification is really self-explanatory, ask the other person to explain what they understood and see if that matches your intention.

If I show a specification to someone and I find myself having to explain it, I write down the explanation and put it in the header. Explaining the examples often leads me to use more meaningful names or insert comments to make the examples easier to understand.

Don't overspecify examples

Many teams made the mistake of extending specifications to include all the possible combinations of input parameters once they put the basic automation infrastructure in place. A common explanation for this was that testers were trying to verify additional examples by reusing the existing automation framework.

 The problem with this approach is that the original key examples get lost in a sea of other values. Specifications become hard to understand, which means that they're no longer self-explanatory.

 A specification that defines three key examples properly is much more useful than one that specifies a hundred examples poorly.

An additional problem with this approach is that executing many more examples to verify the same cases requires more time, so it slows down test execution and gives the delivery team slower feedback.

Lisa Crispin's team ran into this problem while working on automated compliance testing, with rules that are prescribed by the regulators and don't necessarily follow any logic. Crispin collaborated with her product owner to describe algorithms dealing with many permutations, so they wrote a lot of complex executable specifications several sprints ahead of development. Developers were overwhelmed when they started looking at these specifications. Crispin elaborated:

> They [developers] looked at the tests [executable specifications] and were confused; they couldn't see the forest for the trees. They could not use the tests because they did not know what to code. So we found out that the tests should give us the big picture but not necessarily all the detail right away.

A specification should list only the key representative examples. This will help to keep the specification short and easy to understand. The key examples typically include the following:

- A representative example illustrating each important aspect of business functionality. Business users, analysts, or customers will typically define these.

- An example illustrating each important technical edge case, such as technical boundary conditions. Developers will typically suggest such examples when they're concerned about functional gaps or inconsistencies. Business users, analysts, or customers will define the correct expected behavior.

- An example illustrating each particularly troublesome area of the expected implementation, such as cases that caused bugs in the past and boundary conditions that might not be explicitly illustrated by previous examples. Testers will typically suggest these, and business users, analysts, or customers will define the correct behavior.

There is, of course, benefit in reusing the automation structure put in place for key examples to support testers who want to do more testing. Sometimes the easiest way to explore the system behavior with different boundary values is to bolt on more examples to existing specifications. This can make the specifications longer, less focused, and harder to understand. Instead of complicating the main specification, create a separate automated test and point to it from the main one. If you use a web-based system for living documentation, you could use a web link to connect the two pages. With file-based systems, use a file path or a shortcut in the description of the specification. The new test can use the same structure as the original specification and list many additional examples. The main specification of a feature will still be useful as a communication tool and provide quick feedback. Additional tests can explore different combinations of arguments for the purpose of extensive testing. The primary specification can be validated at every change to provide quick feedback. Supplementary tests can run overnight and on demand to give the team confidence in all the additional cases.

Don't try to cover every single case

A common cause for overspecifying examples is a fear by analysts or customers that they will be blamed for any missing functionality. With a collaborative specification process, the responsibility for writing the specifications correct is shared, so there's no justification to do this. André Brissette, the Talia product director at Pyxis, points that out as one of the key lessons learned:

> 66 Decide what to cover and what not to cover depending on the conditions of success for the story. If you think that with those tests you can really cover the conditions of success, then you are OK. If that is not the case, you have a problem. If at the end of the sprint, or in the future, it turns out that you were missing something, one thing is clear: What you made was the condition of success and pretty much the contract between everybody. At that point, it [additional functionality] was not needed. As an analyst, you don't have to take the blame. 99

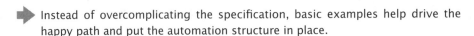

Start with basic examples; then expand through exploring
When: Describing rules with many parameter combinations

To solve the problem described in the previous section, Crispin's team decided to write only high-level specifications before starting to work on a story, leaving detailed tests for later.

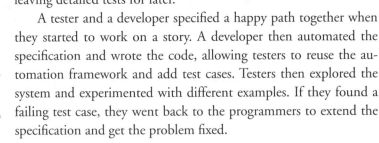

A tester and a developer specified a happy path together when they started to work on a story. A developer then automated the specification and wrote the code, allowing testers to reuse the automation framework and add test cases. Testers then explored the system and experimented with different examples. If they found a failing test case, they went back to the programmers to extend the specification and get the problem fixed.

> Instead of overcomplicating the specification, basic examples help drive the happy path and put the automation structure in place.

Additional examples can then be tried based on risk, and specification can be extended gradually. This is an interesting solution to handle cases where classes of equivalence aren't easy to determine at first and where the implementation drives edge cases.

Specifications should be focused

A specification should describe a single thing—a business rule, a function, or a step of a process. Such focused specifications are easier to understand than the ones that specify several related rules. A specification should also be focused on only the key attributes of relevant examples.

Focus brings two important benefits to specifications: Focused specifications are short, so they're easier to understand than longer, less-focused ones. They're also easier to maintain. A specification that covers several features will be influenced by changes in all of the involved areas of the system. This will cause the automated tests based on the specification to break more often. Even worse, when such a test breaks, it will be hard to pinpoint problems. Here are some tips for improving focus in specifications

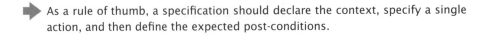

Use "Given-When-Then" language in specifications
In order to: Make the test easier to understand

> As a rule of thumb, a specification should declare the context, specify a single action, and then define the expected post-conditions.

A good way to remember this is *Given-When-Then* or *Arrange-Act-Assert*. Given-When-Then is a common format for specifying system behaviors, popularized by the early behavior-driven-development articles. It requires us to write scenarios of system behaviors in three parts:

- Given a precondition
- When an action happens
- Then the following post-conditions should be satisfied

Some automation tools, such as Cucumber[4] and SpecFlow,[5] use exactly that language for executable specifications. Even with different tools that might use a tabular, keyword-based or free-form text system, structuring specifications to follow a Given-When-Then flow is an excellent idea.

Triggering a single action is crucial. This ensures that a specification is focused on only that action. If a specification lists several actions, a reader will have to analyze and understand how these actions collaborate to produce the final effect in order to understand the results. If a set of actions is important from a business flow perspective, it's probably important enough to be given a name and used as a higher-level concept, so it should be captured in a higher-level concept in the domain code. This higher-level concept can then be listed in the specification.

A specification can still define several preconditions and postconditions (multiple items in the Given and Then sections) as long as they're all directly related to the function specified by the test. The following example of a Cucumber test has two preconditions and two postconditions:

> **Scenario: New user, suspicious transaction**
>
> Given a user with no previous transaction history,
>
> And the user's account registration country is the UK,
>
> When the user places an order with delivery country U.S.,
>
> Then the transaction is marked as suspicious,
>
> But the user sees order status as "Pending."

A potential pitfall with Given-When-Then language is that it's like prose, which often encourages people to think about flows of interactions rather than expressing business functionality directly. Use the advice from section "Scripts are not specifications" earlier in this chapter to avoid such problems.

---

[4] http://www.cukes.info
[5] http://specflow.org

Don't explicitly set up all the dependencies in the specification
When: Dealing with complex dependencies/referential integrity

In data-driven projects that require complex configuration, objects can rarely be created in isolation. For example, the domain validation rules for a payment method might require that it belongs to a customer, that a customer must have a valid account, and so on.

> Many teams made the mistake of putting all the configuration and setup for all prerequisites into the specification. Although this makes the specification explicit and complete from a conceptual perspective, it can also make it difficult to read and understand.

In addition, any change to any of the objects or attributes in the configuration will break the test based on this specification, even if it isn't directly related to the specified rule.

Describing all dependencies explicitly can also hide data-related issues, so this is especially dangerous on data-driven projects (see tip "Avoid creating your own data" in Chapter 7).

Jonas Bandi worked on a project to rewrite a legacy data management system for schools, where one of the biggest problems was understanding the existing data. The team wrote specifications that were setting up the entire context dynamically. The context in the specifications was based on the understanding of the team, not on realistic data variations. The team detected many gaps and inconsistencies in requirements only when they connected the code to the data coming from the legacy system, in the middle of the iterations (see the "Examples should be realistic" section in chapter 7).

The Bekk Consulting team working on the Norwegian Dairy Herd Recording System had a similar issue but from a different perspective. Their project is also data driven, with many objects requiring complex setup. At first, they were defining the entire context in each executable specification. This required people to perfectly guess all the dependencies. If some data was missing, the tests based on the specifications would fail because of data integrity constraints, even though the code was implemented properly.

These issues can be solved better in the automation layer, not in the specification. Move all the dependencies that aren't related to the goal of the specification to the automation layer, and keep the specification focused on only the important attributes and objects. Also see the "Test data management" section in chapter 9 for some good solutions to technical data management problems.

Apply defaults in the automation layer

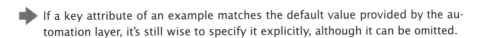 Push the responsibility for creating a valid object to the automation layer.

The automation layer can prepopulate objects with sensible defaults and set up dependencies so that we don't have to specify them explicitly. This allows us to focus on only the important attributes when we write specifications, making them much easier to understand and maintain.

For example, instead of requiring all address details to set up a customer and all credit card attributes to register a valid credit card, we can just specify that a user have $100 available on the card before making a payment. Everything else can be constructed dynamically by the automation layer.

Such defaults can be set in the automation layer or provided in a global configuration file, depending on whether the business users should be able to change them or not.

Don't always rely on defaults
When: Working with objects with many attributes

Although relying on sensible defaults makes specifications easier to write and understand, some teams took that approach too far. Removing duplication is generally a good practice in programming language code but not always in specifications.

 If a key attribute of an example matches the default value provided by the automation layer, it's still wise to specify it explicitly, although it can be omitted.

This ensures that the specification has a full context for the readers and also allows us to change the defaults in the automation layer. Ian Cooper warns:

> Even if it [an attribute of an example] is actually the same as the default, don't rely on that. Define it explicitly. This allows us to change the default later. It also makes it obvious what is important. When you read the specifications, you can see that the example is specifying these values on a product and you can ask, "Why is this important?"

Specifications should be in domain language

Functional specifications are important to users, business analysts, testers, developers, and anyone else trying to understand the system. In order for a specification to be accessible and readable to all these groups, it has to be written in a language that everyone understands. The language used in the documentation also has to be consistent. This will minimize the need for translation and the possibility of misunderstanding.

The Ubiquitous Language (see sidebar) fits both requirements very nicely. Ensure that you use the Ubiquitous Language in specifications, and watch out for class names or concepts that seem to have been invented for the purpose of testing and sound like software implementation concepts.

Ubiquitous Language

Software delivery teams often develop their own jargon for a project, based on technical implementation concepts. This jargon is different from the jargon of business users, leading to a constant need for translation when the two groups communicate. Business analysts then act as translators and become a bottleneck for information. Translation between the two jargons often leads to a loss of information and causes misunderstanding.

Instead of letting different jargons emerge, Eric Evans suggested developing a common language as a basis for a shared understanding of the domain in *Domain Driven Design*.[†] He called this language the *Ubiquitous Language*.

[†] Eric Evans, *Domain-Driven Design: Tackling Complexity in the Heart of Software* (Addison-Wesley Professional, 2003).

By ensuring that specifications fulfill the goals laid out in this section, we get a good target for development, and we get documents that have long-term value as communication tools. They will support us in evolving the system and incrementally building up a living documentation.

Refining in practice

Let's now clean up that bad specification we saw early in this chapter and improve it. First, we should give it a nice descriptive title, such as "Payroll Check Printing," to make sure that we can find it easily later. We should also add a paragraph that explains the goal of this specification. We've identified the following rules:

- The system prints one check per employee, with the employee's name, address, and salary on the check.
- The system prints the payment date on the checks.

- Check numbers are unique, starting from the next available check number, in ascending order.

A check has a payee name, an amount, and a payment date. It doesn't have a name or a salary; those are attributes of an employee. If we print checks as part of letters that will be sent out automatically, we can say that the check also has an address that will be used for automatic envelope packaging. Let's enforce the Ubiquitous Language and use these names consistently.

A combination of a name and address should be enough for us to match employees with their checks—we don't need the database identifiers.

We can make the system more testable by agreeing on an ordering rule, whatever it is. For example, we can agree to print the checks in alphabetic order by employee name. We could suggest this to a customer as a way to make the specifications stronger.

To make the specification self-explanatory, let's pull out the context and put it in the header. Payroll date and the next available check number are part of the context, along with employee salary data. We should also make it explicit what the number is for, so that people who read this specification don't have to figure this out for themselves in the future. Let's call it the "Next available check number." We can also make the specification easier to understand by making the context stick out visually, to show that it prepares the data and does not verify it.

The action that gets kicked off doesn't necessarily need to be listed in the specification. A payroll run can be executed implicitly by the table that checks payroll results. This is an example of focusing on *what* is being tested instead of *how* it's being checked. There's no need to have a separate step that says, "Next, we pay them."

Paycheck Inspector is an invented concept, and it violates the Ubiquitous Language rule. This isn't a special concept in the business domain, so let's explain what it does in a way that means something. Because we want to ensure that whoever automates the validation inspects all printed checks, let's use "All checks printed." Otherwise, someone might use subset matching, and the system might print every check twice and we won't notice.

The cleaned-up version is shown in figure 8.2.

Payroll Check Printing

The system will automaticall print payroll checks:
- one check per employee, with employee's name, address, and salary on the check
- using the payroll date
- the check numbers will be unique
- starting from the next available check number in ascending order
- in the alphabetic order based on employee name

▼ PAYROLL CONTEXT

Payroll date	10/10/2010

Next available check number	1000

Employees in the system

name	address	salary
Jeff Languid	10 Adamant St; Laurel MD 20707	1005.00
Kelp Holland	128 Baker St; Cottonmouth, IL 60066	2000.00

All checks printed in the payroll run

check number	check date	payee	address	amount
1000	10/10/2010	Jeff Languid	10 Adamant St; Laurel MD 20707	1005.00
1001	10/10/201/	Kelp Holland	128 Baker St; Cottonmouth, IL 60066	2000.00

Figure 8.2 A refined version of the bad specification shown in figure 8.1. Note that it's shorter and self-explanatory and has a clear title.

This version is shorter and has no incidental clutter compared to the original. It's much easier to understand. After refining the specification, we can see if the specification is complete by experimenting with input arguments and trying to think of edge cases that might represent valid inputs but violate the rules. (There's no need to consider invalid employee data, because that should be checked in another part of the system.)

One of the heuristics for experimenting with data is to use numerical boundary conditions. For example, what happens if an employee has a salary of 0? This is a valid case; an employee might have been on unpaid leave or suspended or no longer working for us. Do we still print the check? If we keep the rule "One check per employee," any employees that were fired years ago and no longer receive salaries would still get checks printed, with zeroes on them. We could then have a discussion with the business on making this rule stronger and ensuring that checks don't go out when they don't need to.

Depending on whether payroll is the only use case for check printing, we might want to refine this further and split it into several specifications. One would describe generic check printing functionality such as unique sequential check numbers. Another would describe payroll-specific functionality, such as the number of checks printed, correct salary, and so on.

> ### It's not about the tool
>
> Many people complain about FitNesse because of the kind of broken executable specifications shown in figure 8.1. Tools such as Concordion are intentionally built to prevent this kind of problem. Other tools such as Cucumber promote a textual Given-When-Then structure to avoid the trap of tables that are hard to understand.
>
> Before jumping to conclusions that a certain tool is the solution for this, you should know that I've seen similarly bad specifications written with almost all the major tools. The problem isn't in the tools; likewise, the solution isn't in the tools either. The problem is mostly in teams not putting in the effort to make the specifications easy to understand. It doesn't take much more effort to refine the specification, but the result will bring a lot more value.

The benefits of refining are sometimes not obvious instantly because collaboration helps us build a shared understanding of expected functionality. That's why many teams didn't consider refining important and ended up with huge sets of documents that are difficult to understand. Refining from key examples is a crucial step, which ensures that our specifications have long-term value as communication tools and that they will create a good foundation for a living documentation system.

Remember

- Don't just use the first set of examples directly; refine the specification from them.

- To get the most out of the examples, the resulting specification should be precise and testable, self-explanatory, focused, in domain language, and about business functionality.

- Avoid scripts and talking about software design in specifications.

- Don't try to cover every single case. Specifications aren't replacements for combinatorial regression testing.

- Start with one example for each important set of cases and add examples that illustrate particular areas of concern to programmers and testers.

- Define and use the Ubiquitous Language in specifications, software design, and tests.

9

Automating validation without changing specifications

fter we refine the specification of a feature, it becomes a clear target for implementation and a precise way to measure when we've finished. The refined specification also allows us to check in the future whether our system still has the required functionality, every time we change it. Because of the level of detail that we get from illustrating the specifications using examples, it becomes impossible to manually run all the checks within short iterations, even for midsize projects. The solution is obvious: We have to automate as many of these checks as possible.

The right automation for validating specifications with examples is quite different from traditional test automation in software projects. If we have to significantly change the specification while automating it, the telephone game starts all over again and the value of refining the specification is lost. Ideally, we should automate the validation processes for our specifications without distorting any information. This introduces an additional set of challenges on top of the usual test automation issues.

In this chapter I present advice on how to get started with automating validation of specifications without changing them and how to control the long-term maintenance costs of automation. I then cover the two areas that caused the most problems for the teams I interviewed: automating user interfaces and managing data for automated test runs. The practices I present here apply to any tool. I won't be discussing individual tools, but if you're interested in researching more about that topic visit http://specificationbyexample.com and download additional articles. Before we start with that, I'll address a question that's often raised in mailing lists and online forums—do we need this new type of automation at all?

Because automation is a highly technical problem, this chapter is going to be more technical than the others. If you're not a programmer or an automation specialist, you might find it hard to follow some parts. I suggest you read the first two sections and then skip the rest of this chapter. You won't lose anything that interests you.

> ### How does this work?
>
> All the most popular tools for automating executable specifications work with two types of artifacts: specifications in a human-readable form and automation code in a programming language. Depending on the tool, the specifications are in plain text, HTML, or some other human-readable format. The tools know how to extract inputs and expected outputs from those specifications, so that they can pass that on to the automation code and evaluate whether the expectations matched the results. The automation code, with some tools called *fixtures* or *step definitions*, calls the application APIs, interacts with the database, or executes actions through the application user interface.
>
> The automation code depends on the specifications but not the other way around. That's how these tools allow us to automate the validation of specifications without changing them.
>
> Some tools require teams to store examples in programming language code and produce human-readable specifications from that. Technically they achieve the same effect, but such tools effectively prevent anyone who's not proficient with programming language code from writing or updating a specification.

Is automation required at all?

The long-term maintenance cost of executable specifications is one of the biggest issues that teams face today when implementing Specification by Example. The tools for automating executable specifications are improving rapidly, but they're still far from more established unit-testing tools in terms of the ease of maintenance and development tool integration. Automation also introduces additional work for the team. This frequently causes discussions as to whether automation is required at all and whether it costs more than it's worth.

The argument against automation is that it increases the amount of work to develop and maintain software and that teams can get a shared understanding of what needs to be done by illustrating using examples and not automating them at all. Phil Cowans said that this view neglects the long-term benefits of Specification by Example:

> ❝ It feels like you're writing twice as much code to build the same functionality. But the number of lines of code is probably not the limiting factor in your development process, so this is quite naive. You're not taking into account the fact that you spend less time maintaining what you've already built or dealing with miscommunication between your testing and development. ❞

Automation in general is important for larger teams because it ensures that we have an impartial, objective measurement of when we're finished. Ian Cooper has a nice analogy for this:

> When I'm tired, and I wash the dishes, I don't want to dry the dishes. I've washed everything; it's almost done. Missus looks at that and doesn't think that I'm done. For her, "done" is when the dishes have been dried and put away and the sink is clean. It [automation] is forcing developers to be honest. They can't do just the bits that interest them.

Automation is also very important long term because it enables us to check more cases more frequently. Pierre Veragen said that the managers in his company quickly understood this value:

> All of the sudden the managers realized that instead of having something that checks two or three numbers during a test, now we had something that checked 20 or 30 numbers more and we could pinpoint problems easier.

Some teams reduce the cost of automation by moving it to technical tools. While I was preparing for interviews for this book, I was very surprised that Jim Shore, one of the thought leaders in the agile community and an early adopter of Specification by Example, actually gave up on automating executable specifications because of that cost.[1] Shore wrote that in his experience, illustrating using examples brings more value than automating validation without changing the specifications:

> My experience with FIT and other agile acceptance testing tools is that they cost more than they're worth. There's a lot of value in getting concrete examples from real customers and business experts, not so much value in using "natural language" tools like FIT and similar.

From my experience, this push back on automation of executable specifications can save time in the short term but prevents the team from getting some of the most important long-term benefits of Specification by Example.

---

[1] Parts of our email conversation are published online. See http://jamesshore.com/Blog/Alternatives-to-Acceptance-Testing.html, http://jamesshore.com/Blog/The-Problems-With-Acceptance-Testing.html, and http://gojko.net/2010/03/01/are-tools-necessary-for-acceptance-testing-or-are-they-just-evil/. You'll also find the links to opinions of other community members on this topic in those articles. I strongly suggest reading those articles, especially Shore's discussion about alternatives to automation of executable specifications.

When deciding whether to automate the validation of specifications using a technical tool or one for executable specifications, think about which benefits you want to get out of it. If we automate examples with a technical tool, we get easier automation and cheaper maintenance but lose the ability to use them for communication with business users later. We get very good regression tests, but the specifications will be accessible only to developers. Depending on your context, this might or might not be acceptable.

Automating validation of specifications without changing them is a key part of getting to living documentation. Without it, we can't guarantee the correctness of human-readable specifications. For many teams, the long-term benefit of Specification by Example comes from living documentation. Instead of dropping automation that preserves the original specifications, we can work on controlling the cost of maintenance. You'll find many good techniques that teams used to reduce long-term maintenance costs in the "Managing the automation layer" section later in this chapter, as well as in chapter 10.

Starting with automation

Automated validation of executable specifications is quite different from unit testing, recorded and scripted functional automation that developers and testers are often used to. Automating something but keeping it human readable requires teams to learn how to use new tools and to discover the best way of hooking the automation into their system. Here are some good ideas on how to start to implement the automation process and a look at some mistakes the teams I interviewed commonly made while doing that.

To learn about tools, try a simple project first
When: Working on a legacy system

Several teams used a simple project or a spike to learn how to use a new automation tool. If you have a small, relatively isolated piece of work in the pipeline, that trying an automation on might be a good strategy.

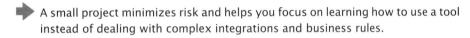 A small project minimizes risk and helps you focus on learning how to use a tool instead of dealing with complex integrations and business rules.

This approach is especially effective if you want to implement Specification by Example at the same time as moving to an agile development process.

At uSwitch, they took this approach when introducing Cucumber, a popular automation tool for executable specifications. They got the entire development team to start converting existing

tests to the new tool. This gave everyone on the team some experience with the new tool quickly. Stephen Lloyd says that it also showed them the power of executable specifications:

> We realized that there is a whole extra level of testing that needed to be done, and that testing at the end of the cycle didn't make sense.

A mini-project gives you a way to learn and practice new skills without much risk to ongoing development, so it might be a lot easier to get approval for that than to experiment with something that's much riskier.

It might be a good idea to get the result reviewed by an external consultant. Once you have done something that can be reviewed, external consultants will be able to provide much more meaningful feedback and discuss better solutions. By then, your team would also have had a chance to play with a tool and go over some basics, so they'll be able to understand more advanced techniques and get more value out of the consultant's time.

Plan for automation upfront

Teams that work on systems that haven't been designed up front for automated testing should expect their productivity to actually drop at first when they start automating executable specifications.

Even without learning how to use a new tool, automated validation initially adds a significant overhead on a project. Automation is front loaded—a disproportional amount of work has to be done when you start automating. This includes creating basic automation components, deciding on the best format of executable specifications and the best way to integrate with the system, resolving issues with test stability and dedicated environments, and many others. We deal with most of those issues in this chapter and in chapter 10, but for now it's important to understand that productivity will drop when you start automating. Once those issues are resolved and the structure of the executable specifications stabilizes, we can reuse the basic automation components when working on new specifications. As the project matures, the automation effort drops significantly and the productivity surges.

In several projects, developers didn't consider this when estimating the effort required to implement a story. But when the automation is just starting, it might take much more effort to automate an executable specification than to implement the required change in production code.

Make sure to plan for a drop in productivity up front. The team should under-commit on scope to allow for automation to be done within an iteration.

Unless this planning is done, automation is going to overrun into the next iteration and interrupt the flow. This is one of the key lessons André Brissette, the Talia product director at Pyxis Technologies, learned:

> If I had to do it all over again, from the start I would be more directive about the need to write tests [executable specifications]. I knew that it was a challenge for a team to write these kinds of tests, so I was patient. Also I could have let more room in the sprint [iteration] for making tests. We'd start, and then I'd talk about executable specifications and the team would say, "We don't really have the time for this learning curve because we're pretty loaded in this sprint." In fact, one of the reasons why they were pretty loaded was because I was filling the sprint with a lot of features. Because of this, it started slowly, and it took many iterations before having a decent set of specifications.
>
> Maybe it would pay off more to break that wall at the beginning and decide to do fewer features at the start. That's the choice that I would make the next time. When you spread the integration of that kind of practice over a long time, you have the cost of it without having the benefit. It ends up being more expensive.

One idea to ensure that the initial automation effort is planned for is to consider the automation toolkit as a separate product with its own backlog and then devote a certain percentage of team's time for that product. Just to make things clear, both the primary product and the automation framework should still be developed and delivered by the same team, in order to ensure that the team is familiar with the automation later. I advise treating it as a separate product purely to limit the impact on the delivery of the primary work.

Don't postpone or delegate automation

Because of the automation overhead, some teams delayed it. They described specifications with examples and then wrote code, leaving the automation for later. This seems to be related to projects where the development and test automation teams were separate or where external consultants were automating tests. This caused a lot of rework and churn.

Developers were marking user stories as done without having an objective automated criterion for that. When the acceptance tests finally got automated, problems often popped out and stories had to be sent back for fixing.

When automation is done along with implementation, developers have to design the system to make it testable. When automation is delegated to testers or consultants, developers don't take care to implement the system in a way that makes it easy to validate. This leads to more costly and more difficult automation. It also causes tests to slip into the next iteration, interrupting the flow when problems come back.

> Instead of delaying automation of executable specifications because of the overhead, deal with the automation problems so that the task becomes easier to do later.

Postponing automation is just a local optimization. You might get through the stories quicker from the initial development perspective, but they'll come back for fixing down the road. David Evans often illustrates this with an analogy of a city bus: A bus can go a lot faster if it doesn't have to stop to pick up passengers, but it isn't really doing its job then.

Avoid automating existing manual test scripts

Creating an executable specification from existing manual test scripts might seem to be a logical thing to do when starting out. Such scripts already describe what the system does and the testers are running them anyway, so automation will surely help, right? Not really—in fact, this is one of the most common failure patterns.

Manual and automated checks are affected by a completely different set of constraints. The time spent preparing the context is often a key bottleneck in manual testing. With automated testing, people spend the most time trying to understand what's wrong when a test fails.

For example, to prepare for a test script that checks user account management rules, a tester might have to log on to an administrative application, create a user, log on as that new user to the client application, and change the password after first use. To avoid doing this several times during the test, a tester will reuse the context for several manual scripts. So she would create the user once, block that account and verify that the user can't log on, reset the password to verify that it is reenabled, and then set some user preferences and verify that they change the home page correctly. This approach helps the tester run through the script more quickly.

With automated testing, the time spent on setting up users is no longer the key problem. Automated tests generally go through many more cases than manual tests.

When they run correctly, nobody is really looking at them. Once an automated test fails, someone has to go in and figure out what went wrong. If the test is described as a sequence of interdependent steps, it will be very hard to understand what exactly caused the problem, because the context changes throughout the script.

A single script checking 10 different things is more likely to fail than a smaller and more focused test, because it's affected by lots of different areas of code. In the previous example with user account management, if the password reset function stops working, we won't be able to set the user preferences correctly. A consequence is that the check for home page changes will also fail. If we had 10 different, smaller, focused, and independent tests instead of one big script, a bug in the password reset function wouldn't affect the test results for user preferences. That makes tests more resilient to change and reduces the cost of maintenance. It also helps us pinpoint the problems more quickly.

> Instead of plainly automating manual test scripts, think about what the script is testing and describe that with a group of independent, focused tests. This will significantly reduce the automation overhead and maintenance costs.

Gain trust with user interface tests
When: Team members are skeptical about executable specifications

Many tools for automating executable specifications allow us to integrate with software below the user interface. This reduces the cost of maintenance, makes the automation easier to implement, and provides quicker feedback (see the "Automate below the skin of the application" section later in this chapter). But business users and testers might not trust such automation initially. Without seeing the screens moving with their own eyes, they don't believe that the right code is actually being exercised.

> When you're starting out with Specification by Example, if your team members doubt the automation, try to execute the specifications through the user interface. Note that you shouldn't change the specifications to describe the user interface interactions, but you can hide those activities in the automation layer.

Getting the business users to trust executable specifications was one of the key challenges on the Norwegian Dairy Herd Recording System project. Børge Lotre, a manager at Bekk Consulting who worked on that project, says that they built the trust gradually as the number of checks in executable specifications increased:

> ❝ They [business users] used to insist on manual testing in addition to Cucumber. I think they are seeing the value of the Cucumber tests because they are not capable of [manually] testing the old requirements each time we add new functionality. ❞

Executable specifications should generally be automated through the user interface only as a last resort, because user interface automation slows down feedback and significantly increases the complexity of the automation layer. On the other hand, executing automated specifications through a user interface might be a good solution to gain trust from the nontechnical users initially. Make the automation layer flexible so that you can switch to integrating below the skin of the application later.

Running executable specifications through the user interface is also a good option when working with a legacy system that doesn't have a clean integration API (in which case the only way to automate tests is end to end, starting with the front-end user interface and validating the results either in the database or by using the user interface again). Making the automation layer flexible is a good idea in this case as well, because you'll probably want to move it below the user interface once the architecture becomes more testable.

Apart from gaining trust, allowing people to see the application screens during automated testing sometimes helps them think about additional examples.

According to my experience and in many of the case studies for this book, executing tests through a user interface doesn't scale well. You might want to reduce the number of tests executed through the UI later, once you gain the trust of the stakeholders.

If you decide to automate specifications through a user interface, apply the ideas described in the "Automating user interfaces" section later in this chapter to get the most out of it and to ensure that you'll be able to move the automation below the user interface when needed.

Managing the automation layer

Controlling the cost of maintenance for a living documentation system is one of the biggest challenges the teams I interviewed faced in the long term. A huge factor in that is managing the automation effectively.

In this section, I present some good ideas that the teams used to reduce the long-term maintenance cost of their automation layers. The advice in this section applies regardless of the tool you choose for automation.

Don't treat automation code as second-grade code

One of the most common mistakes that teams made was treating specifications or related automation code as less important than production code. Examples of this are giving the automation tasks to less-capable developers and testers and not maintaining the automation layer with the same kind of effort applied to production code.

In many cases, this came from the misperception that Specification by Example is just about functional test automation (hence the aliases *agile acceptance testing* and *Acceptance Test-Driven Development*), with developers thinking that test code isn't that important.

Wes Williams said that this reminded him of his early experiences with unit-testing tools:

> I guess it's a similar learning curve to writing JUnit. We started doing the same thing with JUnit tests and then everyone started writing, "Hey guys, JUnit is code; it should be clean." You ran into maintainability problems if you didn't do that. The next thing we learned was that the test pages [executable specifications] themselves are "code."

Phil Cowans listed this as one of the biggest mistakes his team made early on when implementing Specification by Example at Songkick. He added:

> Your test suite is a first-class part of the code that needs to be maintained as much as the regular code of the application. I now think of [acceptance] tests as first class and the [production] code itself as less than first class. The tests are a canonical description of what the application does.
>
> Ultimately the success is more about building the right thing than building it well. If the tests are your description of what the code does, they are not just a very important part of your development process but a very important part of building the product and understanding what you built and keeping the complexity under control. It probably took us a year to realize this.

Clare McLennan says that it's crucial to get the most capable people on the task of designing and building the automation layer:

> When I went back the other day, one of the other developers said that the design of the test integration framework is almost more important than the design of the actual product. In other words, the testing framework needs to have as good a design as the actual product because it needs to be maintainable. Part of the reason why the test system succeeded was that I knew about the structure and I could read the code.
>
> What typically happens on projects is they put a junior programmer to write the tests and the test system. However, automated test systems are difficult to get right. Junior programmers tend to choose the wrong approximations and build something less reliable. Put your best architects on it. They have the power to say: If we change this in our design, it will make it much better and easier to get tested.

I wouldn't go as far as saying that the automation code is more important than production code. At the end of the day, the software is built because that production code will help reach some business goal. The best automation framework in the world can't make the project succeed without good production code. Still, the automation framework will stay with us for a long time, so it should be well designed.

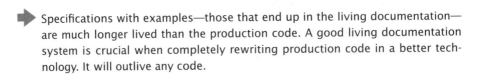

Specifications with examples—those that end up in the living documentation—are much longer lived than the production code. A good living documentation system is crucial when completely rewriting production code in a better technology. It will outlive any code.

 ## Describe validation processes in the automation layer

Most tools for automating executable specifications work with specifications in plain text or HTML formats. This allows us to change the specifications without recompiling or redeploying any programming language code. The automation layer, on the other hand, is programming language code that needs to be recompiled and redeployed if we change it.

Many teams have tried to make the automation layer generic in order to avoid having to change it frequently. They created only low-level reusable components in the automation layer, such as UI automation commands, and then scripted the validation processes, such as website workflows, with these commands. A telling sign for this issue is specifications that contain user interface concepts (such as clicking links or opening windows) or, even worse, low-level automation commands such as Selenium operations.

For example, the Global Talent Management team at Ultimate Software decided at some point to push all workflow out of the automation layer and into test specifications. They were using a custom-built, open source UI automation tool called SWAT, so they exposed SWAT commands directly as fixtures. They grouped SWAT commands together into meaningful domain workflows as FitNesse pages for specifications. This approach made writing specifications easier at first but caused many maintenance issues later, according to Scott Berger and Maykel Suarez:

> There is a central team that maintains SWAT and writes macros. At some point it was impossible to maintain. We were using macros based on macros. This made it hard to refactor [tests] and it was a nightmare. A given [test context] would be a collapsible region, but if you expanded it, it would be huge. We moved to implementing the workflow in fixtures. For every page [specification], we have a fixture behind.

> Instead of describing validation processes in specifications, we should capture them in the automation layer. The resulting specifications will be more focused and easier to understand.

Describing validation processes (how we test something as opposed to what's being tested) in the automation layer makes that layer more complex and harder to maintain, but programming tools such as IDEs make that task easier. When Berger's team described workflows as reusable components in plain-text specifications, they were essentially programming in plain text without the support of any development tools.

We can use programming tools to maintain the implementation of validation processes more efficiently than if they were described in plain text. We can also reuse the automated validation process for other related specifications more easily. See the sidebar "Three levels of user interface automation" later in this chapter for more information on this topic.

 ## Don't replicate business logic in the test automation layer

> Emulating parts of the application business flow or logic in the automation layer can make the tests easier to automate, but it will make the automation layer more complex and harder to maintain. Even worse, it makes the test results unreliable.

The real production flow might have a problem that wasn't replicated in the automation layer. An example that depends on that flow would fail when executed against a real system, but the automated tests would pass, giving the team false assurance that everything is okay.

This is one of the most important early lessons for Tim Andersen at Iowa Student Loan:

> Instead of creating a fake loan from test-helper code, we modified our test code to leverage our application to set up a loan in a valid state. We were able to delete nearly a third of our test code [automation layer] once we had our test abstraction layer using personas to leverage our application. The lesson here is don't fake state; fantasy state is prone to bugs and has a higher maintenance cost. Use the real system to create your state. We had a bunch of tests break. We looked at them and discovered that with this new approach, our existing tests exposed bugs.

On legacy systems, using production code in automation can sometimes lead to very bad hacks. For example, one of my clients extended a third-party product that mixed business logic with user interface code, but we couldn't do anything about that. My clients had read-only access to the source code for third-party components. Someone originally copied and pasted parts of the third-party functionality into test fixtures, removing all user interface bindings. This caused issues when the third-party supplier updated their classes.

I rewrote those fixtures to initialize third-party window classes and access private variables using reflection to run through the real business workflow. I'd never do anything like that while developing production code, but this was the lesser of the two evils. We deleted 90% of the fixture code and occasionally had to fix the automation when the third-party provider changed the way private variables are used, but this was a lot less work than copying and modifying huge chunks of code all the time. It also made tests reliable.

Automate along system boundaries
When: Complex integrations

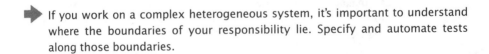 If you work on a complex heterogeneous system, it's important to understand where the boundaries of your responsibility lie. Specify and automate tests along those boundaries.

With complex heterogeneous systems, it might be hard or even impossible to include the entire end-to-end flow in an automated test. When I interviewed Rob Park, his team was working on an integration with an external system that converts voice to data. Going through the entire flow for every automated case would be impractical, if not impossible. But they weren't developing voice recognition, just integrating with such a system.

Their responsibilities are in the context of what happens to voice messages after they get converted to data. Park says that they decided to isolate the system and provide an alternative input path to make it easier to automate:

> Now we're writing a feature for Interactive Voice Response. Policy numbers and identification get automatically transferred to the application from an IVR system, so the screens come up prepopulated. After the first Three Amigos conversation, it became obvious to have a test page that prepares the data sent by the IVR.

Instead of automating such examples end to end including the external systems, Park's team decoupled the external inputs from their system and automated the validation for the part of the system that they're responsible for. This enabled them to validate all the important business rules using executable specifications.

Business users naturally will think about acceptance end to end. Automated tests that don't include the external systems won't give them the confidence that the feature is working fully. That should be handled by separate technical integration tests. In the IVR case, playing a simple prerecorded message and checking that it goes through fully would do the trick. That test would verify that all the components talk to each other correctly. Because all the business rules are specified and tested separately, we don't need to run high-level integration tests for all important use cases.

For more tips on how to deal with large complex infrastructures, see the next chapter.

 ## Don't check business logic through the user interface

Traditional test automation tools mostly work by manipulating user interface objects. Most automation tools for executable specifications can go below the user interface and talk to application programming interfaces directly.

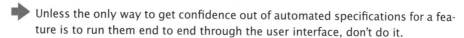 Unless the only way to get confidence out of automated specifications for a feature is to run them end to end through the user interface, don't do it.

User interface automation is typically much slower and much more expensive to maintain than automation at the service or API level. With the exception of using visible user interface automation to gain trust (as described earlier in this chapter), going below the user interface is often a much better solution to verifying business logic whenever possible.

Automate below the skin of the application
When: Checking session and workflow constraints

Workflow and session rules can often be checked only against the user interface layer. But that doesn't mean that the only option to automate those checks is to launch a browser. Instead of automating the specifications through a browser, several teams developing web applications saved a lot of time and effort going right below the skin of the application—to the HTTP layer. Tim Andersen explains this approach:

Automate...below the skin...

> We'd send a hash-map that looks a lot like the HTTP request. We have default values that would be rewritten with what's important for the test, and we were testing by basically going right where our HTTP requests were going. That's how our personas [fixtures] worked, by making HTTP requests with an object. That's how they used real state and used real objects.

Not running a browser allows automated checks to execute in parallel and run much faster. Christian Hassa used a similar approach but went one level lower, to the web controllers inside the application. This avoided the HTTP calls as well and made the feedback even faster. He explains this approach:

> We bound parts [of a specification] directly to the UI with Selenium but other parts directly to a MVC controller. It was a significant overhead to bind directly to the UI, and I don't think that this is the primary value of this technique. If I could choose binding all specifications to the controller or a limited set of specifications to the UI, I would always choose executing all the specifications to the controller. Binding to the UI is optional to me; not binding all specifications that are relevant to the system is not an option. And binding to the UI costs significantly more.

➤ Automating just below the skin of the application is a good way to reuse real business flows and avoid duplication in the automation layer. Executing the checks directly using HTTP calls—not through a browser—speeds up validation significantly and makes it possible to run checks in parallel.

Browser automation libraries are often slow and lock user profiles, so only one such check can run at any given time on a single machine. There are many tools and libraries for direct HTTP automation, such as *WebRat*,[2] *Twill*,[3] and the *Selenium 2.0 HtmlUnit driver*.[4] Many modern MVC frameworks allow automation below the HTTP layer, making such checks even more efficient. These tools allow us to execute tests in parallel, faster, and more reliably because they have fewer moving parts than browser automation.

Choosing what to automate

In *Bridging the Communication Gap*, I advised automating all the specifications. After talking to many different teams while preparing this book, I now know that there are situations where automation would not pay off. Gaspar Nagy gave me two good examples:

> If the automation cost would be too high compared to the benefit of that acceptance criteria—for example, displaying in a sortable grid. The user interface control [widget] will support sorting out of the box. To check whether the data is really sorted you need lots of test data edge cases. This is best left to a quick manual check.
>
> Our application required offline functionality as well. Very special offline edge cases might be hard to automate, and testing manually is probably good enough.

In both these cases, a quick manual check can give the team a level of confidence in the system that was acceptable to their customers. Automation would cost much more than the time it would save long term.

Checking layout examples is, in most cases, a bad choice to automate. Automating them is technically possible, but for many teams the benefits of that wouldn't justify the costs. Automating reference usability examples (such as the ones suggested in the "Build a reference example" section in chapter 7) is practically impossible. Usability and fun require a human eye and a subjective measurement. Other good examples of checks that are probably not worth automating are intuitiveness or asserting how good something looks or how easy it is to use. This doesn't mean that such examples aren't useful to discuss, illustrate with examples, or store in a specification system; quite the contrary. Discussing examples will ensure that everyone has the same understanding, but we can check the result more efficiently by hand.

Automating as much as we can around those functions can help us focus manual checks only on the very few aspects where initial automation or long-term maintenance would be costly.

---

[2] http://wiki.github.com/brynary/webrat
[3] http://twill.idyll.org
[4] http://seleniumhq.org/docs/09_webdriver.html#htmlunit-driver

Although I've mostly presented web applications as examples when talking about user interfaces, the same advice is applicable to other types of user interfaces. Automating just below the skin of the application allows us to validate workflow and session constraints but still shorten the feedback time compared to running tests through the user interface.

After looking into managing automation in general, it's time to cover two specific areas that caused automation problems for many teams: user interfaces and data management.

Automating user interfaces

When it comes to automation, dealing with user interfaces was the most challenging aspect of Specification by Example for the teams covered by my research. Almost all the teams I interviewed made the same mistake early on. They specified tests intended to be automated through user interfaces as series of technical steps, often directly writing user interface automation commands in their specifications.

User interface automation libraries work in the language of screen objects, essentially software design. Describing specifications in that language directly contradicts the key ideas of refining the specification (see the "Scripts are not specifications" and "Specifications should be about business functionality, not software design" sections in chapter 8). In addition to making specifications hard to understand, this makes automated tests incredibly hard to maintain long term. Pierre Veragen worked on a team that had to throw away all the tests after a small change to the user interface:

> User interface tests were task oriented (click, point) and therefore tightly coupled to the implementation of the GUI, rather than activity oriented. There was a lot of duplication in tests. FitNesse tests were organized according to the way UI was set up. When the UI was updated, all these tests had to be updated. The translation from conceptual to technical changed. A small change to the GUI, adding a ribbon control, broke everything. There was no way we could update the tests.

The investment they put into tests up to that point was wasted, because it was easier for them to throw away all those tests than to update them. The team decided to invest in restructuring the architecture of the application to enable easier testing.

If you decide to automate validation for some of your specifications through a user interface, managing that automation layer efficiently is probably going to be one of the key activities for your team. Here are some good ideas on how to automate tests through a user interface and still keep them easy to maintain.

Specify user interface functionality at a higher level of abstraction

Pushing the translation from the business language to the language of user interface objects into the automation layer helps to avoid long-term maintenance problems. This essentially means specifying user interface tests at a higher level of abstraction. Aslak Hellesøy says that this was one of the key lessons he learned early on:

> We realized that if we could write tests on a higher level, we could achieve a lot of benefits. This allowed us to change the implementation without having to change a lot of feature scripts. The tests were a lot easier to read, because they were shorter. We had hundreds of these tests, and just by glancing over them it was much easier to see where the things were. They were much more resilient to change.

Lance Walton had a similar experience, which resulted in creating classes in the integration layer that represented operations of user interface screens and then raising the level of abstraction to workflows and finally to higher-level activities. He explains:

> We went through the predictable path of writing tests in "type this, click this button" style with lots of repetition between tests. We had a natural instinct to refactor and realized we needed a representation of the screens. I very much go with the early XP rules: If you have a small expression that has a meaning, refactor it to a method and give it a name. It was predictable that we'll have to log in for every single test, and that should be reusable. I didn't quite know how to do it, but I knew that was going to happen. So we came up with screen classes.
>
> The next thing to realize was that we kept going through the same sequence of pages—it was a workflow. The next stage was to understand that the workflow still had to do with the solution we designed, so actually let's forget about workflow and focus on what the user is trying to achieve.
>
> So we had pages that contained the details, then we had the task level above that, then we had the whole workflow on top of that, and then we finally had the goal that the user is trying to achieve. When we got to that level, the tests could be composed very quickly, and they were robust against the changes.

Reorganizing the automation layer to handle activities—and focusing tests on specifications, not scripts—helped reduce the maintenance costs of automated tests significantly, Walton said:

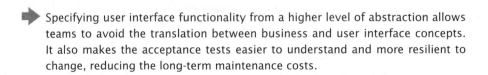

Early on you had to log in to see anything. At one point there was a notion that you could see a whole bunch of stuff before logging in, and you would only be asked to log in when you followed a link. If you have a whole lot of tests that log in at the start, the first problem you have is that, until you remove the login step, all your tests break. But you have to log in after you follow a link, so a whole bunch of tests would break because of that. If you have abstracted that away, the fact that your test is logging in as a particular person doesn't mean that it's doing that immediately—you just store that information and use it when asked to log in.

The tests move smoothly through. Of course, you need additional tests to check when you are required to log in, but this is a different concern. All the tests that are about testing whether the users can achieve their goal are robust even with that fairly significant change. It was surprising and impressive to me that we could make this change so easily. I truly began to see the power we have to control this stuff.

The fact that a user had to be logged in for a particular action was separated from the actual activity of filling in the login form, submitting it, and logging in. The automation layer decided when to perform that action in the workflow (and if it needed to be performed at all). This made the tests based on the specifications much more resilient to change. It also raised the level of abstraction for user interface actions, allowing the readers to understand the entire specification easier.

 Specifying user interface functionality from a higher level of abstraction allows teams to avoid the translation between business and user interface concepts. It also makes the acceptance tests easier to understand and more resilient to change, reducing the long-term maintenance costs.

See the sidebar "Three levels of user interface automation" later in this chapter for an idea how to organize UI test automation to keep all the benefits of refining the specification and reduce long-term maintenance costs.

Check only UI functionality with UI specifications
When: User interface contains complex logic

 Only specify user interface functionality through interactions with user interface elements.

The only example where tests described at a lower technical level didn't cause huge maintenance problems later on was the one I saw from the Sierra team at BNP Paribasin London. They had a set of executable specifications described as interactions with user interface elements. The difference between this case and all the other stories, where such tests caused headaches, was that with those tests the Sierra team specifies only user interface functionality, not the underlying domain business logic. For example, their tests check for mandatory form fields and functionality implemented in JavaScript. All their business logic specifications are automated below the user interface.

Raising the level of abstraction would certainly make such tests easier to read and maintain. On the other hand, that would complicate the automation layer significantly. Because they have relatively few of these tests, creating and maintaining a smart automation layer would probably take more time than just changing the scripts when the user interface changes. It's also important to understand that they maintain a back-office user interface where the layout doesn't change as much as in public-facing websites, where the user interface is a shopping window.

Avoid recorded UI tests

Many traditional test automation tools offer record-and-replay user interface automation. Although this sounds compelling for initial automation, record-and-replay is a terrible choice for Specification by Example. This is one of the areas where automation of executable specifications is quite different than traditional automated regression testing.

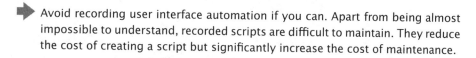

Avoid recording user interface automation if you can. Apart from being almost impossible to understand, recorded scripts are difficult to maintain. They reduce the cost of creating a script but significantly increase the cost of maintenance.

Pierre Veragen's team had 70,000 lines of recorded scripts for user interface regression tests. It took several people six months to re-record them to keep up with significant user interface changes. Such slow feedback would completely invalidate any benefits of executable specifications. In addition to that, record-and-replay automation requires a user interface to exist, but Specification by Example starts before we develop a piece of software.

Some teams didn't understand this difference between traditional regression testing and Specification by Example at first and tried to use record-and-replay tools. Christian Hassa's story is a typical one to consider:

> The tests were still too brittle and had a significant overhead to maintain them. Selenium tests were recorded, so they were also coming in too late. First we tried to record what was there at the end of the sprint. Then

we tried to abstract the recording to make it more reusable and less brittle. At the end, it was still the tester who had to come up with his own ideas on how to test. We found very late how the tester interpreted the user expectations. Second, we were still late in becoming ready to test. Actually it made things worse because we had to maintain all this. Six months later the scripts we used were no longer maintainable.

We used the approach for a few months and tried to improve the practice, but it didn't really work, so we dropped it by the end of the project. The tests we wrote were not structured the way we do it now, but rather the way a classical tester would structure tests—a lot of preconditions, then some asserts, and the things to do were preconditions for the next test.

Three levels of user interface automation

To write executable specifications that are automated through a user interface, think about describing the specification and the automation at these three levels:

- Business rule level—What is this test demonstrating or exercising? For example: Free delivery is offered to customers who order two or more books.

- User workflow level—How can a user exercise the functionality through the UI, on a higher activity level? For example: Put two books in a shopping cart, enter address details, and verify that delivery options include free delivery.

- Technical activity level—What are the technical steps required to exercise individual workflow steps? For example: Open the shop home page, log in with "testuser" and "testpassword," go to the "/book" page, click the first image with the "book" CSS class, wait for the page to load, click the Buy Now link, and so on.

Specifications should be described at the business rule level. The automation layer should handle the workflow level by combining blocks composed at the technical activity level. Such tests will be easy to understand, efficient to write, and relatively inexpensive to maintain.

For more information on three levels of UI tests, see my article "How to implement UI testing without shooting yourself in the foot."[†]

[†] http://gojko.net/2010/04/13/how-to-implement-ui-testing-without-shooting-yourself-in-the-foot-2

Set up context in a database

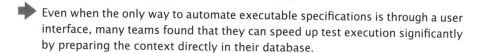

Even when the only way to automate executable specifications is through a user interface, many teams found that they can speed up test execution significantly by preparing the context directly in their database.

For example, when automating a specification that describes how editors can approve articles, we could pre-create articles using database calls. If you use the three layers (described in the previous sidebar), some parts of the workflow layer can be implemented through the user interface and some can be optimized to use domain APIs or database calls. The Global Talent Management Team at Ultimate Software uses this approach but splits the work so that testers can still participate efficiently. Scott Berger explains it:

> The developer would ideally write and automate the happy path with the layer of this database automation that sets up the data. A tester would then pick that up and extend with additional cases.

By automating the whole path early, developers use their knowledge of how to optimize tests. Once the first example is automated, testers and analysts can easily extend the specification by adding more examples at the business rule level.

Setting up the context in a database leads us to the second biggest challenge the teams from my research face when automating executable specifications: data management. Some teams included databases in their continuous validation processes to get more confidence from their systems or because their domains are data driven. This creates a new set of challenges for automation.

Test data management

To make executable specifications focused and self-explanatory, specifications need to contain all the data that's important to illustrate the functionality with examples but omit any additional information. But to fully automate the examples against a system that uses a database, we often need additional data because of referential integrity checks.

Another problem with automated tests relying on data stored in a database is that one test can change the data required by another test, making the test results unreliable. On the other hand, to get fast feedback, we can't drop and restore the entire database for every test.

Managing test data efficiently is crucial to gain confidence from data-driven systems and make the continuous validation process fast, repeatable, and reliable. In this section, I present some good practices that the teams I interviewed used to manage the test data for their executable specifications.

Avoid using prepopulated data
When: Specifying logic that's not data driven

 Reusing existing data can make specifications harder to understand.

When executable specifications are automated to use a database, the data in the database becomes part of the automation context. Instead of automating how the contextual information is put into the database before a test, some teams reused existing data that suits the purpose. This makes it easier to automate the specifications but makes them harder to understand. Anyone who reads such specifications has to also understand the data in the database. Channing Walton advises against this:

> Setting up databases by prepopulating a standard baseline data set almost always causes a lot of pain. It becomes hard to understand what the data is, why it is there, and what it is being used for. When tests fail, it's hard to know why. As the data is shared, tests influence each other. People get confused very quickly. This is a premature optimization. Write tests to be data agnostic.

If the system is designed in a way not to require a lot of referential data setup, then specifications can be automated by defining only a minimal set of contextual information. Looking at this from the other side of the equation, Specification by Example guides teams to design focused components with low coupling, which is one of the most important object-oriented design principles. But this isn't easy to do with legacy data-driven systems.

Try using prepopulated reference data
When: Data-driven systems

Defining the full context for data-driven systems is difficult and error-prone. It might not be the best thing to do from the perspective of writing focused specifications. Gaspar Nagy's team tried to do that and found that specifications became hard to read and maintain:

> We had an acceptance test where we had to set up some data in the database to execute a step. When we did this setup description, it was looking like a database. We didn't say "table" in the text, but they were tables. Developers were able to understand it very well, but you couldn't show this to a businessperson.

For example, we had a table for the countries. We didn't want to hard-code any logic in test automation on what were the countries, so for each of the tests we defined the countries that were relevant for this test. This turned out to be completely stupid because we always used Hungary and France. We could have just loaded all the countries of the world into the database with a "given the default countries are in the system." Having a default data set would be helpful.

Marco Milone had a similar problem while working on a project in the new media industry:

At the beginning, for the sake of getting the tests to run, we weren't doing things well. Setup and teardown were in the test, and they were so cluttered. We started centralizing the database setup and enforced change control on top of that. Tests just did checks; we didn't bother with entering data in the tests. This made the tests much faster and much easier to read and manage.

On data-driven systems, creating everything from scratch isn't a good idea. On the other hand, hiding information can cause a ton of problems as well. A possible solution for this is a strategy implemented by the teams at Iowa Student Loan. They prepopulate only referential data that doesn't change. Tim Andersen explains this approach:

We "nuke and pave" the database during the build. We then populate it with configuration and domain test data. Each test is responsible for creating and cleaning up the transaction data.

Using prepopulated reference data is a good strategy to make test specifications shorter and easier to understand, while at the same time speeding up feedback and simplifying the automation layer.

If you decide to use prepopulated reference data, see the "Run quick checks for reference data" section in chapter 10 for information on how to make tests more reliable.

Pull prototypes from the database
When: Legacy data-driven systems

Some domains are so complex that even with prepopulated reference data, setting up a new object from scratch would be a complex and error-prone task. If you face this on a greenfield project, where the domain model is under your control, this might be a sign that the domain model is wrong (see the "Listen to your living documentation" section in chapter 11).

On legacy data-driven systems, changing the model might not be an option. In such cases, instead of creating a completely new object from scratch, the automation layer can clone an existing object and change the relevant properties. Børge Lotre and Mikael Vik used this approach for the Norwegian Dairy Herd Recording System. They said:

> Getting the correct background for the test so that it is as complete as possible was a challenge because of the complexity of the domain. If we were testing a behavior of a cow and we had forgotten to define a test case where she had three calves, we didn't see the code failing and didn't spot the error before we tested it manually on real data. So we created a background generator where you could identify a real cow and it pulls its properties from the database. These properties were then used as the basis for a new Cucumber test. This not only was useful when we wanted to re-create an error but also turned out be a real help when we start on new requirements.

When the Bekk team identifies a missing test case, they find a good representative example in the real database and use the "background generator" to set up an automated acceptance test using its properties. This ensures that complex objects have all the relevant details and references to related objects, which makes validation checks more relevant. To get faster feedback from their executable specifications, the background generator pulls the full context of an object, which enables the tests to run against an in-memory database.

➡ Find a representative example in the database, and use those properties to set up tests.

When this approach is used to create objects on the fly instead of creating the context for a test (in combination with a real database), it can also simplify the setup required for relevant entities in executable specifications. Instead of specifying all the properties for an object, we can specify only those that are important to locate a good prototype. This makes the specifications easier to understand.

Automating the validation of specifications without changing them is conceptually different from traditional test automation, which is why so many teams struggle with it when they get started with Specification by Example. We automate specifications to get fast feedback, but our primary goal should be to create executable specifications that are easily accessible and human readable, not just to automate a validation process. Once our specifications are executable, we can validate them frequently to build a living documentation system. We'll cover those ideas in the next two chapters.

Remember

- Refined specifications should be automated with as little change as possible.

- The automation layer should define how something is tested; specifications should define what is to be tested.

- Use the automation layer to translate between the business language and user interface concepts, APIs, and databases. Create higher-level reusable components for specifications.

- Automate below the user interface if possible.

- Don't rely too much on existing data if you don't have to.

10

Validating frequently

" Stray too far out of your lane and your attention is immediately riveted by a loud, vibrating baloop baloop baloop. **"**

—David Haldane[1]

In the 1950s, the California Department of Transportation had a problem with motorway lane markers. The lines were wearing out, and someone had to repaint them every season. This was costly, caused disruption to traffic, and was dangerous for the people charged with that task.

Dr. Elbert Dysart Botts worked on solving that problem and experimented with more-reflective paint, but this proved to be a dead end. Thinking outside the box, he invented raised lane markers, called Botts' Dots. Botts' Dots were visible by day or night, regardless of the weather. They didn't wear out as easily as painted lane markers. Instead of relying just on drivers' sense of sight, Botts' Dots cause a tactile vibration and audible rumbling when drivers move across designated travel lanes. This feedback proved to be one of the most important safety features on highways, alerting inattentive drivers to potential danger when they drift from their lane.

Botts' Dots were introduced to software development as one of the original 12 Extreme Programming practices, called *continuous integration* (CI). Continuous integration alerts inattentive software teams when they start to drift from a product that can be built and packaged. A dedicated continuous integration system frequently builds the product and runs tests to ensure that the system doesn't work only on a developer's machine. By flagging potential problems quickly, this practice allows us to stay in the middle of the lane and take small and cheap corrective action when needed. Continuous integration ensures that once the product is built right, it stays right.

---

[1] http://articles.latimes.com/1997-03-07/local/me-35781_1_botts-dots

The same principles apply to building the right product. Once the right product is built, we want to ensure that it stays right. If it drifts from the designated direction, we can solve the problem much more easily and cheaply if we know about it quickly and don't let problems accumulate. We can frequently validate executable specifications. A continuous-build server[2] can frequently check all the specifications and ensure that the system still satisfies them.

Continuous integration is a well-documented software practice, and many other authors have already done a good job of explaining it in detail. I don't wish to repeat how to set up continuous-build and integration systems in general, but some particular challenges for frequent validation of executable specifications are important for the topic of this book.

Many teams who used Specification by Example to extend existing systems found that executable specifications have to run against a real database with realistic data, external services, or a fully deployed website. Functional acceptance tests check the functionality across many components, and if the system isn't built up front to be testable, such checks often require the entire system to be integrated and deployed. This causes three groups of problems for frequent validation in addition to those usual for continuous integration with just technical (unit) tests:

- Unreliability caused by environmental dependencies—Unit tests are largely independent of the test environment, but executable specifications might depend heavily on the rest of the ecosystem they run in. Environment issues can cause the tests to fail even if the programming language code is correct. To gain confidence in acceptance test results, we have to solve or mitigate these environmental problems and make the test execution reliable.

- Slower feedback—Functional acceptance tests on brownfield projects will often run an order of magnitude slower than unit tests. I'd consider a unit test pack slow if it runs for several minutes. Anything close to 10 minutes would be definitely too slow, and I'd seriously start investigating how to make it run faster. On the other hand, I've seen acceptance test packs that had to run for several hours and couldn't be optimized without reducing confidence in the results. Such slow overall feedback requires us to come up with a solution to get fast feedback from selected parts of the system on demand.

- Managing failed tests—A large number of coarse-grained functional tests that depend on many moving parts required some teams, especially when they started implementing Specification by Example, to manage failing tests instead of fixing them straight away.

---

[2] Software that automatically builds, packages, and executes tests when anyone changes any code in the version control system. If you've never heard of one, google CruiseControl, Hudson or TeamCity.

In this chapter, I explain how teams from my research handled these three problems.

Reducing unreliability

An unreliable validation process can undermine a team's confidence in a product and the process of Specification by Example. Investigating intermittent failures that aren't caused by real problems is a huge waste of time. If that happens often, developers will have an excuse not to look at validation problems at all. That will allow real issues to pass undetected, defeating the whole point of continuous validation.

Legacy projects rarely support automated functional testing easily, so executable specifications might need to be automated through unreliable user interfaces or suffer from nondeterminism caused by asynchronous processes. This is especially problematic when developers need convincing to participate in the process and see it only as an improvement on functional testing (in other words, not their problem).

Clare McLennan faced this issue with her team. "Developers didn't care about tests because they weren't stable, but we needed their knowledge to make them stable," she said. This presented a chicken-and-egg problem for her team. To get the developers to participate, she had to show them the value of executable specifications. But to do that, the executable specifications had to be reliable, which required developers to change the system design and make it easier to plug in automated tests.

To get the long-term benefits of Specification by Example, many teams had to invest significant effort into making their validation processes reliable. In this section I present some good ideas for that.

Find the most annoying thing, fix it, and repeat
When: Working on a system with bad automated test support

One of the most important things to understand about making the system more reliable for automated testing is that this won't happen overnight. Legacy systems aren't easy to change; otherwise, they wouldn't be legacy. When something was built without a testable design for years, it won't suddenly become clean and testable.

Introducing too many major changes quickly would destabilize the system, especially if we still don't have good functional test coverage. It would also severely interrupt the flow of development.

> ➤ Instead of trying to solve a problem with one big hit, a more useful strategy is to make many small changes iteratively.

For example, McLennan's team realized that slow test data processing was causing tests to time out. Their database administrator improved the database performance, which led them to discover that some tests were starting before the updated test data was processed, so the system was serving old data. They introduced messages to tell them when the latest data from the database was being served, so that they could reliably start the tests after that and avoid false negatives. When that source of entropy was eliminated, they discovered that HTTP cookie expiry was causing problems. They introduced the concept of business time, so that they could change the time the system thinks it's using. (See the "Introduce business time" section later in this chapter.)

As a strategy to achieve stability under automated testing, McLennan advises an incremental approach:

> ❝ Find the most annoying thing and fix it, then something else will pop up, and after that something else will pop up. Eventually, if you keep doing this, you will create a stable system that will be really useful. ❞

Improving the stability iteratively is a good way to build a reliable validation process without interrupting the delivery flow so much. This approach also enables us to learn and adapt while we're making the system more testable.

Identify unstable tests using CI test history
When: Retrofitting automated testing into a legacy system

On a legacy system that's not susceptible to automated testing, it's often hard to decide where to start with iterative cleanup because there are so many causes of instability. A good strategy for this is to look at the test execution history. Most continuous-build systems today have a feature that tracks test results over a time.

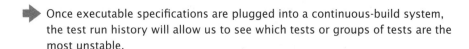

Once executable specifications are plugged into a continuous-build system, the test run history will allow us to see which tests or groups of tests are the most unstable.

I completely overlooked this feature for years because I was mostly working on green-field projects built up to be testable up front or systems where relatively small changes introduced stability. In such projects, tracking the history of test executions is useless: The tests pass almost all the time and are fixed as soon as they fail. The first time I tried to retrofit automated testing into a system that suffered from occasional timeouts, networking issues, database problems, and inconsistent processing, seeing the test history helped me focus my efforts to increase stability. That showed me which groups of tests were failing the most often so that I could fix them first.

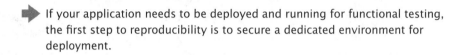

Set up a dedicated continuous validation environment

If your application needs to be deployed and running for functional testing, the first step to reproducibility is to secure a dedicated environment for deployment.

Continuous validation has to work in a reproducible way to be reliable. In some larger organizations it's harder to get a new set of machines than it is to hire a known poisoner as a chef in the company cafeteria, but fighting for better equipment is well worth it. Many teams tried to use the same environment for demonstrating features to business users, manual testing, and continuous validation. This regularly caused data consistency issues.

Without a dedicated environment, it's hard to know whether a test failed because there's a bug, whether someone changed something on the test environment, or whether the system is just unstable. A dedicated environment eliminates unplanned changes and mitigates the risk of unstable environments.

Employ fully automated deployment

Once we have a dedicated environment, we want to ensure that the software is deployed in a reproducible way. Unreliable deployment is the second most common cause of test result instability. For many legacy systems, deployment is a process done overnight that involves several people, lots of coffee, and ideally a magic wand. When we have to deploy once every year, this is acceptable. When we have to deploy every two weeks, it becomes a major headache. For continuous validation, we might need to deploy several times a day, and magic-aided manual deployment is completely unacceptable.

Without a fully automated deployment that can reliably upgrade a system, we'll frequently get into situations where many tests suddenly start failing and someone has to spend hours troubleshooting to find the culprit, only to hear "but it works on my machine" from the back of the room.

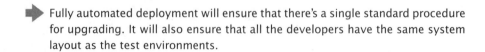 Fully automated deployment will ensure that there's a single standard procedure for upgrading. It will also ensure that all the developers have the same system layout as the test environments.

This eliminates the dependency of executable specifications on a particular environment and makes continuous validation much more reliable. It also makes problems easier to troubleshoot, because developers can use any environment to reproduce problems.

For this to work, it has to be fully automated. No manual intervention should be required—or allowed—at all. (Note that I'm talking about a fully automated deployment that can be executed on demand, not necessarily firing off automatically as well.) Installers that require you to poke around an administration console, half-automated manual scripts, and things like that don't count as fully automated. In particular, this includes automated database deployments. I've seen many teams who claim to have automated deployment, only to find out that someone has to run database scripts manually afterward.

Fully automated deployment brings other benefits as well, such as being able to upgrade production systems more easily. This will save you a lot of time long term. Frequent deployment is a good practice regardless of Specification by Example.

Create simpler test doubles for external systems
When: Working with external reference data sources

Many teams had problems with external reference data sources or external systems that participated in their business workflow. (By *external* I mean outside the scope of a team, not necessarily belonging to a different organization.) In large enterprises with complex networks of systems, a team might work on only one part of the workflow, and its test system will talk to the test systems of other teams. The problem is that the other teams have to do their own work and testing so their test servers might not be always available, reliable, or correct.

 Create a separate fake data source that simulates the interaction with the real system.

Rob Park's team at a large U.S. insurance provider was building a system that looked up reference policy data on an external auto policy server. If the auto policy server went down, all their executable specifications would start failing. For functional testing, they used an alternative version of the external service. The simpler version read the data from a file on a local disk. This allowed Park's team to test their system even when the auto policy server was offline. Creating a separate reference data source also gave the team full control of the reference data. Expired policies wouldn't be served by the real system, so tests that depended on a policy that had expired would start failing.

The simpler version of the reference data source served everything from the configuration file, which avoided the temporal issues. They kept the data in an XML file that was checked into a version control system, so that they could easily track changes and package the correct version of the test data with the correct version of the code. This would be impossible with an external system. A local service that reads from a file is also faster than the external system, speeding up the overall feedback.

A risk with test doubles is that the real system will evolve over time, and the double will no longer reflect the realistic functionality. To avoid that, be sure to check periodically whether the double still does what the original system is supposed to do. This is particularly important when the double is representing a third-party system over which you have no control.

Selectively isolate external systems
When: External systems participate in work

Isolating a system completely isn't always a good idea. When a system participates in a larger workflow where the external systems provide more than just reference data, a test double would have to start implementing parts of the real functionality of external systems. This brings significant overhead in development and more maintenance problems.

Ian Cooper's team at Beazley took an interesting pragmatic approach to solve this problem. They selectively turned off access to some services based on the goal of each executable specification. This made their tests significantly faster but still involved the minimal set of real external systems in each test. The solution didn't completely protect them from external influences, but it made troubleshooting a lot easier. If a test failed, it was clear which external dependency might have influenced it.

 Selectively isolating some external services can make tests faster and troubleshooting easier.

Try multistage validation
When: Large/multisite groups

With legacy systems, running all the executable specifications often takes longer than the average time between two committed changes to the underlying source code. Because of that, it might be hard to associate a problem with a particular change that caused it.

With larger groups of teams, especially if they're spread across several sites, this can cause problems to accumulate. If one team breaks the database, the other teams won't be able to validate their changes until the problem gets fixed. It might take a several hours to find out that there's a problem, determine what it is, fix it, and rerun the tests to confirm that it's fixed. A broken build will always be someone else's problem, and very soon the continuous-validation test pack will always be broken. At that point, we might as well just stop running the tests.

> **Employ multistage validation.** Each team should have an isolated continuous-validation environment; changes should be first tested there.

First integrate a change with the other changes from the same team. If the tests pass there, push changes to the central continuous-validation environment, where they're integrated with all the changes from the other teams.

This approach prevents problems of one team influencing the other teams in most cases. Even if the central environment is broken and someone is fixing it, individual teams can still use their own environments to validate changes.

Depending on how long all executable specifications take to run, we can execute the full test pack in both environments or just run a representative subset of tests in the one of the environments to provide a quick smoke test. The Global Talent Management Team at Ultimate Software, for example, runs most of their tests just in the local team environments. Slower tests don't run on the central environment in order to provide quick feedback.

Execute tests in transactions
When: Executable specifications modify reference data

> Database transactions can provide isolation from outside influences.

Transactions can prevent our process from influencing other processes running at the same time and make tests more reproducible.

If we create a user during our test, the test might fail the next time we run it because of a unique constraint on the username in the database. If we run that test inside a transaction and roll back at the end of the test, the user won't be stored, so the two test executions will be independent.

This is a good practice in many cases, but it might not work with some transactional contexts (for example, if database constraint checks are deferred until a transaction commit or in the case of nested autonomous transactions). Such advanced transactional topics are outside the scope of this book.

In any case, keep transaction control outside the specifications. Database transaction control is a crosscutting concern that's best implemented in the automation layer, not in the description of executable specifications.

Run quick checks for reference data
When: Data-driven systems

In data-driven systems, executable specifications depend extensively on reference data. Changes to the reference data, such as workflow configuration, might break the test even if the functionality is correct. Such problems are difficult to troubleshoot.

> Set up a completely separate group of tests to verify that the reference data is still as we expect it to be.

Such tests can run quickly before executable specifications. If that test pack fails, there's no point in running the others. These tests will also pinpoint reference data problems and allow us to fix them quickly.

Wait for events, not for elapsed time

Asynchronous processes seem to be one of the most problematic areas for executable specifications. Even when parts of a process execute in the background, on different machines, or get delayed for several hours, business users see the whole process as a single sequence of events. At Songkick, this was one of the key challenges to overcome for a successful implementation of Specification by Example. Phil Cowans says:

> Asynchronous processing has been a real headache for us. We do a lot of background processing that is asynchronous for performance reasons, and we ran into a lot of problems because the tests work instantly. The background processing hadn't happened by the time the test moved to the next step.

Reliably validating asynchronous processes requires some planning and careful design in the automation layer (and often in the production system). A common mistake with asynchronous systems is to wait a specific time for something to happen. A symptom of this is a test step such as "Wait 10 seconds." This is bad for several reasons.

Such tests might fail even when the functionality works correctly but the continuous validation environment is under a heavy load. Running these tests on a different environment might require more time, so they become dependent on a particular deployment. When a continuous validation environment is much more powerful than the machines that the developers have, the developers won't be able to validate changes on their systems with the same timeout configuration. Many teams set high timeouts on tests to make them more resilient to environment changes. Such tests then delay feedback unnecessarily.

For example, if a test unconditionally waits 1 minute for a process to end, but it finishes in just 10 seconds, we delay the feedback unnecessarily for 50 seconds. Small delays might not be an issue for individual tests, but they accumulate in test packs. With 20 such tests, we delay the feedback for the entire test pack for more than 15 minutes, which makes a lot of difference.

> ➡ Wait for an event to happen, not for a set period of time to elapse. This will make tests much more reliable and not delay the feedback any longer than required.

Whenever possible, implement such tests to block on a message queue or poll a database or a service in the background frequently to check whether a process has finished.

Make asynchronous processing optional
When: Greenfield projects

When building the system from the ground up, we have the option to design it to support easier testing. Depending on the configuration, the system can either queue a message to process the transaction in the background or directly execute it. We can then configure the continuous validation environment to run all processes synchronously.

> ➡ One good way to deal with test stability is to make asynchronous processing optional.

This approach makes executable specifications run much more reliably and quickly. But it means that functional acceptance tests don't check the system end to end. If you turn off asynchronous processing for functional tests, remember to write additional technical tests to verify that asynchronous processing works. Although this might sound like doubling the work, it isn't. Technical tests can be short and focused just on the technical execution, not verifying the business functionality (which will be separately checked by functional tests).

For some good technical options on automating validation of asynchronous processes, see *Growing Object Oriented Software, Guided by Tests*.[3]

---

[3] Steve Freeman and Nat Pryce, *Growing Object-Oriented Software, Guided by Tests* (Addison-Wesley Professional, 2009).

Don't use executable specifications as end-to-end validations
When: Brownfield projects

Many teams, especially those working with legacy systems, used executable specifications as both functional tests and end-to-end integration tests. This gave them more confidence that the software worked correctly overall but made the feedback a lot slower and increased the maintenance costs for tests significantly.

The problem with this approach is that too many things get tested at the same time. Such end-to-end tests check the business logic of the process, the integration with the technical infrastructure, and that all the components can talk to each other. Many moving parts mean that a change in any of them will break the test. That also means that we have to run through the entire process end to end to validate every single case, even though we could possibly check what we want in only a part of the flow.

 Don't test too many things at the same time with one big executable specification.

Most asynchronous processes consist of several steps that each have some business logic, which needs to be defined using executable specifications. Most of them also include purely technical tasks, such as dispatching to a queue or saving to a database. Instead of checking everything with one big specification that takes long to execute, think about the following when you implement such a process:

- Clearly separate the business logic from the infrastructure code (for example, pushing to a queue, writing to the database).

- Specify and test the business logic in each of the steps separately, possibly isolating the infrastructure, as described earlier in this chapter. This makes it much easier to write and execute tests. The tests can run synchronously, and they don't need to talk to a real database or a real queue. These tests give you confidence that you've implemented the right business logic.

- Implement technical integration tests for the infrastructure code, queue, or database implementations of repositories. These tests can be fairly simple because they don't have to validate complicated business logic. They give you confidence that you are using the infrastructure correctly.

Have one end-to-end integration test that verifies that all the components talk to each other correctly. This can execute a simple business scenario that touches all the components, blocks on a queue waiting for a response, or polls the database to check for the result. This gives you confidence that the configuration works. If you use high-level examples, as suggested in the "Don't look only at the lowest level" section in chapter 5, they're good candidates for this test.

Moving down this list from business logic over infrastructure to end-to-end tests, I'd normally expect to see the number of tests decrease and time to execute individual tests increase significantly. By isolating complicated business logic tests from the infrastructure, we improve reliability.

Getting feedback faster

Most teams found that running the all their executable specifications after every change of the system isn't feasible. A large number of checks (especially if they can only be executed against a website, database, or external services) make the feedback from a full test set too slow. In order to support development efficiently and facilitate change, most teams changed their continuous validation systems to provide feedback in several stages, so that they get the most important information quickly. Here are some of the strategies that the teams I interviewed used to keep their feedback loop shorter.

Introduce business time
When: Working with temporal constraints

Temporal constraints are a common reason for slow feedback in automated functional testing. End-of-day jobs might normally run at midnight, and any tests that depend on them would produce slow feedback, because we'd have to wait 12 hours on average to see the results. Cache headers might affect whether a document is retrieved from the backend system or not, and to test this functionality properly we might have to wait several days for results.

A good solution for this problem is to introduce the concept of business time into the system, a configurable replacement for the system clock.

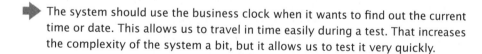

The system should use the business clock when it wants to find out the current time or date. This allows us to travel in time easily during a test. That increases the complexity of the system a bit, but it allows us to test it very quickly.

A quick and dirty way to implement business time is to automate system clock changes on the test environment. Beware of applications that cache time, though, because they might require restarting after system clock updates. Changing the system clock might make test results more confusing if that time is used anywhere else, for example, in test execution reports. A more comprehensive solution is to build the business time functionality into the software.

Introducing business time as a concept also solves the problem of expiring data. For example, tests that use expiring contracts might work nicely for six months and then suddenly start failing when the contracts expire. If the system supports business time, we could ensure that those contracts never expire and reduce the cost of maintenance.

A potential risk with business time is introducing synchronization problems with external systems that we can't influence. To address this, apply the test double or isolation ideas from earlier in this chapter.

Break long test packs into smaller modules

After several months or years of building executable specifications, many teams ended up with tests packs that take several hours to run. Because hundreds of tests are executed, people take it for granted that the feedback will be slow. They don't notice when something starts taking 20 minutes longer than it normally does. Such problems quickly accumulate, and the feedback gets even longer.

 Instead of a big set of executable specifications that takes six hours to run, I'd rather have 12 smaller sets that each take no longer than 30 minutes. Generally, I break those apart according to functional areas.

If I want to fix a problem in the accounting subsystem, for example, I can quickly rerun just the accounting tests to check if the problem is gone. I don't have to wait six hours for all the other tests to finish.

If a single group of tests suddenly starts taking 10 minutes longer, I can easily spot that by looking at the test history for a particular group of tests. A 10-minute increment over six hours isn't as visible as a 10-minute increase over 30 minutes. This allows me to keep the feedback delay under control because I'll start looking for ways to optimize that particular test pack. By splitting a big test pack into several smaller packs, I recently helped a client realize that just one functional area was causing very long delays, and we cut that down from almost one hour to just nine minutes. Divide and conquer!

Avoid using in-memory databases for testing
When: Data-driven systems

Some teams with data-driven systems tried to speed up the feedback by running continuous validation tests against an in-memory database instead of a real database. This allows the system to still execute SQL code but makes all SQL calls run a lot faster. It also makes test runs better isolated, because each test can run with its own in-memory database. But in practice, many teams found that running tests like this costs more than it's worth long term.

An executable specification that includes a database is most likely a functional acceptance test and an end-to-end integration test at the same time. Whoever wrote it like that wants to check SQL code execution as well. Minor SQL dialect differences between the real production database and the in-memory database implementations might make test results misleading. This also often requires maintaining two sets of SQL files and managing data changes in two places.

> If you use an in-memory database, the end-to-end integration test will validate that the system can work correctly against the in-memory database, not the real database that you'll use in production.

I've already mentioned some better solutions to this problem. Running tests in transactions provides better isolation. Mixing end-to-end integration tests and functional acceptance tests might not be the best idea (as mentioned earlier in this chapter), but if you really want to do that, then use the real database and look for ways to speed it up.

The team at Iowa Student Loan used in-memory databases for testing but gave up on that later. Tim Andersen says:

> We used SQL Server for our database and replaced it with Hypersonic to make it run in memory. That saved us 2 minutes of a 45-minute build. Once we added indexes to the database, SQL Server was actually faster. Hypersonic was more maintenance and didn't improve the build time that much.

If the tests are running slowly on realistic data, it probably means that the system is going to work slowly in production, so improving the performance of the database for testing actually makes sense in the grand scheme of things anyway. Note that the context of this tip is data-driven systems where executing specific database code is often required. In-memory databases can be a perfectly good solution for speeding up database-agnostic checks.

Separate quick and slow tests
When: A small number of tests take most of the time to execute

> If a small subset of tests takes the majority of time to run, it might be a good idea to run only the quick tests frequently.

Many teams organized their executable specifications into two or three groups based on the speed of execution. At RainStor, for example, they have to run some of the tests with very large data sets to check the system performance. They have a functional pack that runs after every build and takes less than one hour. They also run customer scenarios overnight, with realistic data obtained from customers. They run long-running suites every weekend. Although this doesn't provide a full validation every time, it significantly reduces the risk of changes introducing problems while still providing relatively quick feedback.

Keep overnight packs stable
When: Slow tests run only overnight

A big problem with delayed execution of slow tests is that any issues in those tests won't get discovered and fixed quickly. If an overnight test pack fails, we find about that in the morning, try to fix it, and get the results the next morning. Such slow feedback can make the overnight build break frequently, which can mask additional problems introduced during the day.

➡ Include tests into packs that run overnight only when they're unlikely to fail.

Night shift   Day shift   A good idea to keep the overnight packs stable is to move any failing tests into a separate test pack (see the "Create a known regression failures pack" section later in this chapter).

Another idea is to add tests into overnight packs only when they've been passing reliably for a while. Test-run history statistics (discussed earlier in this chapter) can help us decide when a test is good enough for an overnight pack.

If these tests are too slow to be executed continuously, a possible solution is to execute them periodically on demand until they become stable enough for delayed execution. Adam Knight at RainStor uses this strategy:

> "Tests were executed manually until they were deemed reasonably stable and then executed through the nightly test [pack]. Having the separation of tests has benefited us in many ways. If a test fails, we get it fixed. A significant failure becomes our top priority."

By adding specifications into the overnight packs only when they're unlikely to fail, the team at RainStor reduced the risk of the packs with slower feedback failing because of features currently in development. This significantly reduced the maintenance costs for overnight packs. They'll still catch unexpected and unpredictable changes, which appear rarely. Considering that, slower feedback for such features is a good trade-off for lower maintenance costs.

Create a current iteration pack

A common special case of breaking long tests into smaller packs is creating the current iteration pack. This pack contains the executable specifications that are affected by the current development phase.

> Having a current iteration pack, clearly separated, allows us to get very quick feedback on the most volatile and the most important area of the system for our current changes.

When the current iteration pack is split from the rest of the tests, we can safely include in it even the tests for the functionality that was planned but not yet implemented. Running all the tests for the current iteration will enable us to track the development progress easier and know exactly when we're finished. The current iteration pack might fail as a whole most of the time, but this won't affect the main regression validation.

A variant of this is to create a pack for the current release if we need to validate such specifications more frequently. Note that many automation tools allow us to create parallel hierarchies so the same specification can belong to multiple packs at the same time.

Parallelize test runs
When: You can get more than one test environment

> If you're privileged enough to work in a company where setting up an additional test environment isn't a problem, once you divide a big test pack into several smaller ones, try to run them in parallel. This will give you the fastest feedback possible.

If some tests have to run in isolation and can't be executed in parallel, it's worth splitting them out into a separate pack as well. At LMAX, Jodie Parker organized continuous integration and validation in this way:

> Commit build ran all unit tests and statistical analysis within 3 minutes. If that passed, sequential boxes executed tests that needed to be run one after another or not in parallel. Then 23 virtual machines ran acceptance tests in parallel. After that, a performance test kicked off. They [executable specifications] typically ran between 8 and 20 minutes.

At the end, if the tests passed a certain amount, the QA instance was available to deploy to run smoke tests and exploratory tests and provide feedback to development. If the commit build failed, everyone had to stop (a complete embargo) and fix it.

If you're not paranoid about security, or don't work under regulatory constraints that prevent you from deploying the code outside your organization, emerging cloud computing services can help with parallel test runs. Deploying the code remotely takes some time, but this allows you to run tests on a very large number of machines concurrently. At Songkick, they use Amazon's EC2 cloud to run acceptance tests. Phil Cowans said that helped them cut down build time significantly:

> Running the full test suite on a single machine would take 3 hours but we parallelize. We just learned how to do this on EC2 to bring it down to 20 minutes.

Some continuous build systems, such as *TeamCity*,[4] now offer test execution on EC2 as a standard feature. This makes it even easier to use computing clouds for continuous validation. There are also emerging services that offer automation through cloud services, such as Sauce Labs, which might be worth investigating.

Try disabling less risky tests
When: Test feedback is very slow

The team at uSwitch has a unique solution for slow feedback of long-running test packs. They disable less risky tests after the features described by those tests are implemented. Damon Morgan said:

> Sometimes you write acceptance tests (which are very good to drive development) that aren't that important to keep around once a feature has been developed. Something that is not moneymaking—e.g., sending delayed emails—is not a truly core part of the site but adds functionality to it.... They [executable specifications] were very good to help us drive the development, but after that, keeping them running as a regression pack wasn't that useful to us. It was more hassle to maintain them than to throw them away. We do have the tests in our source control; they are just not running. If we have to extend the functionality, we can still modify an existing test.

---

[4] http://www.jetbrains.com/teamcity

For me, this is quite a controversial idea. I'm of the opinion that if a test is worth running, it's worth running all the time.[5]

Most of the tests at uSwitch run through the web user interface, so they take a long time and are quite expensive to maintain, which is what pushed them in this direction. With a system that doesn't make you run tests end to end all the time, I'd prefer trying to automate the tests differently so that they don't cost so much (see the "Automate below the skin of the application" section in chapter 9).

One of the reasons why uSwitch can afford to disable tests is that they have a separate system for monitoring user experience on their production website, which tells them if users start seeing errors or if the usage of a particular feature suddenly drops.

Managing failing tests

After covering faster feedback and more reliable validation results, it's time to tackle something much more controversial. As the size of their living documentation system grew, many teams realized that they sometimes need to live with failing tests occasionally. In the following section, I present some good ideas for dealing with failing tests that you might not be able to fix straightaway.

In *Bridging the Communication Gap*, I wrote that failing tests should never be disabled but fixed straightaway. The research for this book changed my perspective on that issue slightly. Some teams had hundreds or thousands of checks in continuous validation, validating functionality that was built over several years. The calculation engine system at Weyerhaeuser (mentioned in the "Higher product quality" section in chapter 1) is validated by more than 30,000 checks, according to Pierre Veragen.

Frequently validating so many specifications will catch many problems. On the other hand, running so many checks often means that the feedback will be slow, so problems won't be instantly spotted or solved. Some issues might also require clarification from business users or might be a lesser priority to fix than the changes that should go live as part of the current iteration, so we won't necessarily be able to fix all the problems as soon as we spot them.

This means that some tests in the validation pack will fail and stay broken for a while. When a test pack is broken, people tend not to look for additional problems they might have caused, so just leaving these tests as they are isn't a good idea. Here are some tips for managing functional regression in the system.

---

[5] To be fair, I picked this idea up from David Evans, so if you want to quote it, use him as a reference.

Create a known regression failures pack

Similar to the idea of creating a separate pack of executable specifications for the current iteration, many teams have created a specific pack to contain tests that are expected to fail.

> When you discover a regression failure and decide not to fix it straightaway, moving that test into a separate pack allows the tests to fail without breaking the main validation set.

Grouping failing tests in a separate pack also allows us to track the number of such problems and prevent relaxing the rules around temporary failures that will cause problems to pile up.

A separate pack also allows us to run all failing tests periodically. Even if the test fails, it's worth running to check if there are any additional failures. At RainStor, they mark such tests as bugs but still execute them to check for any further functional regression. Adam Knight says:

> One day you might have the test failing because of trailing zeros. If the next day that test fails, you might not want to check it because you know the test fails. But it might be returning a completely wrong numeric result.

A potential risk with a pack for regression failures is that it can become a "get out of jail free" card for quality problems that are identified late in a delivery phase. Use the pack for known failures only as a temporary holding space for problems that require further clarification. Catching issues late is a warning sign of an underlying process problem. A good strategy to avoid falling into this trap is to limit the number of tests that can be moved to a known regression pack. Some tools, such as Cucumber, even support automated checking for such limits.

Creating a separate pack where all failing tests are collected is good from the project management perspective, because we can monitor it and take action if it starts growing too much. One or two less-important issues might not be a cause to stop a release to production, but if the pack grows to dozens of tests, it's time to stop and clean up before things get out of hand. If a test spends a long time in the known regression pack, that might be an argument to drop the related functionality because nobody cares about it.

Automatically check which tests are turned off
When: Failing tests are disabled, not moved to a separate pack

Some teams don't move failing tests into a separate pack, but they disable them so that a known failing test won't break the overall validation. The problem with this approach is that it's easy to forget about such disabled tests.

A separate pack allows us to monitor the problems and ensure that they eventually get fixed or that we don't waste time troubleshooting a similar problem again until the issue gets fixed. We can't do this easily with tests that are disabled. An additional problem is that someone might disable a high-priority failure without understanding that it should actually be fixed straightaway.

➡ If you have tests that are disabled, automatically monitor them.

The team at Iowa Student Loan has an automated test that checks to see which tests are disabled. Tim Andersen said:

> People were turning tests off because we needed a decision or we were writing a new test and weren't sure how this old test fit in. There were conversations that never got followed up on, or people just forgot to turn the test back on. Sometimes the tests were turned off because people were working on it and there was no code behind it yet.
>
> We used FitNesse to find the tests that were turned off, and we had a page that checked all of those test names. We'd use that to list the tests that were intentionally turned off and put a JIRA [an issue-tracking system] ticket next to each test. So a turned-off list acts as another test. It has to match what you say you turned off. At the end of an iteration, we follow up on those tests that were turned off. We could say, "This is no longer applicable, let's just delete the test," or "Oh, there's a difference and we didn't really hear back from the business," and in these cases we'd have to fix the test.

If you opt for temporarily disabling broken tests instead of moving them out into a separate pack, make sure that you can monitor them easily and prevent people from forgetting about the disabled tests. Otherwise, the living documentation system you build will quickly get outdated. Disabling executable specifications is a quick and dirty temporary fix for a broken test, but it defeats the whole point of frequent validation.

Once we have specifications that are continuously validated, it becomes easy to assert what a system does from a functional perspective, at least for the parts of it that are covered with executable specifications. The specifications then become a living documentation system that explains the functionality. In the next chapter, I present some good ideas on how to get the most out of your set of executable specifications by evolving a documentation system.

Remember

- Validate executable specifications frequently to keep them reliable.

- Compared to continuous integration with unit tests, the two main challenges for frequent validation of executable specifications are fast feedback and stability.

- Set up an isolated environment for continuous validation and fully automate deployments to make it more reliable.

- Look for ways to get faster feedback. Split quick and slow tests, create a pack for current iteration specifications, and divide long-running packs of executable specifications into smaller packs.

- Don't just disable failing tests—either fix the problems or move the tests to a pack for low-priority regression issues that's closely monitored.

11

Evolving a documentation system

In chapter 3, I introduced the concept of living documentation and explained why it's important, without discussing how to build it. We now have enough context information to deal with that issue.

A living documentation is more than a directory full of executable specification files. To experience the benefits of living documentation, we have to organize specifications so they make sense together and add relevant contextual information that will allow us to understand individual parts.

Ideally, a living documentation system should help us understand what our system does, which means that the information must be

- Easy to understand
- Consistent
- Organized for easy access

In this chapter, I present the techniques that the teams from my research used to fulfill those three goals.

Living documentation should be easy to understand

By rigorously refining the specification, as described in chapter 8, we create executable specifications that are focused and self-explanatory and make use of the domain language of a project. As a living documentation system grows, we add information to its specifications and merge or split them. Here are some useful ideas for keeping the living documentation easy to understand as it grows.

Don't create long specifications

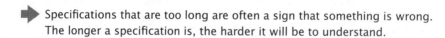

Documentation grows as you add functionality to the underlying system; you create new specifications and extend the existing ones. Watch out for specifications that become too long as a result.

> Specifications that are too long are often a sign that something is wrong. The longer a specification is, the harder it will be to understand.

Here are some examples of things that might be wrong when a specification is too long:

- The concepts aren't explained at the appropriate level of abstraction. Ask yourself, "What are we missing here?" and try to identify the missing concepts that would allow you to break the test apart. Identifying missing concepts can lead to design breakthroughs. See "Look for implied concepts" in chapter 7 for more on this.

- Instead of being focused on a single function, the specification describes several similar functions. Break it apart into separate specifications. See "Specifications should be focused" in chapter 8 for more details.

- You're describing the functionality using a script, not a specification. Restructure the information and focus it on what the system is supposed to do instead of how it's done. See "Scripts are not specifications" in chapter 8 for further information.

- The specification contains a lot of unnecessary contextual information. Clean it up by focusing on important attributes that illustrate the goal of this particular test.

Don't use many small specifications to describe a single feature

As a system evolves, our understanding of the domain changes. Concepts that start out differently might start to look similar—we discover that they are two sides of the same coin. Similarly, we might break complex concepts into smaller elements that suddenly start looking similar to existing concepts. In these cases, multiple specifications in a living documentation system that describe the same feature should be merged.

Rakesh Patel's team at Sky Network Services went too far in breaking down the specifications at one point. A single specification no longer described an entire feature. Patel said:

> If you have lots of examples in one file, it makes that file a bit more difficult to work with because you see a lot of similar code and you might be in a wrong part of it. I used to prefer having a lot of different files with different examples, but then you have a lot of files so that becomes hard to track as well.

If someone has to read 10 different specifications to understand how a feature works, it's time to think about reorganizing the documentation.

Look for higher-level concepts

In the course of adding functionality to the system, we sometimes end up with similar specifications that have only minor differences.

Step back and look at what your specifications describe from a higher level of abstraction.

Once we've identified a higher-level concept, a whole set of specifications can typically be replaced with a single specification that focuses only on the attributes that are different. This makes the information easier to understand, find, and access. Identifying missing concepts might also lead to breakthroughs in system design, similar to the process described in the "Look for implied concepts" in chapter 7.

Avoid using technical automation concepts in tests
When: Stakeholders aren't technical

Instead of creating a communication tool, some teams focused on functional regression testing with their executable specifications and wrote technical acceptance tests. This allows developers to write tests quicker, but it also makes the tests harder to read and often impossible to understand for anyone who isn't a developer. Johannes Link had such an experience on his first project using FIT:[1]

> We ended up with lots of tests with lots of duplication. Developers could understand the tests, but they were cryptic for anyone from the business side. They took longer to run and longer to maintain than just JUnit tests. We threw away some of them and rewrote them in JUnit.

---

[1] The first automation tool for executable specifications

➡ Specifications described in a technical language are ineffective as a communication tool. If business users care about an executable specification, then it should be described in a language they understand. If the business users don't care about a specification, it should be captured with a technical test tool.

A living documentation system that contains technical automation concepts, such as the command to wait until a given time for a process to complete, is a signal for a team to revisit the design of the underlying software system. The need to use technical concepts in living documentation often points to problems with system design, such as reliability of asynchronous processes (see "Listen to your living documentation" at the end of this chapter).

Using technical language is acceptable only when the stakeholders are technical as well and can understand what's going on in the technical language (such as SQL queries, DOM identifiers, and so on). Note that even if the stakeholders are technical, using such technical language tends to describe how something is tested rather than what the functionality is. Although such tests might initially be quicker to write, they might cause maintenance problems in the long term. See "Scripts aren't specifications" in chapter 8 for more information.

Mike Vogel used DbFit, a database test script extension for FitNesse that I wrote, to describe acceptance tests in a project with technical stakeholders who could understand scripts. In hindsight, he thinks this was a mistake:

> In the beginning they were happy because they could quickly use Db-Fit and not write custom fixtures, so they had automated tests from day one. Later on, as the complexity of the solution increased, there was no time in the release plan to go back and create test fixtures to make the tests simpler and more understandable and to make the system more testable. We ended up with too brittle, too complicated tests.

Living documentation should be consistent

Living documentation is probably the longest living artifact of a project. Technologies will come and go, code will be replaced with other code, but the living documentation system describes how the business works. We'll add content to it over several months or years and we need to be able to understand it later. One of the biggest challenges for many teams was keeping the structure and the language of their living documentation consistent. Stuart Taylor explains it nicely:

> 66 There's a danger when you start writing very clear BDD tests [executable specifications] that you'll end up with 57 ways to navigate to a page because it's different every time. It's important to keep refactoring the language and get it to a point that it's not so abstract that it's cumbersome, but it's not so detailed that it isn't BDD. 99

A consistent language also allows us to automate executable specifications more efficiently. For Gaspar Nagy, this is one of the key guidelines for development:

> 66 It's very important to use consistent wording and consistent expression language for acceptance criteria. It's easier for developers to spot that it's the same structure as before and easier for automation. 99

To keep a living documentation system consistent, we have to constantly refine it and keep it in sync with the current model that's applied to the underlying software system. As concepts evolve in software, that needs to be reflected in the living documentation system as well. This maintenance has costs, but without it there's no living documentation.

 ## Evolve a language

Almost all the teams ended up evolving a kind of a specification language, a set of reusable patterns for specifications. For some teams, this language evolved over several months and was often instigated by maintenance problems.

Andrew Jackman explained that the Sierra team at BNP Paribas started evolving a language when they noticed that their automation layer grew too much:

> 66 We have so much fixture code now that it's becoming a maintenance issue. We had a lot of very specific fixtures that used a very wordy description that worked for only one test, but we tried to boil it down to a generic language. We developed a mini domain-specific language in FIT for our web tests. That has reduced a lot of fixture code. 99

Some teams evolved the basics of this language quickly. Rob Park's team at a large U.S. insurance provider is a good example:

> 66 The language evolved very quickly. The first three or four fixture [automation] classes were individual. We were making it work and focusing on the conversational part. We immediately noticed some kind of duplication in the step files [automation classes] and we started moving away from that. For each story we'd have one Gherkin file [executable specification], but we had five or six story cards for the same feature.

For the most part, the steps were very similar, so we found that having a single step file for the all of the stories that belonged to that one piece of business functionality was really better. Otherwise, even though they were one-liners, we had a lot of duplication.

> Evolving a language helps reduce the cost of maintaining the automation layer because reusing existing phrases to describe new specifications leads to consistency of specifications.

The fact that a living documentation system is automated and connected directly to software ensures that the software model aligns with the business model. Because of that, evolving a language for the living documentation system is a great way to create and maintain the ubiquitous language (as discussed in chapter 8).

Base the specification language on personas
When: Web projects

Some teams described user stories through personas, especially when developing websites. In those cases, the specification language can come from the activities that different personas can perform.

> Personas can help simplify executable specifications and make them easier to maintain.

The team at Iowa Student Loan aligned the language used in their specifications with personas. Tim Andersen said:

Instead of users as an amorphous blob, we talked about different people and what their motivations to use the system are, how they use the system, and what they want to get out of it. We put names on different people. Boris was a borrower. Carrie was a co-signer.

Personas helped us because they made us think about how the system needs to behave from the perspective of a user. There are a bunch of positive side effects of using personas that we didn't anticipate—for example, personas were test helpers [automation components] that were able to interact with our system at a more appropriate entry point.

Personas don't make as much sense for projects that have little user interaction. Based on the success of using personas on a previous project, Andersen tried to apply the same concept to a technical data processing system. He eventually gave up and changed the language to a process flow model.

> Data comes from multiple sources and is loaded into a phone system so people can make phone calls. The phone data is updated, and we send it back to the entities who sent it to us. It is a batch process. Nobody actually uses it; it just runs. Personas weren't a good fit. We tried to get tests defined with personas and we got blank stares from the businesspeople. So I deleted all my persona code, and we changed it to be process based using the Given-When-Then keywords. That made it a lot clearer, and it made more sense to everyone.

Evolving the ubiquitous language around the activities of user personas allows us to ensure that our understanding of what individual personas need is aligned with how they use the system. This drives the structure and language used in specifications and helps us make the documentation system consistent.

Collaborate on defining the language
When: Choosing not to run specification workshops

➤ If you decide not to run big workshops and instead use one of the alternative approaches, make sure to collaborate on defining the language.

Christian Hassa says that collaborating on a language was one of the biggest challenges for his team:

> Building a domain language that was consistent and bound well was completely impossible without guidance. Testers wrote things that developers had to rephrase. Sometimes this was because the way testers were writing them down was unclear or not easy to bind [automate]. When the tester had written already a lot of things, we had to rephrase a lot of things. If we tried to bind [automate] the first example immediately, we would notice that it was not easy to do.
>
> It's like doing pair programming compared to doing code reviews afterwards. If you do pair programming, the pair will tell you immediately if he thinks you are doing something wrong. If you do reviews, you say: Yes, next time I'll do it differently, but this time let's leave it like this.

Instead of catching consistency problems and having to go back and fix them, Christian Hassa suggests getting developers and testers to write specifications in pairs as a way to prevent such problems. This is similar to the way a pilot and a co-pilot in an airplane work to prevent problems. The risk of someone writing bad specifications is significantly reduced because the other person validates the specifications as they're writing them and watches out for problems.

The Sierra team at BNP Paribas has a relatively stable language, one that evolved over many years, and their business analysts use this language to write new specifications themselves. To avoid inconsistent language or specifications being hard to automate, they ask the developers to review anything that has a structure significantly different from the existing specifications. When working on the Norwegian Dairy Herd Recording System, the Bekk Consulting team used a similar process. Their business users write specifications with examples, but the developers review the work and advise on how to make them more consistent with the rest of the living documentation system.

 ## Document your building blocks

 It's good practice to document the building blocks for specifications; this helps people reuse components and keep the language consistent.

Some teams have built a separate documentation area for their building blocks. At Iowa Student Loan, they have a page with all the personas. It doesn't have any assertions, but instead shows which specification building blocks are already available. The page is built from the underlying automation code, creating a living dictionary of the living documentation.

But there's an even easier way to build good documentation about your project language. When asked what advice they would give a new team member on writing a good specification, almost all the research participants suggested looking at examples of existing specifications. A nice way to document specification building blocks is to extract good representative examples from the existing set of specifications. Because these specifications are already executable, this documentation of building blocks is guaranteed to be accurate and consistent.

Because living documentation supports a team as it builds a project over a long period of time, there's a danger that parts will stay in jargons that are no longer used. One part might use a language that the team used three years ago; another might be using terminology from two years ago, and so on, depending when the specifications were originally written. This pretty much defeats the point of having a documentation system, because we'll need to have people translate the old language into the new one.

It doesn't take a lot of effort to keep the entire documentation consistent when the language evolves, and a consistent documentation will give the team much more value over the long term.

Living documentation should be organized for easy access

Living documentation systems grow quickly. As a project moves forward, the implementation team will frequently add new specifications to it; it isn't uncommon to have hundreds of specifications in a documentation system after a few months. I interviewed several teams that had more than 50,000 checks in their living documentation systems built up over the course of several years.

For the living documentation to be useful, users have to be able to find a description of a required function easily, which means that the whole documentation set has to be nicely organized and that individual specifications have to be easy to access.

Phil Cowans says that, for him, one of the biggest lessons about living documentation was that teams should think about high-level structure early:

> We didn't think about the high-level structure of the tests. We were just adding new tests when we needed. As a result, it's hard to find which tests cover which functionality. Getting the description of what the feature set of the site is and organizing the test suite along those lines (rather than just the last thing we built) would have helped. I think that's useful in terms of developing a product and maintaining a code base that's relatively easy to understand.

If we have to spend hours trying to piece together the big picture from hundreds of seemingly unrelated files every time we want to understand how something works, we might as well read the programming language code. To get the most out of living documentation, information has to be easy to find. Here are some tips on how to do that.

 ## Organize current work by stories

Many tools for automating executable specifications allow us to group specifications into hierarchies, either as website sections and subsections or file directories and subdirectories.

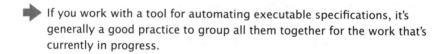

> If you work with a tool for automating executable specifications, it's generally a good practice to group all them together for the work that's currently in progress.

Grouping specifications into hierarchies allows us to quickly execute all those specifications as a test pack, as suggested in "Create a current iteration pack" in chapter 10.

A user story will typically require us to change several functional areas. For example, a story about enhanced registration might affect a back office report for users and how the system does age verification. It might also require us to implement new integrations with PayPal and Gmail. All these functions should be described by separate and focused executable specifications. We also want to have a clear definition of when each story is done; everything related to a story should be grouped together to facilitate easy execution of all those tests.

See the suggested organization in figure 11.1: the Current Iteration branch.

Reorganize stories by functional areas

User stories are excellent as a planning tool, but they aren't useful as a way to organize existing system functionality. Six months after PayPal integration is implemented, the fact that it initially came into the system as part of story #128 is largely irrelevant (unless you need traceability for regulatory purposes, for example). If anyone wants to understand how PayPal integration works, they'll need to remember the exact story number so they can find it.

> Most teams reorganize their executable specifications into hierarchies by functional areas once they've been implemented. This makes it easy find an explanation of a feature by navigating through the hierarchy based on business functionality.

In figure 11.1, this is shown in the branch under Feature Sets. Once story #128 is implemented, we should move the specification of how PayPal integration works into payments, put back-office user reports into user management, and so on. Organizing a living documentation system in this way enables us to quickly find all the existing examples related to MasterCard payments when we want to discuss a change request in that feature.

If you still want to know how some functionality was part of a particular story, there are tools that will allow you to cross-reference the same specification from different hierarchies.

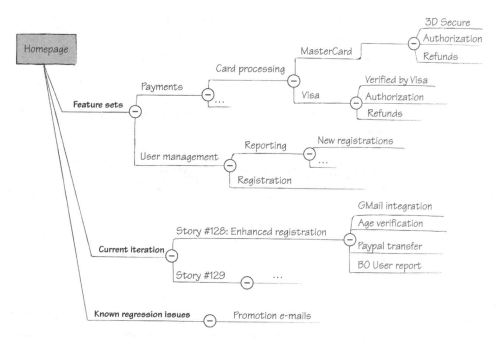

Figure 11.1 Living documentation hierarchy organized by functional areas (such as Payments and User Management). Specifications for the current iteration are organized by stories and features. Known issues waiting for more information are also in a separate holding place.

Organize along UI navigation routes
When: Documenting user interfaces

Replicate your user interface navigation structure in your living documentation system.

Ian Cooper's team at Beazley implemented an innovative organization for their living documentation system. Instead of functional areas, they replicated the user interface navigation structure in their living documentation system. Cooper says:

> FitNesse tests allowed us to pick a story and find out what's involved in a story. But it was exceptionally hard to navigate in that form. How did you know where to find the story that represented a part of the software?
>
> We restructured it so that the FitNesse page looks like a help page. I'm in this page, and I've got a FitNesse test to tell me everything I can do on this

page. And if I click a link next to this dialog, it will take me to another page that explains the dialog. That made it much easier to find out where to go to get information on how something works. 99

This approach is intuitive for systems with clearly defined navigational routes, such as back-office applications. But it might cause maintenance problems if the UI navigational routes change often.

Organize along business processes
When: End-to-end use case traceability required

Structuring the living documentation system along the lines of business processes makes it easy to trace the functionality provided by a system in end-to-end use cases.

Mike Vogel worked on a software system to support pharmaceutical research where the team organized their living documentation system along the lines of business processes. He explains this approach:

66 We organized our [FitNesse] tests to align with our use cases. Our use cases are organized in a hierarchy, with the top-level use case naming a system goal. Each top-level use case is also the definition of the end-to-end business processes for that goal. A use case refers to lower-level use cases, which are subprocesses.

The table of contents of our requirements document is identical to the table of contents to our tests. This made it easier to understand how the tests align with the business processes. It also created direct traceability from business requirements to tests, which is critical to meet regulatory requirements in our domain. 99

These aren't the only ways to organize a living documentation. Another good approach is to organize information along the chapters of a help system or user guide. Use these ideas as inspiration to find the best way to set up the hierarchies for your team.

Use tags instead of URLs when referring to executable specifications
When: You need traceability of specifications

Many living documentation tools now support tags—freeform textual attributes that we can assign to any page or file. Metadata like this is generally better for traceability than for keeping specifications in a hierarchy by user stories or use cases. When the domain model changes, the living documentation should ideally follow those changes. Specifications will often get moved, merged, split, or changed. Keeping track of this is impossible if you rely on a strict static hierarchy for traceability, but it can easily be done if story/case numbers are assigned to specifications as tags.

Tags are also useful if you want to refer to a living documentation page from another tool, for example, from an issue-tracking-system ticket or a planning-tool schedule. Using a URL based on the current location of a page would prevent us from moving it later because the link would be broken.

> Assigning a tag and linking to search results for that tag makes the system much more resilient to future changes.

Even if you don't use a web-based tool and instead keep specifications in the project directory, you can still use tags with the help of a simple script. This is what the Norwegian Dairy Herd Recording System team at Bekk Consulting did. Børge Lotre explains this approach:

> To share Cucumber tests with customers we use Confluence and link the Cucumber tests directly from Subversion into Confluence. This prevents us from restructuring the file hierarchy of the Cucumber tests without hassle, but utilizing tags has proven to help us overcome this shortcoming. Now we use tags to document which requirements are covered by which Cucumber tests.

Avoid referring to a particular specification in the living documentation system directly, because that prevents you from reorganizing the documentation later. Metadata, tags, or keywords that you can dynamically search for are much better for external links.

A living documentation system is more than just a pile of executable specifications. Information that's buried deep inside an unmanageable list of tests is useless as documentation. To experience the long-term benefits of Specification by Example, we have to ensure that the documentation is organized in a way that makes it easy for anyone to quickly find a specification of a particular function and test it.

I've presented the most common ways of organizing the specifications here, but you don't have to stop with these. Find your own way of structuring documents that makes it intuitive for your business users, testers, and developers to find what they're looking for.

Listen to your living documentation

At first, many teams didn't understand that living documentation closely reflects the domain model of the system it describes. If the design of a system is driven with executable specifications, the same ubiquitous language and domain models will be used in both the specifications and software.

Spotting incidental complexity in executable specifications is a good indicator that you can simplify the system and make it easier to use and maintain. Channing Walton refers to this approach as "listen to your tests." He worked on an order-management system at UBS where the acceptance criteria for workflows was complex. He says:

> If a test is too complicated, it's telling you something about the system. Workflow testing was very painful. There was too much going on and tests were very complicated. Developers started asking why the tests were so complicated. It turned out that workflows were overcomplicated by each department not really knowing what the others are doing. Tests helped because they put everything together, so people could see that another department is doing validations and handling errors as well. The whole thing got reduced to something much simpler.

Automating executable specifications forces developers to experience what it's like to use their own system, because they have to use the interfaces designed for clients. If executable specifications are hard to automate, this means that the client APIs aren't easy to use, which means it's time to start simplifying the APIs. This was one of the biggest lessons for Pascal Mestdach:

> The way you write your tests defines how you write and design your code. If you need to persist patient data in a part of your test to do that, you need to make a data set, fill a data set with four tables, call a huge method to persist it, and call some setup methods for that class. That makes it really hard to come to the part where it actually tests your scenario. If your setup is hard, the tests will be hard. But then, persisting a patient in real code is going to be hard.

Markus Gärtner points out that long setups signal bad API design:

> When you notice a long setup, think about the user of your API and the stuff you're creating. This will become the business of someone to deal with your complicated API. Do you really want to do this?

Living documentation maintenance problems can also provide a hint that the architecture of the system is suboptimal. Ian Cooper said that they often broke many tests in their living documentation system with small domain code changes, an example of shotgun surgery. That led him to investigate how to improve the design of the system:

> It's an indicator that your architecture is wrong. At first you struggle against it, and then you begin to realize that the problem is not FitNesse, but how you let it interact with your application.

Cooper suggested looking at living documentation as an alternative user interface to the system. If this interface is hard to write and maintain, the real user interface will also be hard to write and maintain.

If a concept is defined through complex interactions in the living documentation, that probably means that the same complex interactions exist in the programming language code. If two concepts are described similarly in the living documentation, this probably means the domain model also contains this duplication. Instead of ignoring complex specifications, we can use them as a warning sign that the domain model should be changed or that the underlying software should be cleaned up.

Remember

- To get the most out of your living documentation system, keep it consistent and make sure that the individual executable specifications are easy to understand and easy to access for everyone, including business users.

- Evolve the ubiquitous language and use it consistently.

- As the system evolves, watch out for long specifications or several small ones that explain the same thing with minor variations. Look for concepts at a higher level of abstraction that would make these things easier to explain.

- Organize the living documentation system into a hierarchy that allows you to easily find all the specifications for the current iteration and any feature that was previously implemented.

PART 3

Case studies

12

uSwitch

Switch.com is one of the busiest UK websites. The website compares prices and services for a variety of companies and products, including energy suppliers, credit cards, and insurance providers. The complexity of their software system is driven by high scalability as well as complex integrations with a large number of external partners.

uSwitch is an interesting case study because it illustrates how a company working in a Waterfall process with separate development and testing teams on a problematic legacy environment can still transition to a much better way of delivering quality software. uSwitch has completely overhauled their software delivery process over the course of three years.

At uSwitch, I interviewed Stephen Lloyd, Tony To, Damon Morgan, Jon Neale, and Hemal Kuntawala. When I asked them about their software process, their general answer was, "Someone suggests an idea in the morning and then it gets implemented and goes live." Early in my career, I worked for a company with a software process that could be described the same way—and that experienced fireworks on the production systems almost daily. But in the case of uSwitch, the quality of the product and the speed with which they deliver features is enviable.

Although uSwitch didn't set out to implement Specification by Example in particular, their current process contains the most important patterns described in this book, including deriving scope from goals, collaborating on specifications, and automating executable specifications. To improve the software development process, they focused on improving product quality by constantly looking for and addressing obstacles to quality.

When looking for a better way to align development and testing, they automated tests in human-readable form. After that, they discovered that tests can become specifications. Moving to executable specifications got them to collaborate better. In the course of refining the process, they had to make continuous validation more reliable, which led them to improve how they refine the specifications. When looking for better ways to engage business users, they started to derive scope from goals.

Starting to change the process

In 2007, uSwitch was using a Waterfall development process, working on long projects with big designs up front. A new CTO pushed the teams to "go agile" in 2008, and they introduced three week iterations with Scrum. In October 2008, the average time to market for a new feature at uSwitch was six to nine weeks. Although this was a huge improvement over Waterfall, the effort involved in each sprint consisted of roughly 40% of unplanned work. Scrum works best with cross-functional teams, but because of the way their development was organized, they never got to that point.

The QA team was separate from the development team. The testers used QTP, which the developers could not access for commercial reasons. Because of that, developers developed and testers tested without communicating with each other. As a result, developers found it difficult to know when they were finished. Because the criteria for a release was that the QTP tests had to pass, testing was often a bottleneck in the process.

The deployment process at the end of a sprint took an average of three days, mostly because of testing, and they still had numerous quality problems. When the team moved to short iterations, QTP tests started to require a lot of maintenance. According to Hemal Kuntawala, "Nobody knew what they did, and they were a complete waste of time."

This led to a companywide effort to focus on quality. Everyone was asked to start thinking about quality. They recognized the problem with developers throwing things to testers without explanation and decided to merge the testing team and the development team. They removed the different job titles; testers became "developers" with a particular specialty. In the same way that tasks requiring specialist database knowledge could go to a more experienced database developer, testers were taking on tasks that required specialist testing knowledge. But they were no longer solely responsible for testing. Programmers started to look into better ways to write unit tests and functional tests. The team decided to use Selenium instead of QTP to make tests more lightweight and accessible to everyone. This enabled developers and testers to collaborate better, but because Selenium is quite technical, this change didn't give them a better way to communicate with the business users.

Because uSwitch didn't have any reliable documentation about a system that had been built over a period of 10 years, legacy business rules often caused problems in understanding. Kuntawala says:

    ❝One day we had a legacy business rule in Energy [a subsystem] that I didn't know about. It was frustrating. I wanted a way for us to know about business rules and how the application works without diving into the code and the unit tests. Not everything was unit tested anyway. Googling around, we found Cucumber to bridge the gap between tests and portraying what we wanted to achieve—the goal of the feature. We could write what we wanted in plain English, and it would fit in with the outside-in approach that developers were trying to achieve.❞

To get everyone familiar with the new tool, they started to convert Selenium tests to Cucumber. This was still test automation—checking for problems after the fact—but it sparked a move to test-first executable specifications. Jon Neale explained:

    ❝The Given-When-Then format of Cucumber tests forced us to rewrite the stories and really nail down what we were building, showing us that we've forgotten stuff.❞

The team started taking business stakeholders through different Cucumber scenarios, not only to verify edge cases but also to identify which scenarios were important, reducing the scope and avoiding just-in-case code.

By the time they finished converting Selenium tests to Cucumber and reviewing them with the business users, they realized that testing at the end of the iteration didn't make sense. Neale said:

    ❝We realized that we could gain quite a lot by sitting down and having specification workshops and drawing out exactly what we wanted to achieve and how we were going to achieve it.❞

The team then introduced specification workshops as a way of collaborating with the business users to nail down the acceptance criteria for future requirements. This significantly improved communication within the group. The developers (at this point testers were also called developers) learned about the domain. Business users learned about edge cases and more obscure user routes because developers were asking about them.

    This change also affected the division of labor. Previously, work was mostly organized by technical tasks. With such technical chunks of work, they found it hard to work out a specific acceptance criteria for each task. The team moved the focus away from the implementation tasks to the value that a feature should deliver. They started describing stories from the user perspective, which made it easier to discuss and specify the acceptance criteria for chunks of work.

This new organization also allowed them to release software more often. Because technical tasks depended on each other, developers were reluctant to deploy a task until everything in a larger block of work was complete. By focusing on user stories, they worked on independent, smaller chunks that could be released more often.

Optimizing the process

As the number of executable specifications grew, the team noticed that the test results were unreliable. Problems with the environment often caused the tests to fail, even when the functionality in the system was correct. They had no stable environment to run tests against. They had a development environment, a testing environment, and a staging environment, but none of these was appropriate for running executable specifications frequently.

Because the developers used the development environment to try things out, it was often broken. The testing environment was used for manual testing and deployed on demand. Any number of changes could occur between two deployments, so when a test failed it wasn't clear what caused the problem. Business users were also manually testing on this environment, which could affect automated Cucumber test results. The staging environment was a mirror of production and was used for final deployment testing. uSwitch created one more environment, to be used exclusively for continuous validation. This was a solution to stability problems: a dedicated environment that could be used for testing without interrupting other work. This environment was deployed automatically by their continuous build system. With this environment, the feedback from executable specifications was received quickly and became significantly more reliable.

Once they eliminated environment problems as a source of instability, they could see which tests or parts of software were unstable by design. Because all the tests were executing through the user interface, an increase in the number of executable specifications running the tests caused a bottleneck. Some of the tests were slow, and some were unreliable. The tests were written at a technical level, which caused maintenance issues.

The team started rewriting tests, breaking them apart, and raising the level of abstraction. They started removing unreliable tests and looking into the causes of instability in order to improve them. Kuntawala says that this was quite a big step for them:

> When we first started writing tests, they would rely on browser-specific things, for example, DOM identifiers on the page, which would change. Once we got used to the syntax and the power of Cucumber, we started writing tests in a real business language. Previously you would say stuff like, "User enters 100 in box _id." Now you would say, "The user enters a valid amount." A valid amount would be defined in a separate test. Once

you have it written, you don't have to test that explicitly in every other test. A test for valid amounts would also try negative numbers, letters, and so on, but it was abstracting away from having that test in every other test. This was quite a big step. 🙶🙶

In order to reduce long-term maintenance costs, the uSwitch team started refining the specifications, evolving a consistent language for specifications, and looking for missing concepts to raise the level of abstraction.

With a relatively good functional coverage in executable specifications and a stable continuous validation environment, the uSwitch team had a lot more confidence in their code. But their test suite was running slowly and didn't give them the quick feedback they expected. They decided that not every test was worth running for an automated regression check. Some tests were good to drive development but were unrelated to the functionality that increased profit.

One example was sending delayed emails. They were automatically running executable specifications while implementing the feature but disabled them once the feature was developed. Such low-risk tests wouldn't run as part of the continuous validation process. This gave them quicker feedback and reduced test maintenance costs. The next time someone picked up a development task related to that part of the system, they would reenable the test and clean it up if needed.

Running tests or validating that the system was ready to go live was no longer the bottleneck; now deployment to production was the slowest part of the process. The developers paired with the operations engineers to understand what was slowing them down. It turned out that pre-deployment test execution was causing delays. Some tests were timing out on the staging environment, which required the operations engineers to rerun the entire test pack. By identifying differences in the environments and rewriting the tests to make them more resilient, the developers reduced the execution time for the entire test pack from two hours to about 15 minutes.

Pairing up also helped to get operations engineers involved in the process. Previously, they could report that a test pack had failed, but their report lacked details. Once they understood how to interpret test results, they could provide the developers with a much more meaningful report if something went wrong.

The next change was getting the business users more involved with the development. Although the team was using user stories for planning at this point, they were writing the user stories themselves. The business users started writing stories with the development team, taking more ownership over specifications. They would generally define the benefit ("so that") and the developers would then define the solution ("I want"). The business users also became responsible for running specification workshops. This improved communication on the team. Damon Morgan explained:

““They were previously divorced from the process. They would ask, "Can we have this?" and we'd write it down in some odd language that they didn't necessarily get. They would see it move across the board, and it didn't really mean anything to them. Once we got into specifications [workshops] and talked to them a lot more about what should be actually delivered, having executable criteria for those stories and working with them to write the stories, they took much more ownership of the whole thing. We wouldn't get stories coming back from the business in terms of "you didn't do this right." It would be more in terms of "as a team, we didn't think about this scenario."””

With more involvement from the business users, the team at uSwitch built trust and confidence. This meant that there was no need for long-term prioritization and big chunks of work. It also meant that the business users would be more open to suggestions from the development team.

With closer collaboration and more trust, the business users were open to approaching the development scope differently. The team then started breaking down required functionality into minimal features that would be releasable and still give the business some value.

One example is the process of rewriting the energy directory, a four-level page hierarchy that contains an index of energy suppliers and plans. Instead of releasing it all at once, they were rewriting it one page at a time, hooking up that page to the rest of the services, and releasing it. Although this approach increased integration costs—because new pages had to be integrated with the old pages—they got a lot of value out of releasing earlier. One of the reasons for rewriting the directory was search engine optimization: Releasing one page at a time meant that Google could index some pages sooner. Also, the team found that smaller releases mitigated the risk of mistakes. If there was a problem, it could be attributed to a particular release. By having smaller releases, it was easier to pinpoint its cause.

Once the team started producing potential deliverables more frequently than the iterations themselves, the sign-off at the end of an iteration became a bottleneck. Instead of one big demonstration at the end, they started showing new features to the business users and getting sign-off as soon as a releasable piece of functionality was done.

The team noticed there was no more need for formal specification workshops, and they were replaced with informal chat sessions. Handling smaller pieces of work and receiving fast feedback allowed the team to proceed when they had enough information to start working, even though they didn't necessarily have enough information to complete the task. According to Damon Morgan:

> At the beginning the [specification workshop] meetings were a lot longer and bigger, and we were trying to spec out a lot more. Now it's really "We're going to start work on this feature now," and it's a relatively small feature so we'll speak with the parties involved. The whole team will get together to kind of do a mini-specification workshop—but it really is just a conversation; you don't even need to go into a room to have it. And you come up with the criteria for that, you start building it, and you show it a lot quicker. It's normally built and delivered in two days, and you move on to the next thing. We're much more iterative in the way we build stuff.

Because the process allowed developers to learn a lot more about the business domain than they used to, they didn't have as many problems caused by misunderstood business requirements, and they could get the right work done with less up-front information. Stephen Lloyd said:

> As a team we are much better integrated and we understand what the business wants a lot more than we used to. So the whole purpose of specifying out exactly what they require is less important because we understand the domain much better now than we did a year ago.

Finally, the team at uSwitch started deploying on demand and moved away from iterations altogether. To help with this process, they started regularly monitoring their production systems, tracking error rates and usage of new features. This additional visibility provided a safety net against unnoticed deployment problems.

The current process

After all those changes, the development process is much simpler. It's lightweight and based on flow, rather than iterations.

New ideas come into the backlog when someone suggests them during a daily stand-up meeting. Anyone can suggest a new idea—including business users or developers. A new idea is briefly discussed at the stand-up meeting and prioritized. The person who suggests it might draw some rough diagrams about it or prepare a business case for it before the meeting, in order to explain the idea better. Apart from that, unless contracts with external partners need to be signed, there isn't a lot of up-front preparation.

When the story becomes one of the top-priority items, the team thinks about what steps would lead to completion. Everyone with an interest in that story will meet to briefly discuss exactly what's needed and write down the acceptance criteria. In the past, the team had tried to produce Cucumber tests during these meetings, but they decided the syntax of Cucumber tests was getting in the way: One person would have to type and the others would be watching, causing an interruption in the flow of discussion.

The development team and the marketing and email teams sit closely to each other, so they can work without a lot of detail up front. Developers will start working on the story and frequently talk to the business users, asking for more information or revisiting the acceptance criteria.

Acceptance criteria gets converted into Cucumber tests and automated during development. Developers will use exploratory testing to understand the existing parts of the system better before changing them. Sometimes they use customer session logs to understand how real users interact with a particular feature of the website. Based on that, they develop Cucumber tests and capture user journey paths that they need to consider while developing. They usually use browser automation toolkits to automate tests through the user interface. There's no manual scripted testing anymore, but they do a lot of exploratory testing, including trying out different paths through the system and trying to break it.

Once all the Cucumber scenarios pass, the change gets deployed to a release environment and then pushed to the production at some point that same day.

In general, the uSwitch team doesn't track many technical project metrics. Instead, they only look into lead time and throughput. They're much more focused on the business performance of the system and on the value added by a feature. To do so, they monitor user experience metrics such as conversion rates and feature usage rates on the production website.

At the time of my interview, the uSwitch team was moving away from estimations. Estimates are useful when the business users don't trust the development team or when they want to invest in larger pieces of work; now, neither scenario applies to uSwitch. The business users have a greater view of development and trust developers more than before. They also generally work on small increments. Estimating how long a piece of work is going to take isn't necessary.

The result

At uSwitch, the average turnaround time for a feature—from the time it gets accepted for development until it goes live—is currently four days. When I interviewed the team, they couldn't remember a single serious production issue over the previous six months. Boomerangs happen rarely—one every few months. During Hemal Kuntawala's presentation at the Agile Testing UK user group in 2009,[1] one of the development

---

[1] See http://skillsmatter.com/podcast/agile-testing/how-we-build-quality-software-at-uswitch. com and http://gojko.net/2009/10/29/upgrading-agile-development-at-uswitch-com-from-concept-to-production-in-four-days

managers from uSwitch said that "quality has increased substantially and conversion rates have grown."

The entire development process is now driven by expected business values of features. Instead of big plans and large releases, they build small increments, release them often, and monitor whether the increment added value to the business. Because their business model depends on immediate web conversion rates, they can easily achieve this kind of evaluation.

You can see some interesting metrics on how this process evolved in slides from Mark Durrand and Damon Morgan's presentation at Spa2010.[2]

Key lessons

To me, one of the most important aspects of this story is that uSwitch decided to focus on improving quality instead of trying to implement any particular process (for more on this, see "Focus on improving quality" in chapter 4). Instead of a big bang approach, they constantly looked for the most important thing to improve and began work there. When they were comfortable with the resulting change, they inspected the process again and moved on to the next issue.

The realization that testing was a bottleneck and that QTP was too expensive and bulky for developers to work with led the team to adopt Specification by Example through functional test automation, an approach I suggested in "Start with functional test automation" in chapter 4. They first adopted Cucumber as a way to automate functional tests but then realized that they could get a lot more out of it because it enabled them to automate tests while keeping them in a human-readable form. This turned the testing process on its head.

Another big lesson from this story is that change, though initially driven by a tool, is mostly cultural. uSwitch removed the division between the testers and the developers and dropped the tester role, making all team members understand that an issue with quality is everyone's problem. They started focusing on delivering business value instead of implementing technical tasks, which allowed them to increase the involvement of the business users during the development process. Without such close involvement of the business users, it would have been impossible to decide what to build, agree on it, implement it, and verify it within such a short turnaround.

More involvement from the business users meant that they started to understand and trust the development team a lot more, and the developers learned more about the domain. Formal specification workshops were an important step to building this knowledge. Once communication was improved and developers had learned a lot more about the domain, formal workshops became unnecessary. This is an example of how the process can be optimized once team knowledge has built up.

---

[2] www.slideshare.net/markdurrand/spa2010-uswitch

In my mind, the most controversial step taken by uSwitch was the decision to disable less important tests after the functionality was implemented. I've seen and heard most of the other ideas with other teams, but they're the only ones who don't run all the tests from their living documentation system frequently. Executable specifications for them are truly executable—there's a potential to execute them but not an obligation. The team found that there's a lot of value in executing them while they develop a feature but that slower feedback as the result of an ever-growing test suite costs more in the long term than protection against functional regression in less-risky areas. This is perhaps because they have other means to protect against problems in production, in particular the continuous user experience monitoring system.

13

RainStor

RainStor is a UK company that builds high-capacity data archiving and management systems. RainStor is an interesting case study because they deal with a technical domain where complexity comes from high data volumes and high-performance requirements, combined with advanced compression and data management algorithms.

The company has fewer than 30 employees, and about half of them work in Research and Development, so they have to be efficient in building and supporting their software. All the developers and testers work as part of the same Scrum team, although they're now thinking about splitting it into two.

Their journey to Specification by Example was almost organic, without any big plans or buzzwords, driven mostly by the testers. When I interviewed Adam Knight, senior test and support team leader at RainStor, he said, "Nobody else in the company knows what Acceptance Test-Driven Development means." Although their process has almost all the key elements of Specification by Example, they just think about it as their homegrown way of developing software. They illustrate requirements using examples, automate them into executable specifications, and validate them frequently to build a living documentation system. The changes they implemented allowed the development team to triple in size over three years, at the same time making them more effective.

Changing the process

Three years ago, a new CEO decided to implement Scrum and expanded the team of four developers by hiring two testers and a test manager. Although they adopted iterations and daily stand-up meetings, the process was actually a mini-waterfall, according to Knight. He explained:

> We had requirements as a large document put in at the start of the sprint. It was supposed to be both the requirements document and the technical specification. There was too much technical detail in it. It was set in stone at the start of an iteration. The development would go ahead against that, and testing was based on the contents of that document. The document was not maintained with the decisions made during the development process, so towards the end our test cases differed from the implementation.

In addition to the problems in coordinating development and testing, they had a problem with the way tests were executed. Although they had some automated tests, testers were running most of the validations manually. As the product grew, it became obvious that manual testing wouldn't scale. Even if they added more people to run manual checks, their software handles very high volumes of data, and manually checking queries that return tens of thousands of records wasn't feasible.

Knight took over as a test manager in late 2007. He wanted to make testing more efficient and to support development, preventing the need for manual testing as the product developed. They implemented a simple automated test harness, which allowed them to push testing much earlier in the process. They could define tests at the same time as they were developing the relevant feature. This helped them align development and testing.

Functional test automation gave them immediate value, because they no longer had testing tasks pile up toward the end of an iteration. It also gave developers quicker feedback as to whether a piece of work is done, removing the interruptions to the flow caused by testing spilling into the next iteration.

Once the team aligned testing and development, they started noticing problems with scope creep and knowing when they were finished. They often had to rewrite the requirements after development started. Boomerangs were coming back from the previous iterations in the form of stories titled "Finish off ...." During the summer of 2008, Knight brought in David Evans as a consultant to help them understand how to improve.

As a result, they started to describe scope with user stories instead of using large, detailed technical requirements up front. This enabled them to start thinking about acceptance criteria from a business perspective and deriving the tests from that, instead of receiving requirements in the form of functionality to implement. Knight said that this allowed them to understand the scope better and have a clear picture of when they're finished developing a feature.

They started to break down stories into smaller deliverable items, which gave them more visibility of what could realistically be delivered in an iteration. This helped the team to better manage the expectations of their business users.

The team then started to use examples to illustrate conditions of satisfaction, even for requirements such as performance. Knight explained:

> We used well-defined acceptance criteria for performance measurement. For example, the system has to import a certain number of records within 10 minutes on so many CPUs. Developers would either get access to dedicated testing hardware or testers would run tests and provide feedback.

Focusing on user stories allowed the business users to engage better in defining the expectations from an upcoming piece of work, and illustrating those expectations with examples allowed the team to measure objectively whether they've achieved the targets.

As their customer base started to grow, they were getting more customer-specific scenarios to implement. In late 2008 the team decided to reach out to the customers as the final stakeholders and involve them in the specification process. Knight added:

> Generally a customer would have an implementation they would like to put in. They would give us the requirements, and we'd work with them on getting realistic data sets and expected targets. We'd put this in the testing harness and use that to drive the development.

Putting the customer-specific scenarios with sample data into the system as acceptance tests ensured that the team met their targets. It also meant that the team didn't have to waste time coming up with a separate set of acceptance criteria and prevented any wasteful rework caused by potential misunderstandings.

This process worked best when they could involve actual customers with realistic requirements. RainStor primarily works with reselling partners, who sometimes request functionality without a specific business case. "That is the most difficult kind of requirement," said Knight. In such cases, they push back and ask for examples, sometimes organizing workshops with the customers to go through high-level examples on relatively developed prototypes. They use those high-level examples to drive the scope later. Working on paper prototypes also helps them look at the system outputs first, promoting outside-in design.

The current process

At the moment, the Research and Development team at RainStor works in five-week iterations. Sprints start on a Tuesday, with a sprint kick-off meeting in which they briefly go through the stories planned for the iteration. They use the rest of the day to elaborate those stories. The developers, the testers, the technical writers, and the product manager collaborate to flesh out the requirements and define some basic acceptance criteria for each story. The testers write down the acceptance criteria based on the notes they took during that meeting and publish them for the whole team to see.

Once the conditions of satisfaction for a story are published, development and testing start in parallel. Developers work on implementing the existing specifications with examples and testers work on creating more detailed test cases. For some stories, they might not have any examples automated at the start. In such cases, the developers initially work on delivering the basic functionality while the testers automate the simpler examples. The testers then go on to develop further tests, and the developers deliver the functionality that ensures that these tests pass.

As the functionality is implemented, the testers perform exploratory tests and start to run automated tests against the new version of the system. When the full functionality is implemented for a story, the testers ensure that all the tests pass and then integrate them into the continuous validation system.

Top three ah-ha moments

I asked Adam Knight to single out top three key lessons he learned about Specification by Example. Here's what he said:

- As you develop a harness of automated tests, those can become your test documentation if you set them up properly to reveal the purpose behind it. Metadata made the tests much more readable. We produced HTML reports that listed tests that were run and their purpose. Investigation of any regression failures was much easier. You could resolve conflicts much more easily, because you could understand the purpose without going back to documentation.

- The acceptance criteria and specifications with examples created as part of the story process became the requirements. You can have a lightweight story to get started. Once you have the tests, passing those tests tells you that the requirements have been met. You don't have to refer to anything to find the requirements. That allowed us to spot if future requirements were conflicting and what the changes were impacting. It allowed us to maintain the requirements on an ongoing basis. We were always in a position to know how the product sits against the requirements that we implemented. If a test starts failing, we know which requirement wasn't met.

- The test and test results were part of the product. You need to store them in the version control with the product. We test different branches and versions and we need to execute the tests appropriate to the branch.

Some tests work with very large data sets or check performance, so they divide the automated validation into three stages: regular builds, overnight builds, and weekend builds. Regular builds take less than one hour. Slower checks run overnight. Checks with very large data sets, often customer scenarios, run only over the weekend. Because of such slow feedback, they add tests to the overnight or weekend packs only once they're stable. When developers release parts of the functionality, they run tests on their machines if possible. Testers run tests that require specialist hardware and offer feedback to developers.

In the last week of the iteration, they close up any unfinished issues. The team ensures that all the tests are running in the appropriate automated pack; they chase stakeholders about open issues and fix them. On the last Monday of an iteration, they run final regression tests and hold a retrospective.

Because RainStor is a relatively small company, their vice president of product engineering is responsible for analysis, along with many other things. He's not always available to attend the specification workshops, so the testers sometimes step in to help and take over some of his analysis tasks. Testers are responsible for gathering a list of questions and getting clarification before writing specifications with examples.

Key lessons

Although the development team size more than tripled over the last three years, RainStor still has a relatively small team. The same people have to develop a product, support the existing customers, and help grow the customer base. They have to be effective to do so with such a small number of people. Here's what they accomplished and how:

- Implementing executable specifications eliminated the need to maintain two sets of documents. It helped align testing and development and eliminate a lot of wasteful rework.

- Switching to user stories helped them engage their business users better.

- Deriving scope from business goals with high-level examples ensured that they build the right product and not waste time developing unnecessary features.

- Engaging customers into collaboration on specifications helped them make the process even more effective, because they get acceptance criteria from the very start, which ensures that they achieve the targets.

They gradually improved over the course of three years without any big plans or enforcing any particular process. Similar to many other stories, they always looked for the next big thing to improve, looked for ideas in the community to see which ones could help, and then figured out how to implement them in their particular context. This led them to implement several unique practices such as running tests manually until they become stable and creating living documentation from metadata with a custom-built tool.

Their particular context makes it unlikely that they'd be able to use any of the more popular tools to get the same effect, so they built a tool that helps them do the job efficiently. They started with the process and built a tool to support it.

For me, the key lesson here is to focus on the important principles when improving and to use popular community practices just as an inspiration.

14

Iowa Student Loan

Iowa Student Loan is a financial services company that pushes the ideas of Specification by Example to the limit. They're an interesting case study because their living documentation system gave the business a competitive advantage. It enabled them to efficiently deal with a major business model change.

The Iowa Student Loan development team builds and maintains a complex system, from the public website, which takes loan requests, to the back-office systems for underwriting and origination. Apart from that, the main driver of complexity on their projects is the data-driven nature of the domain.

I interviewed Tim Andersen, Suzanne Kidwell, Cindy Bartz, and Justin Davis, who worked on several different projects while the company was improving its software process. It was interesting to track how they rolled out practices from a smaller project into rewriting the entire underwriting platform.

Changing the process

In 2004, the Iowa Student Loan development team implemented Extreme Programming by the book to improve the quality of their software. When their next project went to production, they prepared to handle bugs similarly to the way they did things in the past. Over the next 12 months, the new system only had half a dozen bugs. This proved to the management that agile development, especially writing tests first, was a good idea and that it significantly improves quality.

The tests were, however, very technical. The team used HTTPUnit (a unit-testing framework for websites). Programmers translated use cases to HTTPUnit tests, which weren't readable by anyone. When the system went live, they noticed that they were missing documentation. They hired a consultant, J. B. Rainsberger, to help them figure out what they were doing wrong and to give them ideas on improving with tools and practices. One of the tools he introduced was FitNesse.

The team was wrapping up the first project in which they used FitNesse as a way to capture the specifications in July–August 2006. This project allowed the team to learn how to use the tool and also led them to rethink how they write executable specifications. The business analysts had technical knowledge, so the specifications they wrote with developers turned out very technical. As a result, the business users couldn't understand them. Justin Davis explains that problem:

> I could look at tests and read them as a business analyst, and we were still writing them, but they were very disconnected from the other business members of the team.

This was just the start of a larger effort to rewrite the entire underwriting platform and automate a lot of the work that was previously done manually on paper. The next project would take three years with a team of six developers, two testers, a business analyst, and an on-site business user. They brought in a consultant to help them communicate better with the business users. Tim Andersen says:

> David Hussman said that we should work harder on developing tests that make sense, so that when businesspeople read them, we don't have to explain the tests to them. That was pretty hard to do. It took a shift in our thought process, and we had to be a lot more business savvy. It required a lot more understanding and conversation about how the system should work instead of just technical requirements.

They started to describe the system with user personas, which allowed them to consider how different groups of users were interacting with the system.

Instead of using generic users, they started thinking a lot more about why different groups of people use the system, what they want to get out of it, and how they use it. This allowed the business stakeholders to engage better and provide more meaningful information to the team. You can see some nice examples of the personas they used in Tim Andersen's presentation from the Code Freeze 2010 conference.[1]

Optimizing the process

Because their executable specifications were previously very technical, the automation layer was complicated and hard to maintain. Tests described technical components as parts of larger flows, so they had to be automated by faking portions of the user workflows. Tim Andersen says that the test results also weren't reliable:

---

[1] http://timandersen.net/presentations/Persona_Driven_Development.pdf

> We were able to show the test working, and then we weren't able to show working software. Our tests were lying (false green bar). For example, a borrower can borrow money if he is less than 18 years old. We'd have a test that if they are less than 18 on that day, it would say, "You're not allowed to borrow without a co-signer." If you change the date of birth to be over 18 years, it would say "OK, you can borrow without a co-signer." Our test was green, but when we actually opened a browser and tried it in development, it didn't work. Even though we coded the validation rule, it wasn't hooked up in the right place. Our test code was setting up a loan within a fantasy state.

The business users didn't trust the test results from executable specifications, so they didn't consider them important, which was another barrier to get them more engaged in the process. Andersen says:

> There was a lot of frustration on both sides. We asked, "How come they aren't reviewing the tests; how come they aren't valuing the tests?" At the same time the business team was frustrated: "How come the developers have a passing test but it doesn't work?" They did not believe in those tests.

The team restructured the automation layer for executable specifications to go through production flows, not trying to fake state. The new way of automating specifications fit in nicely with the ways they were describing the system with personas. Andersen says:

> "Fantasy state" is the term I kept using to let other developers know that I didn't trust a test that wasn't using the correct entry point. Other symptoms of fantasy state are "thick fixtures"; fixtures shouldn't have much logic in them and should be pretty lightweight. Using personas helped us find the right level of abstraction to identify the appropriate entry point in our application. Before we used personas, we often picked an inappropriate entry point, which led us to heavy fixtures that were prone to fantasy state.

The team organized the automation along the activities that would be available to a persona. Each persona was implemented as a fixture in the automation layer, talking to the server using HTTP calls, essentially going in the same way a browser would but without launching a browser. This enabled them to significantly simplify the automation layer, and it also made test results much more reliable. Some tests started failing after that, and the team discovered bugs that had previously passed unnoticed. Around May 2007, the test results became a lot more reliable and the automation layer was easier to maintain. Andersen adds:

> Changing our test code to leverage the application to set up the state of a loan exposed these bugs so we could fix them, and our false green bar symptoms vanished. It also had an impact by dramatically reducing the cost of test maintenance.

Once the executable specifications were talking about the business functionality on a level that the business users could understand, the automation layer became a lot simpler—it was connecting to the business domain code. It also made the specifications a lot more relevant, because they no longer had misleading false positives from tests that looked at only a part of the flow.

The feedback started to slow down as the number of tests grew. Many slow technical tests were executed through a browser. Andersen said that looking at the system from the perspective of personas helped reduce those problems:

> We used FitNesse as a tool to make WatiJ [a UI automation library] configurable. Before using personas, we kind of fell back to the browser tests as a last resort because "we have to test this somehow to make sure that it really works." Those browser tests multiplied like rabbits.

The team rewrote the browser tests to use personas, which significantly improved the feedback time. Instead of launching a browser every time, the new automation layer issued HTTP requests directly. They also looked into running tests with in-memory databases instead of SQL Server, but they decided to improve the performance of the real SQL database using indexes instead. The team organized executable specifications into several modules to get better visibility on what was slowing down the tests.

Instead of always creating new specifications, the team started thinking about integrating change requests with existing specifications. This reduced the number of tests and helped avoid unnecessary setup tasks. Andersen explains:

> We started thinking about scenarios. A new feature might not be a feature by itself; it might be a change to a set of scenarios. Instead of writing a new test for each requirement, we were thinking about that in the context of our current system and what tests we need to change versus what new tests we need to write. That helped keep our build time constant.

This led them to start reorganizing the specifications to reduce the number of tests. They would look for smaller partial specifications and consolidate them into bigger ones. They would break apart large specifications into smaller, more focused ones. "You basically have to refactor your tests and your test code as much as you would refactor your old code," says Andersen.

Iowa Student Loan was an early adopter of Specification by Example, so they had to deal with immature tools, which got in the way of collaboration several times. Because the team was using open source tools, they were able to modify the tools to suit their development process.

Once they started putting executable specifications into a version control system, the business analysts could no longer change them on their own without access to development tools. The developers wrote a plug-in for FitNesse that handled version control system integration, allowing them to still run a wiki where business analysts can change specifications.

As the number of tests grew, the team started to have problems with functional regression. Bugs that should have been caught by existing tests slipped through, because the relevant tests were disabled. Some tests were disabled because developers were unsure of how they fit into the new functionality; some were disabled when the team was waiting on a decision from business stakeholders. People then forgot to reenable these tests or follow up on the discussions. Developers at Iowa Student Loan wrote an automated check for disabled tests (see the "Automatically check which tests are turned off" section in chapter 10), which reminded them at the end of every iteration what they had to follow up on.

They used JIRA to manage requirements and FitNesse to manage executable specifications, so rearranging FitNesse pages broke links in JIRA. They extended FitNesse to support keywords and used keywords to link executable specifications and JIRA web pages. On another project, they took a different approach and created a business framework. The business framework is a set of pages in FitNesse designed to be a stable documentation entry point, which then has internal links to tests. This was a start of a good living documentation system. Justin Davis explains:

> One of the goals of the business framework was to create a front to FitNesse that the business team could use while also allowing developers to understand the order of the things in the current system. In effect, it provides a map to how the system behaves. So if you have a context there in terms of knowing how the system works, you can go to this framework to find what you want. The system flow would be there, and you can choose which steps you'd like to view tests and requirements for.

Introducing the business framework and making sure that the executable specifications actually get validated frequently and stay relevant enabled them to create a useful living documentation system. They had a relevant source of information on what the system does, which anyone could access.

Living documentation as competitive advantage

With such a good living documentation system, they were able to handle very big changes efficiently. Three months before the end of the project, the business model of the company suddenly had to change. They normally fund loans through a bond sale. Because of the credit crisis in 2008, the bond sale failed. The business is technology driven, so this business model change had to be reflected in their software. Andersen says that the living documentation system helped them understand what was required to support this business change:

> Typically, we use bond proceeds to fund private student loans. However, we changed our business model and made all of the funding portion of the system configurable so that we could use lenders to provide funds and continue to provide loans to the students. It was a dramatic overhaul of a core piece of the system. Before this new funding requirement, our system didn't even have the concept of a lender because we were able to assume Iowa Student Loan was the lender.
>
> We were able to use our existing acceptance tests and repurpose them to say, "OK, here's our funding requirement." For all of the tests we had, we discussed the impact and provided funding so they would still work. We had some interesting discussions based on scenarios where there is no more funding available, or funding is available but not for this school or this lender, so we had some edge cases for these requirements, but it was really making the new funding model more flexible and configurable.

Once they understood the impacts of this new business model on the software, they were able to implement the solution efficiently. According to Andersen, such change would be impossible to implement quickly without a living documentation:

> Because we had good acceptance tests, we were able to implement a solution within a month. Any other system that didn't have the tests would halt the development and it would have been a rewrite.

This is when the investment in the living documentation system paid off. It supported them in analysis, implementation, and testing of the impact of a business model change, at the same time enabling them to quickly verify that the rest of the system is unaffected.

Key lessons

The Iowa Student Loan development team started out by focusing on a tool and quickly realized that it doesn't help them achieve the goal of bringing business users into the process. So they started approaching the specifications from the perspective of a user. This enabled them to communicate with their business users better and reduce the costs of maintenance for tests. When the tool prevented them from collaborating effectively, they modified it. This is another argument for using open source tools.

Implementing Specification by Example at Iowa Student Loan was driven not by the need to improve quality or automate tests but by the need to build a relevant documentation system in order to be more effective and engage business users better. They invested heavily into building a good living documentation system, which paid off well. It helped them implement a business model change, which was very powerful.

15

Sabre Airline Solutions

Sabre Airline Solutions offers software and services to help airlines plan, operate, and sell their products. They are an early adopter of Extreme Programming and Specification by Example and an interesting case study because they applied SBE on a massive project, with a relatively large distributed team.

The project was Sabre AirCentre Movement Manager, a software system that monitors airline operations and alerts the relevant teams when it finds issues, allowing them to adjust schedules to minimize the impact to customers and the airline. According to Wes Williams, an agile coach at Sabre, two previous projects to build similar systems failed because of the domain complexity and quality issues. Specification by Example enabled them to complete this project successfully.

Changing the process

Because of the complexity of the domain, the teams at Sabre were looking for a collaborative way to specify and automate acceptance testing soon after implementing Extreme Programming. Williams said that they initially tried to do it with a technical unit-testing tool. That approach didn't help with collaboration and it wasn't reusable, so they abandoned it.

They started looking for a tool to drive collaboration. In 2003, Williams found FIT, the first widely available tool for automating executable specifications. His team started implementing acceptance testing with FIT, but they focused on the tool, not the practices. Williams says that it didn't give them the improvement in collaboration they expected:

> We liked the idea that a customer could define the test and drive the value you deliver in an application. In reality, we never got a client to write FIT tests in HTML. The tests got written most of the time by a developer. We had a hard time getting the customers to do it. Testers were using QTP. That never drove collaboration, and developers never ran QTP tests or got involved in writing them.

The developers were the only ones who wrote executable specifications, and they understood that didn't give them the benefits they expected. To improve the communication and collaboration, everyone had to be involved. A single group of people was unable to do that on their own.

A senior vice president of product development, influenced by the development team, brought in consultants from ObjectMentor to train everyone. They made the wider group aware of the goals of Specification by Example and the benefits they could get out of it. Although they didn't get everyone on board immediately, the training helped them get more people enthusiastic about the practices. Williams says:

> Not everyone adopted it. Still, there was a core group of people who believed in it, and they learned a lot. Those who didn't continued to fight against it.

That core group of people started with a relatively simple web project—an internal system for aggregating software build information. They wanted to try out the practices and get their heads around the tools, which were a lot worse in 2004 than they are now. The team selected FitNesse to manage executable specifications collaboratively. They wrote executable specifications either just before the development or roughly at the same time. The business stakeholder for the project was an internal manager, who got involved in reviewing the tests. The team initially looked at the automation layer as second-grade test code and cared little about making it clean, which caused numerous maintenance problems. They also ended up with a lot of duplication in test specifications. Williams says:

> We learned that we should try to keep fixtures as simple as possible and that duplication is bad. It [automation layer] is code, like any other code.

Developers didn't care much about making the automation layer or executable specifications maintainable because they just associated them with testing. By the end of the project, they realized that this approach led to huge maintenance problems. Similar to the team at Iowa Student Loan, the first project allowed the Sabre Airline team to learn how to use a tool and see the effects and limitations of the way they automated executable specifications. This gave them ideas about how to improve the next project.

After the smaller team better understood the limitations of tools and realized why they should invest more in writing maintainable specifications with examples, they started to roll out the process to a large and risky project. This was a rewrite of a C++ legacy system to Java, with lots of deliveries. The project was data driven and had to support global distribution. At the end, it took 30 people two years to deliver the whole thing. They were split in three teams on two continents.

Because of the risk, they wanted to significantly improve the coverage and frequency of testing. This led them to start using the practices implemented on the smaller project. Williams says:

> Proper manual testing of a large application like this would take months. We wanted to prevent defects and not have to spend months testing. We did continuous testing. You can't even do manual sanity testing daily on applications this big.

Because they now had in-house experience with FitNesse, the people working on the previous project started to automate functional tests. They involved the business users in specifying the tests, expecting that this would ensure that their targets were met.

Improving collaboration

The group was split into three teams. The first team was working on the core features, the second on the user interface, and the third on integrations with external systems. It took about four months for the first version of the user interface to be delivered. Once the business users started to look at it, the core features team noticed that their software missed many customer expectations. Williams explained:

> The customer thought completely differently about the application when they saw the user interface. When we started writing acceptance tests for the UI, they had much more in them than the ones written for the domain. So the domain code had to be changed. But the customer assumed that that part was done. They had their FitNesse test there, they drove it, and it was passing. People assumed that the back end would handle everything that the UI mockup screens had on them. Sometimes the back end didn't support queries or data retrieval in a form that was usable to the front end.

They realized the problem was in the division of work between the teams. The customers naturally thought about the system at a more detailed level once they could see something visually, so they couldn't engage properly in defining the specifications for the work of the teams that didn't deliver any user interfaces.

About six months after the project started, the group decided to reorganize the work so that teams deliver end-to-end features. This allowed the business users to engage with all the teams. Williams added:

> Once we divided in the feature groups, we were in such a mature state on our user stories and the core of application that we didn't have story explosions. The surprises that came up were much lower.

When each team worked to deliver a whole feature end to end, it was much easier for business users to collaborate with the team to specify the conditions of satisfaction and engage in illustrating them with examples.

After the group reorganized the work, the teams realized that they need faster feedback on implemented stories, so they halved the length of an iteration to one week. Although they were writing acceptance tests before implementation, they still considered them tests, not specifications. Testers were charged with writing acceptance tests, but they couldn't keep up with such short iterations. To help remove this bottleneck, the group who implemented FitNesse on a previous project suggested that developers should help write acceptance tests. Williams says that the testers were initially reluctant to allow that:

> It was a struggle at the beginning to say that it's OK for a developer to write a test, because testers thought that they did such a better job of testing. I think they come from a completely different perspective. Actually, I've found since then that when a developer and a tester talk about the test together, it comes out significantly better than if one of them does it on their own.

Williams realized that this required a change of culture. As a coach, he tried to bring people together and let them expose the problems. When a tester got behind on testing, he would bring in a developer to help. When testers complained that developers didn't know how to write tests, he suggested pairing and writing tests in a group.

> They both went away and came back surprised with, "Wow—what I would have written on my own was nothing like what came out of this!" You need to get them through this experience.

Williams was surprised by how much trust was built between the testers and the developers as a result of that:

> ❝ The trust was amazing. They realized that they do a better job together, that they are on the same page, and that the other person is not trying to make things bad for them. At the end, you have a much more collaborative environment. ❞

Getting people to work together not only helped them address bottlenecks in the process but also resulted in better specifications, because different people were approaching the same problem from different aspects. Collaboration helped both groups share knowledge and build trust in the other group gradually, which made the process much more efficient long term.

The result

Although the previous two attempts to rewrite the legacy system failed because of quality problems, this project went live initially with a very big customer and had very few issues. They discovered only one critical issue, which was related to failover. Williams said that Specification by Example was "one of the key pieces" for the success.

Key practices for data-driven projects

Wes Williams shared his top five tips for writing good specifications in a data-driven environment:

- Hide incidental data.

- Remove the duplication.

- Look for the duplication when you do incremental development—look at the old similar tests and clean up.

- Refactor tests similarly to the code.

- Isolate yourself and don't depend on third parties where you can't control the data. In the airline world, the system is going to talk to some host system at the end. They might have a test system as well, but you can't control the data. You need to have tests that talk to them, but these are completely separate tests. During the automated acceptance testing, this is what you want to mock.

Key lessons

Developers were driving the adoption of SBE as a way to reach out to testers and business users, but they quickly found out that focusing on a tool within a closed group wouldn't succeed. It was crucial to get everyone engaged. Although the training didn't get everyone on board, it gave them a common baseline, and it identified a core group of people who were genuinely interested in trying out the new ideas.

They used a smaller and less risky project to get their heads around the tools and discover good ways to write and maintain the specifications and the automation layer. A small group of people involved in that project acted as a catalyst for the larger group on the big project.

While the teams were delivering components of the system, the business users couldn't engage properly with the teams working on background components, which caused a lot of rework and missed expectations. Once they restructured into feature teams, the problem went away.

Getting testers and developers to collaborate on writing acceptance tests produced much better specifications and helped to build trust between those two groups.

Specification by Example helped them conquer a complex domain by providing a clear target for development and continuous validation.

16

ePlan Services

ePlan Services is a 401(k) retirement pension service provider based in Denver, Colorado. It's a technology-driven business, relying heavily on an effective software delivery process. According to Lisa Crispin, an agile tester who works there, they use living documentation to deal with a complex domain and to facilitate the transfer of knowledge both for software development and for business operations.

The business model of the company is to offer services to small employers, which benefit from a cheaper cost of operation, resulting in a significant competitive advantage. Business process automation is a key factor. In 2003, they realized that their software delivery process would have to change to support the business. "We weren't getting the software out of the door; there were too many problems with the quality," says Crispin.

The need to deliver a cheaper service and automate their business processes got ePlan Services on a path of improving their software development process, in which they implemented most of the ideas of Specification by Example.

Changing the process

The company convinced Mike Cohn to take over the development team, and he helped them implement Scrum. Early on, they spent two days at the end of every iteration doing manual testing. All members of the team, including testers, developers, and database administrators, were running manual test scripts. This meant that one fifth of their iteration was spent on testing. Because of that, they decided to implement test automation. According to Crispin, unit testing was the first thing they had to get right:

> Most of the bugs testers found before were unit-level bugs. You spent all your time with that and didn't have time for anything else.

While the developers were getting used to unit testing, the testers started with functional test automation. Without the help from the developers, the testers could automate tests only through the user interface. Eight months later, they had hundreds of unit tests and enough automated functional smoke tests to eliminate the need to do manual regression checking for unit-level bugs. Crispin says that this allowed them to start looking at the bigger picture:

> We found really quickly that once developers had mastered TDD, we didn't have these bugs any more. We had more time for exploratory testing. Anything that we reported as a bug was usually because the developer didn't understand the requirement. Bugs in production were often something that we didn't understand.

Like in so many other cases, without efficient test automation the team had little time to deal with anything else. Once the technical unit-level bugs were no longer causing trouble, they could see the other problems as well.

Although they had some automated functional tests in place, this wasn't enough to prevent problems. Those tests were very slow, so they ran overnight and only checked happy-path scenarios. The team started looking at alternative ways to automate functional tests, to run more checks more quickly. They found FitNesse, but that required developers to help with automation. Crispin says that getting the developers engaged was a challenge:

> Programmers are used to being rewarded for writing production code. On Mike Cohn's suggestion, I just picked a story, went to a developer working on it, and asked if we could we pair up writing FitNesse tests on it. In the next sprint I picked a different story and a different person. We found a bug right away, where he didn't really understand the requirement. So developers immediately saw the value.

Collaborating on writing tests brought testers and developers together to discuss requirements and helped them write better tests. Crispin says that this eliminated most of the big problems:

> Within a year after we started doing agile, we felt comfortable that really bad bugs weren't going to production.

They also realized the importance of collaboration. Crispin says:

> The biggest benefit from this is getting us to talk together so that we have a mutual understanding of the requirements. That's more important than test automation. After we saw the benefits of collaboration, the product owner got excited about it as well and heard about Acceptance Test-Driven Development.

Efficient functional test automation required the developers to get involved, which resulted in much tighter collaboration between the developers and the testers. It also gave the team visible benefits, which helped to build a business case for further improvements. This inspired the team to take the process even further and prevent bugs from coming into the system instead of catching them with automated tests later.

Working to improve the process even more, they started using acceptance tests as specifications and collaborating on them. Crispin worked with their product owner up front to prepare examples. They had some early success, but they still looked at the examples as functional tests. When the team was working on automating compliance testing, one of the most complicated parts of the system, they over-specified tests and had to think much more about what they wanted to achieve with this approach. Crispin explained:

> The product owner and I sat down and wrote all these FitNesse tests to test algorithms. There are so many permutations, so we wrote a lot of very complex tests a couple of sprints in front. When the developers started coding, they looked at the tests and were confused. They couldn't see the forest for the trees.

They realized that the developers couldn't handle too much information up front. After several experiments, the team decided only to write a high-level test up front to give the developers the big picture. When a developer picked up a story, he would pair with a tester on writing a happy-path scenario test and automate it. A tester could then extend the specification by adding more examples. Testers used this automated framework for exploring the system. If they found a case that failed the test, they'd go back to the developer to get it fixed. This changed the way they look at acceptance tests as specifications, according to Crispin:

> We had a vague idea at first that we could write acceptance tests ahead of time so that they could be the requirements. What changed over time is how much detail we need to put into tests up front, how many test cases is enough. I'm a tester; I could probably test something forever and

keep thinking of things to test, but we have only two weeks. So we had to figure out how to internalize the risk analysis and say: Here are the tests we really need; here are the really important parts of the story that have to work. 99

As they shifted from thinking about automated tests to thinking about automated specifications, it became clear that the structure of what they specify and automate is primarily a communication tool, not a regression check. They simplified and refined them to ensure that developers have enough specifications just in time when they need them.

Good test design

Lisa Crispin is a well-known agile tester and the co-author of *Agile Testing*. I asked her about what makes good acceptance test design. This was her response:

- Good test design is key long term. People start testing and make a big suite of tests. All of the sudden, the effort they spend maintaining them is more than they are worth.

- Each test has to be clear about the essence of the test.

- As soon as you have some duplication, you have to extract it.

- Programmers or someone with strong code design skills needs to help design these tests. Once you have a template, it's easy to put in details.

Living documentation

Looking at examples more as specifications than tests, the team realized how powerful they are as documentation. Crispin says that having a living documentation system saved them a lot of time when they investigated issues:

66 We'd get a call: "We have this loan payment and the amount of interest we applied isn't correct. We think there is a bug." I can look at the FitNesse test and put in the values. Maybe the requirements were wrong, but here's what the code is doing. That saves so much time. 99

At one point, the person who was a manager and senior developer at ePlan decided to move back to India and wouldn't be available for a couple of months. Crispin says that they started looking at applying Specification by Example to extract the unique knowledge he had about the system:

> When there was a strange problem, he always knew how to fix it. So we really had to get the knowledge that he had about the legacy parts of the system. We then decided that one person will get some time during each sprint to go over parts of their business process and document them.

This led them to start documenting the other parts of the system as well. Although they wrote tests for anything they were developing, there were still parts of the legacy system without test automation, and this sometimes caused problems. Creating an automated living documentation for these areas helped them discover inconsistencies in business processes. Crispin explains that:

> I had been with the company for four years at that point, but I never understood how the cash accounting worked. I learned that we have five different bank accounts outside of the automated application. The money in these accounts is moved around via emails and phone calls, but the cash amounts must balance. When they don't, the accountant needs a way to research why. After the accountant explained this process to us, we documented it for future reference on our wiki. We were then able to produce reports with useful information about money in and out of the system. Now, when the cash is out of balance, she can use the reports to find out why.

Building a living documentation system to share the knowledge helped the development team learn about the business processes, and it gave the business users visibility of what they were actually doing. Writing things down exposes inconsistencies and gaps. In this case, it made people think harder about what they're actually doing from a business perspective.

Current process

All these changes were implemented a while ago, and with a living documentation system the team has a relatively stable process. At the moment, the team consists of four programmers, two testers, a Scrum master, two system administrators, a database administrator, and a manager. They work in two-week sprints. Two days before the start of a sprint, the team meets with the product owner and the stakeholders. The product owner introduces all the stories planned for the next sprint, and they write high-level tests on a whiteboard. This enables the team to provide feedback on the plan and ask questions before the real sprint planning session.

With such a complex business and a small team, the product owner is a bottleneck. To enable him to work upstream with the business users, the testers take over some analysis responsibilities. The product owner often creates a "story checklist" upfront, containing the purpose of a story and rough conditions of satisfaction. For stories that involve user interfaces, he adds a UI mock-up into the story checklist. For stories that deal with complex algorithms, he adds a spreadsheet with examples.

Ultimately, the product owner also took on more work unrelated to software, so he often doesn't have enough time to prepare for the meeting. To work around that, the testers get his approval to get in touch with the upstream stakeholders directly and work with them on the specifications.

The iteration starts with a planning meeting, when they go through all the stories again and the product owner answers any open questions. They create screen mockups and illustrate requirements with examples. Testers merge that information with the story checklist, if it's available, and then refine the specifications and put them on a wiki site.

On the fourth day of the sprint, the two testers meet with the product owner and go over all the specifications and test cases in detail, to make sure they understand everything correctly. This allows the product owner to review the specifications and what the team is going to do in the iteration.

As soon as the specifications start appearing on the wiki, the developers start implementing the stories, and they show the results to the business users as soon as they are finished.

Ah-ha moments

I asked Crispin about her key ah-ha moments related to Specification by Example. She replied:

- I didn't own quality. My job was to help the customer understand quality and help the whole team define quality and make sure that it happens.

- Developers need to be engaged.

- The process requires patience. We had to take baby steps and couldn't take everything at once.

- A tool such as FitNesse can really help with collaboration. You think of it in a technical sense, that it's going to help you automate, but it changes the team culture and helps you communicate better.

- The real value of this is that we're talking.

Key lessons

Because of their business strategy, ePlan Services relies heavily on business process automation and efficient software delivery. As a way to improve quality and speed up software delivery, they had to move away from manual software testing. They initially focused on functional test automation but then found out that the shared understanding that comes from collaboration leads to much better software.

At first, they thought about the collaboration from a testing perspective and over-specified tests, making it hard for developers to use those documents as a target for development. Instead of covering every possible combination of values, they moved to specifying key examples, which made the process more efficient and provided developers with good specifications, just in time when they needed them.

Once they had a comprehensive set of executable specifications for a part of the system, they realized how useful it is to have living documentation, especially as a way to capture specialist knowledge. When they started documenting other parts of their business, a consistent living documentation system exposed inconsistencies and errors in their existing business processes.

A living documentation system made the software delivery process much more efficient and enabled them to discover inconsistencies in their business processes.

17
Songkick

Songkick is a UK-based startup that operates Songkick.com, a consumer website about live music. They are an interesting case study for two reasons. Unlike all the other companies featured in this book, they implemented Specification by Example while still at a startup phase, without having to deal with a large legacy system in the background. Also unlike most other projects covered in this book, user interaction is one of the most critical aspects of their product, and new features are developed with a strong emphasis on the user experience, based on observation of how users interact with the site.

The complexity of the system mostly comes from the number of user experience subtleties and the number of features they build to give users a rich experience. Songkick implemented Specification by Example to focus on delivering software that matters and to be able to grow their development team.

"As a startup you can't afford to not be delivering value all the time," says their CTO Phil Cowans. Here's what he pointed to as the biggest benefits of SBE:

> Getting to what we actually intended to build quicker because we use the same language in the tests as we do when we decide what to build and go through the process of understanding our customers. That helps reduce communication issues. We aspire to never having a situation where developers turn around and say: What we built works; you just didn't ask for the right thing.

For a startup, delivering software that adds real value efficiently is much more important than it is at more mature companies. The practices of Specification by Example help Songkick get more value for their investment in software development.

Changing the process

Their project started two and a half years ago. After the first year, the team started growing "beyond the size where everyone can sit around a table and develop the code together," according to Cowans. To deal with a code base that's getting more complex and a growing team, they decided to implement test-driven development. He says:

> Before moving to TDD we relied on trusting that everything we'd previously built still worked when we released new code. But very soon it became clear we'd need more confidence that when we'd finished something, it did what we thought it would and didn't cause regressions. It seemed pretty obvious that we were going to start slowing down if we didn't find some way to avoid constantly tripping over each other's toes and find a better way of communicating requirements and avoiding regression.

Within three months, they felt that TDD was a natural way to do things. At the same time, they started looking into Kanban and the ideas of user stories, which led them to start applying TDD principles to business functionality and effectively start implementing SBE. As a team, they like to experiment with different ways of working, so they just tried it out without much fuss. Cowans explains:

> We were in touch with the guy—who's now a full-time employee but who was an adviser at that point—who had used Kanban on earlier projects. Through him we had some evidence that working in terms of user stories could be successful, and it seemed to make sense. The decision to make that part of our process was really just a matter of "there are some people using this technology to do this; let's just try it and see how it works." It became something that we found very natural to do.

The team started to derive scope from goals to drive the user stories from the business value. They also used Cucumber to create executable specifications. Cowans says that the focus of the process shifted from unit tests to business specifications as they got better with Cucumber:

> Initially we set out to use a mix of Rails test framework and Cucumber. We used Cucumber to drive out the high-level user stories and unit tests to specify the detailed behavior. Over time, we were using Cucumber more and more and found ways to specify things more in Cucumber.

The new way of specifying helped the team focus on building software that really matters. Cowans says:

> It helps people stay focused on why we're doing something and see the value of what we're doing. It helps people avoid wasting time building things we don't need. Everyone approaches the problem from the same direction, which ensures that the development team and the rest of the company think about the problem in the same way.

Similar to the team at ePlan Services, Songkick first implemented (unit) test-driven development and then extended that to business features. They didn't actually hit quality problems that made them change the process, but they did that proactively to be more efficient.

Cowans says that the key challenges for his team, when implementing Specification by Example, were understanding what to test, how to avoid making the executable specifications brittle, and how to make continuous validation faster.

Once the team got comfortable with how to use the tools, they went too far with focusing on the user interface functionality, because that was easy to think about. Cowans says:

> We spent too long testing trivial bits of the user interface, because that was easy to do. We didn't spend enough time digging into edge cases and alternative paths through the application.

They also automated executable specifications in a way that was closely tied to the user interface, so the test results were brittle. Cowans says that in some cases this pushed them to testing after development instead of using tests as specifications:

> Someone changing some punctuation on the web page and breaking the test is not good. It's frustrating because it makes it difficult to predict the effects of a change. So it's difficult to update the entire test suite in advance. As a result, in some cases people would code first and test later.

To address these problems, the team started to make tests more semantic and pushed the translation between the domain language and user interface concepts into the automation layer, Cowans explained.

> You develop a familiarity with the process and start understanding where dependence on the UI is likely to cause a problem in the long term. Developing more domain-focused step definitions [in the automation layer] helped to get around that, giving us higher-level ways to work with the markup.

The changes they implemented were effectively the start of refining the specification and looking for ways to express the specifications in the business language, not in the language of user interface terms.

According to Cowans, it took about six months for the team to get comfortable with the process and the tools they use for Specification by Example:

> It's probably in the last nine to six months that it has felt like this is a part of what we do. Within the last nine months no one has really questioned how we specify work; it's just there in the background.

The team realized exactly how important their executable specifications are when they had to rewrite a part of the system dealing with activity feeds. An existing set of business-focused specifications that were automated as tests gave them the confidence that they didn't introduce bugs or reduce functionality while rewriting the feeds. Cowans says:

> Everyone on the team became aware at that point that this can save us a lot of time. My gut feeling is that we saved 50% of the time doing the refactoring because of the tests.

For a startup, saving 50% of the time on a task means a lot. Their set of executable specifications effectively protects the system from regression issues. According to Cowans, they have so few issues in production that they don't need a bug-tracking system. This allows them to focus on delivering new features instead of maintaining the system.

No living documentation yet

At the time I interviewed Cowans, the number of executable specifications in their system had grown enough for them to start thinking about reorganizing the specifications, essentially starting a living documentation system. Cowans says:

> When setting this up we didn't think enough about the high-level structure of the tests. As the application evolved, we ended up just adding new tests as needed in an ad hoc way. As a result, when modify-

> ing existing code it's hard to find which tests cover which functionality. Deciding on a high-level description of the feature set of the site and organizing the test suite along those lines, rather simply adding new tests for each new feature we built, would have helped. I think that's also useful when it comes to developing a product and maintaining a code base that's relatively easy to understand. You end up with a shared language to describe how things fit in with what's already there.

Current process

Songkick's development process is based on Kanban flow. They have a product team responsible for the roadmap and a development team responsible for implementation. The product team consists of the head of product development, a creative director, and an interaction designer. The development team has nine developers and two testers. In the development team, two people focus more on the client side and user interfaces, and the rest are more focused on middleware and backend. Cowans, who is the CTO, is also part of the development team. According to him, the company tries to build in as much collaboration between product and development as possible, so the boundaries between the teams are fairly blurred.

Once a feature is of sufficiently high priority that it's likely to be built, the product team meets to investigate the user experience and the technology required to implement it. The outputs of this meeting are wire frames, notes about specific cases, and a first guess at the list of user stories for the feature.

When the development team has enough capacity to start implementing the feature, they organize an initial meeting with the product team and any developers or testers likely to work on the feature. At this meeting they break down the feature into user stories and jointly brainstorm the acceptance criteria for each story. The acceptance criteria are defined as a set of things to check, with detailed examples to be filled in later.

The testers own the requirements, including the user stories and the associated list of acceptance criteria. They are responsible for maintaining that as additional information comes through during development. Because of the importance of usability and user interaction, they manually test the core functionality of every feature after development, in addition to running all the executable specifications. So testers start thinking about a test plan after the initial meeting.

The developers write specifications with examples, and the testers review them, advising on what else should be covered. The developers then automate them, implement the required functionality with TDD and make that branch of code available to the testers.

The testers then run their manual tests, start doing exploratory testing, and provide feedback to the developers. Once the testers and the developers agree that a feature is ready, it goes into a queue for integration.

Features from the queue are integrated into the master branch. The entire continuous validation suite is then executed, the code is deployed to a staging environment, and the testers run final core functionality manual tests. After that, the code goes live to a production environment.

Ah-ha moments

I asked Cowans about the key ah-ha moments for him from related to their implementation of Specification by Example. He says:

- It's quite easy to test what you can see, but ultimately you need to have a deep understanding of what the software does rather than what the user interface looks like. Thinking in terms of user stories and paths through the application really helps.

- Treat your test suite as a first-class citizen. It needs careful maintenance as much as the application code itself.

- The tests are the canonical description of what the application does. Ultimately, success is as much about building the right thing as building it well. If the tests are your description of what the code does, they're not just an important part of your development process but an important part of the wider process of building the product. They can help you understand what you've built and keep complexity under control.

- It's important to have everyone in the process involved; it's not just something that developers do. Ultimately it [Specification by Example] gives you tests written by the developers that the product owner can read. You should make good use of that.

Key lessons

The key lesson from Songkick for me was that if you don't have a massive legacy system to slow you down, it's possible to go from TDD to Specification by Example quickly. At Songkick they just approached it an extension of the TDD process to cover business functionality.

The team builds and maintains a web system, so they initially automated tests in a way that was too closely tied to the user interface. This caused lots of maintenance problems and led them to start refining the specifications and automating user interface checks at a higher level of abstraction.

It took them about one year to start thinking about living documentation and seeing how important that can be when parts of the system are rewritten.

As a startup, Songkick benefits greatly from focusing on delivering the things that really matter. A shared understanding from collaborating on specifications ensures that they all focus on delivering the right product. The second most important benefit for them comes from executable specifications, because they discover problems early and can focus on rolling out new functionality rather than wasting time troubleshooting and fixing bugs.

18

Concluding thoughts

I began my research for this book because I was seeking external confirmation. I wanted to document that there are many teams that produce great software using agile techniques. I hoped that they were using BDD, agile acceptance testing, or what I would come to call Specification by Example. I thought I already knew how these processes worked and that I would find other people applying them in the same way I was. But the more research I did, the more unexpected lessons I learned. I found that many teams working in different contexts used a variety of practices and techniques to get to the same results. This proved that there's no such thing as a "best practice." Software development is incredibly contextual, and what might seem like a good idea for one team might be completely wrong for another.

Looking back, it surprises me how much I've learned about delivering high-quality software effectively. Some of these discoveries were completely new to me. Some were the result of viewing something with which I was familiar from a wider perspective, which gave me a much deeper understanding of the real forces behind the practices. To conclude this book, I'd like to present the top five things I've learned.

Collaboration on requirements builds trust between stakeholders and delivery team members

In *Bridging the Communication Gap*, I wrote that specification workshops have two main outputs. One is tangible: the examples or specifications. Another is intangible: a shared understanding of what needs to be done that's the result of a conversation. I stipulated that shared understanding might be even more important than the examples themselves. But it turns out the situation is much more complicated; there's another intangible output that I discovered when researching this book.

The examples of uSwitch, Sabre, Beazley, and Weyerhaeuser show that collaboration on specifications sparks a change in the culture of teams. As a result, development, analysis, and testing become better aligned and teams become better integrated.

To quote Wes Williams, after collaborating on specifications, "the trust was amazing."

Many companies I worked with use a software development model that's based on a lack of trust. Business users tell analysts what they need but don't trust them to specify it properly and require sign-off on specifications. Analysts tell developers what they need but don't trust them to deliver, so testers need to find some way to check independently that developers are honest. Because developers don't trust testers—they don't cut code—whenever testers report a problem, it's marked as impossible to reproduce, or it appears with a note "It works on my machine." Testers are trained not to trust anyone, almost like master spies.

A model based on mistrust creates adversarial situations and requires a lot of bureaucracy to run. Supposedly, requirements have to go through sign-off because users want to ensure what the analysts will do is right—in truth, sign-off is required so analysts can't be blamed for functional gaps later on. Because everyone needs to know what's going on, specifications go through change management; really, this ensures that nobody can be blamed for not telling others about a change. It's said that code is frozen for testing to provide testers with a more stable environment. This also guarantees that developers can't be blamed for cheating while the system was being tested. On the face of it, all these systems are in place to provide better quality. In reality, they're only alibi generators.

All these alibi generators are pure waste! By building up trust among business users, analysts, developers, and testers, we can remove the alibi generators and the bureaucracy that comes with them. Collaborating on specifications is a great way to start building up this trust.

Collaboration requires preparation

Although I stipulated that a good way to implement the process in iterations is to hold a pre-planning meeting, I didn't have anything more to say about preparing for workshops in *Bridging the Communication Gap*. I introduced the pre-planning phase because we spent too much time at the start of each workshop trying to identify important attributes for a set of examples; the real discussion started once we had something to work with. Now I see that the pre-planning meeting is a part of a much wider practice.

After talking to teams who formalized a preparation phase in different ways, I have learned that the collaboration on examples is a two-step process. In the first step, someone prepares the basic examples. In the second step, these examples are discussed with the team and extended. The goal of the preparation phase is to ensure that basic questions are answered and that there's a suggested format for examples when the team starts to discuss them. All these things can be done by a single person or two people, making the larger workshop much more effective.

For teams who worked on projects where the requirements were vague and required a lot of upfront analysis, the preparation phase started two weeks before the collaborative workshop. This allowed analysts to talk to business users, collect examples from them, and start refining the examples. Teams that had more stable requirements started working on examples a few days before, collecting the obvious open questions and addressing them. All these approaches help to run a bigger workshop more efficiently.

There are many different ways to collaborate

I suggested big, all-team workshops as the best way to collaborate on specifications in *Bridging the Communication Gap*. Again, after talking to teams in different contexts, I know that the reality is much more complex.

Many teams found that, at the start, big workshops were useful as a means to transfer the domain knowledge and align the expectations of developers, testers, and business analysts and stakeholders. But the majority of teams stopped doing big workshops after a while because they discovered that they're hard to coordinate and cost too much in terms of people's time.

Once the right process is in place, trust improves, and developers and testers learn more about the domain, smaller workshops or ad hoc conversations seem to be enough to produce good specifications. Many teams approached this from a "whoever has an interest in the story" perspective, involving only the people who would actively work on a task. When the others need to change the functionality, they would learn about what the software does from the living documentation system.

Looking at the end goal as business process documentation is a useful model

If we think of business process documentation as the end goal of Specification by Example, many of the common automation and maintenance problems disappear. For example, the flaw in creating overly complex scripts that mimic the way the software is built becomes obvious; scripts always end up being hard to maintain and the communication value of such scripts is marginal.

As a community, we noticed this a few years ago, and many practitioners advised teams not to write acceptance tests as workflows. Although this is good advice for a majority of cases, that doesn't help when the domain is about workflows, as in processing payments. David Peterson wrote Concordion as a response to all the misuse of workflows in FIT and got a bit closer to the point by advising people to write specifications instead of scripts. Again, it's a useful rule of thumb but hard to explain to people who deal with websites. The problem is the misalignment of models in acceptance tests or specification and the models in business;[1] one small change in the business domain has a shotgun effect on tests, which makes them hard to maintain.

If we focus on documenting business processes, the model in the specifications will be aligned with the business model and changes will be symmetric. A small change in the business domain model will result in a small change in specifications and tests. We can document business processes well before we start writing software, and they'll stay the same when we change technologies. Specifications that talk about business processes are worth much more over the long term. Business users can participate in documenting business processes and provide much better feedback than they would on acceptance tests that pertain to software.

This also tells us what to automate and how to automate it. It's easy to spot the flaws in changing specifications to include invented testing concepts or fit it into user interface interactions. If the specifications document business processes, the automation layer exercises those business processes on software. This is where the technical workflows, scripts, and simulated user interactions need to go. Automation itself isn't a goal: It's a tool to exercise the business processes.

In order to create reliable documentation, we have to validate it frequently. Automation offers one inexpensive way to do so, but it isn't necessarily the only way. Some things, such as usability, can never be properly automated; but we can still try to validate parts of specifications frequently. This addresses the problem of specifying things that are hard to automate, an issue that many teams avoid.

Long-term value comes from living documentation

Almost everyone I spoke with experienced the short-term benefits of faster deliveries and better quality. But teams who "cleaned up their tests" also got fantastic long-term benefits from them. As a consultant, I've helped many teams implement these practices, but because I don't generally stay with anyone for long, I did not notice the long-term effects. Luckily, some of the earliest adopters of these practices have now been using them for six or seven years, and they have seen great benefits in the long term as well.

Iowa Student Loan was able to change a business model quickly because they had reliable documentation. The team at ePlan Services was able to survive the absence of a key team member. The team working on the Sierra project uses "tests" as supporting documentation when they get support requests. At that point, I think it is wrong to call what they used "tests," because they don't use them for testing software: They're documentation that was built to be reliable and relevant.

Most of these teams adopted living documentation by trial and error, when they

---

[1] See http://dannorth.net/2011/01/31/whose-domain-is-it-anyway

were looking for easier ways to maintain tests. They restructured tests to make them more stable, aligning the models in tests and in the business. They restructured the folders containing tests to make it easier to find all the things that are relevant for a particular change. They practically evolved a documentation system structured in a way that's similar to how business users think about system features.

At this point I feel relatively confident in making the bold assumption that new teams can get these benefits quicker if they intentionally create a living documentation system rather than arrive there after years of trial and error.

With that in mind, I invite you and your team to try this yourselves. After you've tried it, please share your experiences with me. You can contact me by sending an email to gojko@gojko.com.

Appendix A

Resources

Books

Gojko Adzic, *Bridging the Communication Gap: Specification by Example and Agile Acceptance Testing* (Neuri, 2009).

Gojko Adzic, *Test Driven .NET Development with FitNesse* (Neuri, 2008).

David Anderson, *Kanban: Successful Evolutionary Change for Your Technology Business* (Blue Hole Press, 2010).

Mijo Balic, Ingrid Ottersten, and Peter Corrigan, *Effect Managing IT* (Copenhagen Business School Press, 2007).

Mike Cohn, *Agile Estimating and Planning* (Robert C. Martin Series) (Prentice Hall, 2005).

Lisa Crispin and Janet Gregory, *Agile Testing: A Practical Guide for Testers and Agile Teams* (Addison-Wesley Professional, 2009).

Kev Darling, *F-16 Fighting Falcon (Combat Legend)* (The Crowood Press, 2005).

Mark Denne and Jane Cleland-Huang, *Software by Numbers: Low-Risk, High-Return Development* (Prentice Hall, 2003).

Eric Evans, *Domain-Driven Design: Tackling Complexity in the Heart of Software* (Addison-Wesley Professional, 2003).

Steve Freeman and Nat Pryce, *Growing Object-Oriented Software, Guided by Tests* (Addison-Wesley Professional, 2009).

Donald C. Gause and Gerald M. Weinberg, *Exploring Requirements: Quality Before Design* (Dorset House Publishing Company, 1989).

Capers Jones, *Estimating Software Costs: Bringing Realism to Estimating*, 2nd ed. (McGraw-Hill Osborne, 2007).

Craig Larman and Bas Vodde, *Practices for Scaling Lean & Agile Development: Large, Multisite, and Offshore Product Development with Large-Scale Scrum* (Pearson Education, 2010).

Richard Monson-Haefel, *97 Things Every Software Architect Should Know: Collective Wisdom from the Experts* (O'Reilly Media, 2009).

Rick Mugridge and Ward Cunningham, *Fit for Developing Software: Framework for Integrated Tests* (Prentice Hall, 2005).

Mary Poppendieck and Tom Poppendieck, *Lean Software Development: An Agile Toolkit* (Addison-Wesley Professional, 2003).

James Shore and Shane Warden, *The Art of Agile Development* (O'Reilly Media, 2007).

Gerald Weinberg, *Quality Software Management: Vol. 1, Systems Thinking* (Dorset House Publishing, 1992).

Online resources

Here are the URLs of all the online resources mentioned in the book. You can find all these links and more on the accompanying website: http://www.specificationbyexample.com.

Tools

Concordion: http://www.concordion.org.

Cucumber: http://cukes.info.

FitNesse: http://fitnesse.org.

GreenPepper: http://www.greenpeppersoftware.com.

JBehave: http://jbehave.org.

Robot Framework: http://www.robotframework.org.

SpecFlow: http://www.specflow.org.

TextTest: http://www.texttest.org.

Twist: http://studios.thoughtworks.com/twist-agile-test-automation/.

Videos

Gojko Adzic, "Challenging Requirements,"
http://gojko.net/2009/12/10/challenging-requirements/.

Dan North, "How to Sell BDD to the Business,"
http://skillsmatter.com/podcast/agile-testing/how-to-sell-bdd-to-the-business.

Hemal Kuntawala, "How we build quality software at USwitch.com," http://skills
matter.com/podcast/agile-testing/how-we-build-quality-software-at-uswitch-com.

Björn Regnell, "Supporting Roadmapping of Quality Requirements,"
http://oredev.org/videos/supporting-roadmapping-of-quality-requirements.

Presentations

Tim Andersen, "Persona Driven Development," http://www.umsec.umn.edu/
events/Code-Freeze-2010/PDD; http://timandersen.net/presentations/Persona_
Driven_Development.pdf.

Mark Durrand and Damon Morgan, "Creating a Lean business from the inside out:
Technical innovation at uSwitch.com to reduce waste," http://www.slideshare.
net/markdurrand/spa2010-uswitch.

Articles

Gojko Adzic, "Agile in a Start-up Games Development Studio,"
http://gojko.net/2010/05/19/agile-in-a-start-up-games-development-studio/.

Gojko Adzic: Are tools necessary for acceptance testing, or are they just evil?
http://gojko.net/2010/03/01/are-tools-necessary-for-acceptance-testing-or-are-
they-just-evil.

Gojko Adzic, "Examples make it easy to spot inconsistencies,"
http://gojko.net/2009/05/12/examples-make-it-easy-to-spot-inconsistencies/.

Gojko Adzic: How to implement UI testing without shooting yourself in the foot,
http://gojko.net/2010/04/13/how-to-implement-ui-testing-without-shooting-
yourself-in-the-foot-2/.

Gojko Adzic: Improving testing practices at Google,
http://gojko.net/2009/12/07/improving-testing-practices-at-google/.

Gojko Adzic, "QUPER model for better requirements," http://gojko.net/2009/11/04/quper-model-for-better-requirements/.

Gojko Adzic, "Shock therapy agile adoption at 7Digital," http://gojko.net/2009/12/08/shock-therapy-agile-adoption-at-7digital/.

Michael Bolton, "Acceptance Tests: Let's Change the Title, Too," http://www.developsense.com/blog/2010/08/acceptance-tests-lets-change-the-title-too/.

Michael Bolton, "Testing vs. Checking," http://www.developsense.com/blog/2009/08/testing-vs-checking/.

Alistair Cockburn, "Sacrifice One Person," http://alistair.cockburn.us/Sacrifice+one+person+strategy.

Craig Larman and Bas Vodde, "Acceptance Test-Driven Development with Robot Framework," http://code.google.com/p/robotframework/wiki/ATDDWith RobotFrameworkArticle.

Craig Larman and Bas Vodde, "Feature Teams Primer," http://www.featureteams.org/feature_team_primer.pdf.

Dan North, "Whose domain is it anyway?" http://dannorth.net/2011/01/31/whose-domain-is-it-anyway/.

Björn Regnell, Richard Berntsson Svensson, and Thomas Olsson, "Supporting Roadmapping of Quality Requirements," *IEEE Software* 25, no. 2 (Mar/Apr 2008): 43–47

James Shore, "Alternatives to Acceptance Testing," http://jamesshore.com/Blog/Alternatives-to-Acceptance-Testing.html.

James Shore, "The Problems with Acceptance Testing," http://jamesshore.com/Blog/The-Problems-With-Acceptance-Testing.html.

Lance Walton, "Writing Maintainable Acceptance Tests," http://www.casual miracles.com/blog/2010/03/04/writing-maintainable-acceptance-tests/.

Comics

Chris Matts, "Real Options at Agile 2009," http://www.lulu.com/product/file-download/real-options-at-agile-2009/5949486.

Training courses

Gojko Adzic: http://neuri.co.uk/training.

Object Mentor: http://objectmentor.com/omTraining/omi_training_index.html.

Lisa Crispin and Janet Gregory: http://www.janetgregory.ca/training.htm.

Elisabeth Hendrickson: http://www.qualitytree.com/workshops/.

Pyxis Technologies: http://pyxis-tech.com/en/our-offer/training.

TechTalk: http://www.techtalk.at/training.aspx.

Rick Mugridge: http://www.rimuresearch.com/Coaching.html.

Index